The Montgomery-Arnold invasion of 1775 had initial success. Montgomery took Montreal without much difficulty, then joined Arnold in front of Quebec. But Arnold's men had had a rougher time of it in traversing the Maine wilderness. Many of them had deserted and many of those left were sick, underfed, and poorly armed. Carleton had difficulties too, but he also had some big guns, with trained men to use them, and spies who provided him with accurate intelligence. The Americans attacked Quebec in a raging northeaster and were mowed down by the defenders. Montgomery was killed, Arnold wounded. That was the end of the invasion and the beginning of a retreat that turned into a succession of disasters.

This is a meticulously detailed account that does justice to both sides. Carleton emerges as an able, astute, and decent man; Montgomery as an authentic hero; Arnold as a brilliant, courageous leader, who was also embittered and self-serving.

The story of an American army invading a peaceful neighbor and of a country preserved by the wisdom and courage of the British colonial government is a strange contrast to the events in the thirteen colonies—and Robert Hatch tells it compellingl

THRUST FOR
CANADA

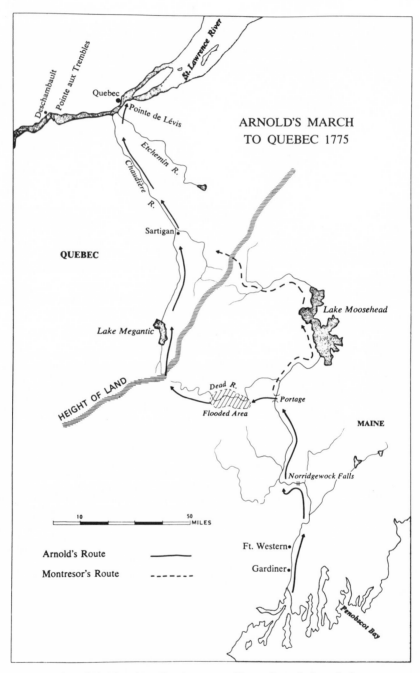

Arnold's March to Quebec 1775. From *Canada Invaded*
by George F. G. Stanley (Hakkurt, Toronto 1973).

THRUST FOR CANADA

THE AMERICAN ATTEMPT ON QUEBEC IN 1775–1776

ROBERT McCONNELL HATCH

ILLUSTRATED WITH PHOTOGRAPHS
AND MAPS

HOUGHTON MIFFLIN COMPANY
BOSTON 1979

Library of Congress Cataloging in Publication Data

Hatch, Robert McConnell.
Thrust for Canada.

Bibliography: p.
Includes index.
1. Canadian Invasion, 1775–1776. I. Title.
E231.H37   971.02'4   79-13639
ISBN 0-395-27612-8

Printed in the United States of America

V 10 9 8 7 6 5 4 3 2 1

To Margaret
with gratitude

Acknowledgments

My thanks are due to John H. G. Pell and John W. Krueger of Fort Ticonderoga for allowing me the benefit of their own researches and supplying me with a wealth of information about General Schuyler, the army he commanded, the logistical problems with which he wrestled, and the illnesses that beset his troops. I am grateful to Dr. Douglas W. Marshall of the University of Michigan for providing me with maps of the campaign and for introducing me to the Gage Papers at the William L. Clements Library; to John Humphrey of Roxbury, Connecticut, for material on Colonel Seth Warner; and to Harold W. Felton and John W. Farr of Falls Village, Connecticut, for help with three from their corner of New England who took part in the campaign, Colonel Charles Burrall, Captain John Stevens, and Chaplain Ammi Robbins.

I am indebted to the late Colonel Edward P. Hamilton for material on General Thomas, to Colonel John A. Williams of Essex Junction, Vermont, J. Robert Maguire of Shoreham, Vermont, and Dr. H. N. Muller, President of Colby-Sawyer College in New London, New Hampshire, for filling me in on the Valcour Island engagement, and to Colonel Williams for showing me where ships of the two navies fought one another in their contest for Lake Champlain. Also to the Reverend Honorius Provost of the Séminaire de Québec for conducting me to landmarks associated with the battle on December 31 and with the siege that followed; to

Colonel George F. G. Stanley of Sackville, New Brunswick, for help in several particulars; to René Chartrand, Military Curator for National Parks in Canada, and to Colonel Frederick P. Todd of Cornwall-on-Hudson, New York, for supplying me with specifics about the Royal Highland Emigrants; and to James T. Flexner for clues to the authorship of a British journal kept during the siege of St. Jean.

My thanks also to White Nichols of the Arnold Expedition Historical Society, Duluth Wing of Eustis, Maine, and Roland A. Martin of Locke Mills, Maine, for information about Arnold's march; and to John G. Senter of Nashua, New Hampshire, the Reverend Benjamin Minifie of Newport, Rhode Island, and Edwin W. Connelly, project coordinator for the documentation and restoration of Rhode Island burial grounds, for data on Dr. Isaac Senter, Captain John Topham, and Major Henry Sherburne, all of whom hailed from Newport. The Reverend David W. Works of Topsfield, Massachusetts, and Richard W. Hale, late Archivist of the Commonwealth of Massachusetts, came to my rescue in the hunt for early documents.

I appreciate the support and encouragement of Dr. J. Duane Squires of New London, New Hampshire, and the help given me by Dr. Robert C. Black III of Denver, Colorado, Homer T. Gregory of Branford, Connecticut, Robert W. Kenyon of Warwick, Rhode Island, the Reverend Paul S. Koumrian of Ayer, Massachusetts, Edson L. Merrill of Randolph, New Hampshire, and the Reverend Ronald G. Whitney of Springfield, Massachusetts.

I have been blessed with two wise and perceptive editors, Grant Ujifusa and Robie Macauley, with a consummate manuscript editor in Frances L. Apt, and with a meticulous secretary, Phyllis Hinchman. I am most appreciative of the expertise of Victoria Smith Schilling, who assisted me with the translation of several French diaries and other source materials. And I have marveled anew at the patience of my wife, Helen, who has endured with unflagging good cheer what must have seemed an interminable round of libraries and old battle sites.

I am indebted, immeasurably, to the staffs of the following: the Public Archives of Canada, the National Archives of Quebec, the

Public Record Office, the British Museum, Nottingham University, the Houghton and Widener Libraries at Harvard University, the Library of Congress, the New York Public Library, the Boston Athenaeum, the William L. Clements Library at the University of Michigan, the American Antiquarian Society, the Archives of the Commonwealth of Massachusetts, the Fort Ticonderoga Museum Library, the Arnold Expedition Historical Society, the Company of Military Historians, and the Connecticut, Massachusetts, New Hampshire, New York and Vermont Historical Societies. All have been generous of their time and unfailingly helpful.

R. M. H.

Contents

Illustrations

THRUST FOR
CANADA

I

Furor Over a Well-Intentioned Measure

1

CHURCH BELLS burst upon the bright September stillness, and the guns on the ramparts gave a thunderous salute, as *Canadian*, a long sea voyage behind her, rounded Ile d'Orléans and swept into full view of the city of Quebec. This was no ordinary homecoming. General Guy Carleton, governor of the province and its advocate in Parliament, was returning after four years in England, during which he had taken a wife, sired two offspring, and fathered a bill that would change the map of Canada, please some but not all of his subjects, and help ignite the American Revolution.

In 1774, Guy Carleton was fifty years old. He was lean and trim, resplendent in his regimentals, correctly military in mien, but an unlikely spouse for the young wife who clutched his elbow. Lady Maria, who had entered into wedlock after a sheltered upbringing on an ancestral estate in England and amid the French nobility at Versailles, could have passed for his teen-age daughter. Although resolutely self-possessed, she could not conceal her excitement as she scanned the steeples and rooftops surmounting a sheer wall of rock and wedged along the shoreline at its base.

The city occupied a headland between the St. Lawrence, nearly a mile wide where *Canadian* dropped anchor, and its tributary, the St. Charles. The Lower Town was a welter of quays, warehouses, and weathered stone buildings crammed between the cliff and the river. Lady Maria could detect a steeple her husband said was that of the old French church of Notre Dame des Victoires and, behind it, a road toiling up the cliff to the Upper Town. He pointed out the place where they would live — the Château St. Louis, built almost a century before by the Comte de Frontenac near the crest of the soaring rock. He identified the cathedral and adjoining seminary with their lush lawns and shade trees, the spires of the religious houses, the orchard of the Récollect Fathers, easily distinguishable amid the massed stone buildings, and a short distance upriver, commanding the St. Lawrence from a promontory called Cape Diamond, a mighty bastion anchoring the far reaches of the wall that hemmed the city.

The governor and his lady were welcomed by the lieutenant governor, Hector Theophilus Cramahé, plainly relieved to have his superior home again after four worrisome years, and by the Bishop of Quebec, Jean Olivier Briand, who embraced the governor and was invited to ride with him in the gubernatorial coach. The regiments of the garrison, ablaze in white and scarlet, flanked the road as the coach ground up the cliff to the Upper Town and came to a halt before the Château St. Louis, a rambling two-story structure that may have given Lady Maria pause as she bundled her infants into its musty recesses. That night candles were lit in honor of the governor and his lady in the windows of all the religious houses and in many private homes as well, especially those of the aristocracy, known as the *noblesse*. The clergy of the city came to thank him for his support during his sojourn in London. The *noblesse* asked him to assure the king that "he will have no subjects more faithful and more submissive than the Canadians." [1] Carleton was pleased beyond measure. Five days after his arrival he wrote Lord Dartmouth, Secretary for the Colonies, that he found the Canadians uniformly appreciative of "the King's great goodness toward them in the late Act of Regulation for the Government of this Province" and that "all ranks of People amongst them vie with each other in testifying their Gratitude." [2] It was indeed an auspicious homecoming.

Carleton was Canada's second military governor after the conquest. In defeating New France, Britain had brought to a close a succession of wars, culminating in Wolfe's conquest of Quebec in 1759 and the surrender of the province a year later. But Canadian society remained overwhelmingly French. It included small farmers, or *habitants*, whose antecedents had been sent out to colonize the province and who lived in rural parishes bordering the St. Lawrence, the Richelieu, and the Chaudière. There was a much smaller class known as *seigneurs*, most of them members of the *noblesse*, whose forebears had been given large tracts of land in a semifeudal arrangement designed to encourage colonization. There was also an urban bourgeoisie of tradesmen and artisans in Quebec, Trois Rivières, and Montreal. All classes were held together by the Church, which must now cope with a Protestant king. Half the clergy were Canadian-born, half were French. The bishops had always been French. When Bishop Pontbriand died, in 1760, his post remained vacant for six years, and the Church had to depend on the combined energies of three vicars general, none of whom had episcopal prerogatives. Finally, the British government allowed one of them, Jean Olivier Briand, of Quebec, to become Bishop Pontbriand's successor.

Canada as Carleton knew it had its beginnings in 1535, when Jacques Cartier sailed out of Saint-Malo with a small fleet to penetrate the St. Lawrence and drop anchor at the Indian village of Hochelaga on the site of what would one day be Montreal. Others followed, to harvest fish along the coast and open a fur trade with the Indians. In the early seventeenth century, a trading corporation known as the Company of the Hundred Associates was authorized to develop the fledgling colony. Explorers ranged the hinterland west of the Ottawa, Jesuit missionaries journeyed far into the interior risking torture and death to convert the Indians, but progress was slow and there were many discouragements. In 1663, Louis XIV proclaimed the colony a royal province ruled by a governor and council. Associated with the governor was an intendant, who watched over the king's financial interests and who often contrived to pad his own. The bishop, too, was influential. Bishop François Xavier de Laval-Montmorency and his successors saw to it that power was shared by both Crown and Church, so the province had theocratic as well as semifeudal overtones. All but inevitably, it ran into conflict with the English colonies to the south.

Border wars followed one another with mounting bloodshed. French and Indian scalping parties reduced New England farms to ashes, laid siege to blockhouses, devastated whole communities. The city of Quebec was threatened by the colonists, Louisburg was taken, a Jesuit mission on the Kennebec was sacked and its priest shot. It was an ugly, hate-ridden contest, reaching its pitch in the French and Indian War, which culminated in 1760 and yielded Canada to Britain. The Church, at the mercy of a Protestant king, feared for her very life. The *seigneurs* looked to the governor to restore sinecures in the army and civil government that would supplement the meager income derived from their land. The *habitants*, bewildered and battle-weary, wished only to be left in peace.

The Treaty of Paris, in 1763, allowed the Canadians to "profess the worship of their religion according to the rites of the Romish church, as far as the laws of Great Britain permit," although tithes, a mainstay of the Church, were forbidden. A singularly enlightened policy by eighteenth-century standards, this became a milestone in the long struggle for religious liberty and won Britain the nearly solid support of the Canadian clergy.

The province was deprived of its links with the Great Lakes and the Mississippi and was restricted to a parallelogram bounded on the east by Labrador, on the south by the English colonies and what is now New Brunswick, and on the west by Lake Nipissing. A vast Indian reserve was set apart west of the Ottawa. British law was introduced, and an elected assembly promised. The government of the province was entrusted to two career soldiers who became warm friends of French Canada, Brigadier General James Murray and his successor, Guy Carleton.

Murray, who had commanded the left wing of Wolfe's army in the battle that won Quebec, was governor from 1763 to 1766. He soon ran afoul of fellow Englishmen who had emigrated to Canada to make their fortunes in commerce and who sought to protect their interests through a British code of law and a legislative assembly restricted to Protestants. But the French wanted a restoration of French civil law and no assembly at all, and they had Murray's support. A stubborn and fiery Scot, he became embroiled in a quarrel with both the British merchants and the military and was recalled after three years. However, his brief administration set a precedent of magnanimity toward French Canada that won the allegiance of both the clergy and the *noblesse*.

Guy Carleton was the antithesis of Murray. Where Murray was outspoken, Carleton watched his tongue. Where Murray was an explosive Scot, Carleton was an Ulsterman who let his anger fester. Where Murray was forthright, Carleton could be secretive. Murray was a professional army man who was too blunt to be a diplomat. Carleton, although a soldier, was a cautious and instinctively humane statesman.

Carleton's antecedents had emigrated to Ulster from northern England and had prospered as landowners. Born at Strabane, County Tyrone, in 1724, he seemed destined from boyhood for the army and was commissioned an ensign in the British infantry at eighteen. His rise through the ranks was halting compared with that of his friend James Wolfe, who, although three years his junior, had become a captain while Carleton remained a lieutenant. But Wolfe was impressed with Carleton, recognizing gifts that he would one day put to use. He had wanted Carleton in his command when he was serving as Lord Amherst's brigadier in 1758. However, Carleton had made slurring references to the Hanoverian troops, an unpardonable affront to the king's ancestry, and instead of joining Wolfe at Louisburg was assigned to a British unit in Germany. Prior to the Quebec campaign, Wolfe included Carleton's name on a list of officers submitted for the king's approval. His Majesty is said to have drawn a line through it, but Wolfe persisted and, with the help of William Pitt, managed to have his friend appointed deputy quartermaster general. Carleton was wounded in the battle for Quebec. He was wounded twice more, at Port Andro and Havana, and had been raised to brigadier by the time he surfaced, at forty-two, as Murray's successor.

Carleton turned out to be as pro-French as Murray. He preferred the company of the French *noblesse* to that of the English-speaking merchants. He took to Bishop Briand and, although himself a Protestant, favored the interests of the Church. A year after becoming governor, he wrote Lord Shelburne that the French with their high birth rate should multiply indefinitely, whereas the harsh winters should discourage immigration from England and persuade some of the English-speaking merchants to quit Canada. Lord Shelburne did not have to read between the lines to see that the sooner this took place, the happier the governor would be.[3]

Conditioned by army thinking and eighteenth-century class distinctions, Carleton found the English-speaking merchants hard to take. Most of them were self-made, with no claim to titled forebears. They had come out to Canada to make money in wheat, lumber, sealskins, beaver pelts — any commodity that would yield a profit. Because their London creditors were sparing with subsidies, they had to gamble heavily on their investments. A lean fur season or a plunging market could leave them bankrupt. For their own protection they needed a supportive governor, English civil law, and an assembly they could control.

Peaking at 360 in 1770, the English-speaking population included some who had lived in the American colonies and a few who had been born there. Although most of them made no trouble for the governor, a minority lobbied for an assembly and bombarded Parliament with nettlesome petitions. Their leader was a hulking, raw-boned Englishman named Thomas Walker, who had emigrated from Boston and had acquired the Bostonians' knack for raising hackles. When, as a justice of the peace, he had flouted the military by signing a warrant for the arrest of an officer involved in a dispute over billeting, friends of the accused, armed and in blackface, invaded his home, thrashed him mercilessly, and sliced off part of one ear. But Walker, who seems to have thrived on persecution, became more strident than ever, and surrounded himself with a coterie of lieutenants that included James Price, William Heywood, and Joseph Bindon in Montreal, and John McCord, Zachary Macaulay, Edward Antill, and John Dyer Mercier in Quebec.

Late in 1773, Walker and his associates took their case to Lord Dartmouth through a former attorney general of the province, Francis Masères. A petition to the king was drawn up by a committee in Quebec, whose chairman, John McCord, was coached by Walker. Sixty-one English-speaking merchants signed it, but not one French Canadian. Walker then returned to Montreal, where a second petition was signed by sixty-six English-speaking merchants. Both petitions asked for an assembly, but unlike previous appeals, which had requested an exclusively Protestant body, indicated a willingness to accept whatever representation His Majesty saw fit to grant. Even Masères, a Huguenot who detested all things Roman Catholic, agreed to the admission of some French delegates. The petitions had the support of the Lord Mayor and Corporation of London as well as some of the merchants' colleagues in the city, but in higher echelons, where Carleton was at work, they were virtually ignored. The governor knew that the Canadian French cherished their civil law and had no objection to being ruled by a governor and council. Their legal system, tailored to their special needs, derived from ancient edicts and customs and was elastic enough to protect the land tenure and inheritances of the *seigneurs* when administered by a knowledgeable judge. English civil law seemed inflexible by comparison, and the *noblesse* recoiled at the thought of submitting their affairs to a jury composed of artisans and shopkeepers. An assembly was foreign to their experience and could do them great harm if confined solely or chiefly to Protestants.

The *noblesse* inherited their *seigneuries* from forebears who had been favored by the king. Many of their antecedents had been army veterans, like the officers of the Carignan-Salières regiment, who were awarded extensive holdings in the Richelieu Valley. At first the *seigneuries* had been owned by the *noblesse*, by government officials, and by ecclesiastical orders, but early in the eighteenth century many had been taken over by enterprising *habitants*. Others were acquired by Britons after the conquest. Members of the *noblesse* were ordinarily *seigneurs*, but in time more and more *seigneurs* were not of the *noblesse*.

The *seigneur* depended on the *habitant* to cultivate his land. For an annual return paid in cash or produce, *seigneurs* parceled out their acres in thin strips that reached back from the river as much as a mile and a half and embraced meadowland and woodlot. The *habitant* might be expected to patronize his *seigneur*'s mill when grinding corn and his ovens when baking bread, and, if he fished in the river bordering his land, to forfeit one fish in every eleven. He must donate a day or more of free labor every year. Nevertheless, the rents were low, the profits marginal. Many *seigneurs* were financially hard-pressed, and it was not uncommon to see a *seigneur's* wife toiling beside him in the fields while his sons took to the woods to eke out a shaky livelihood in the fur trade. Some had depended on civil and military sinecures to supplement their meager incomes and were impoverished without them. Carleton sympathized with their plight and was increasingly disturbed by a rebellious spirit among the *habitants*. He had a staunch supporter in Bishop Briand, who had found the *habitants* "docile, submissive, easy to lead" when he arrived in Canada as a young priest, but had recently noted signs of "indocility, obstinacy, rebellion." [4] Both hoped for a return to the unquestioning obedience the *habitants* had previously shown their clergy and their *seigneurs*.

With a benign countenance and the compact body of a peasant, Jean Olivier Briand was gentle in pastoral relations, indefatigable in the pulpit, and, when the Church's interests were at stake, as tenacious as his Breton forebears. He possessed a humility that might have qualified him for sainthood. He had not sought the office of bishop nor did he relish its perquisites. He was said to have remarked that his predecessor, Bishop Pontbriand, had assigned him many unwelcome tasks during his lifetime and must be continuing the treatment from beyond the grave. But he gave the episcopate his best, moving modestly among his flock, and set the tone of his administration by renting out the bishop's palace and making his own quarters in the seminary. He was ever conscious of his debt to Murray for his favors to the Church, and to Carleton for safeguarding the episcopal succession by allowing him a coadjutor. He made sure that his clergy gave both governors their unequivocal support.

2

When Carleton went to London in 1770 to work for a bill that would regularize the government of Quebec, he was met with a welter of inconclusive reports. Three years earlier, the Privy Council had asked him to make a study of Canada's judicial system with the advice of his own council, his chief justice, William Hey, and his attorney general, Francis Masères. They had recommended the restoration of French civil law, although Hey and Masères had been less than enthusiastic over this provision. Further studies were made, but they failed to settle some thorny questions. If an assembly were allowed, how could it include Roman Catholics without their gaining control of the province? If only members of the Protestant minority were made eligible for membership, how could this be made palatable to the French majority, who outnumbered the British by thirty to one? How would Britain's Protestant electorate react to a policy of toleration toward the Roman Catholic Church in a Crown colony? Would the British public approve of restoring French civil law without trial by jury or habeas corpus? In the winter of 1774, after four years of continual revision, Lord Dartmouth announced that a Quebec Bill was on its way to Parliament. But it was to be rewritten four times after that, before being introduced in May. Promptly passed by the House of Lords but subjected to a spirited attack in Commons, it was enacted just before the warm weather threatened to empty the House of all but its diehard members.

The Quebec Act enlarged the province to include the Great Lakes, the hinterland north of the Ohio to its junction with the Mississippi, up the Mississippi to its source, and north of the Great Lakes to Hudson Bay territory — the whole vast Indian reserve set apart by the Treaty of Paris. The annexed lands would be off limits to homesteaders and would form the heartland of the Canadian fur trade and a sanctuary for the trade's Indian dependents. The province would also include the seal-producing Labrador coast and the islands at the mouth of the St. Lawrence, formerly part of Newfoundland.

The act promised "the free exercise of the religion of the Church of Rome." Tithes were reinstated. The oath of allegiance was replaced with a less offensive pledge that made no reference to the king's supremacy over the Church or to the inflammatory doctrine of transubstantiation, thereby enabling Roman Catholics to take part in government and hold office without compromising their religious faith.

French civil law was restored without habeas corpus or trial
by jury. Unwilling to permit an assembly controlled by French
Canadians, yet recognizing the injustice of limiting membership to
Protestants or providing for an unassailable Protestant majority,
Parliament ruled that it would be "inexpedient" to have any assembly for the time being. The province would be governed by the
governor and council, the latter to consist of from seventeen to
twenty-three members, both Protestant and Catholic, appointed by
the king with the advice of the Privy Council. Revenues would
be derived from import duties on liquor and molasses.

The Quebec Bill had been introduced at the tag end of a session
that was wrestling with the even more vexatious problem of the
American colonies. Many members of Parliament, weary and out
of sorts after long weeks of rancorous debate, had left for the country. By the time the vote was taken, only seventy-six out of a
possible 558 votes were cast. In speaking for the bill, Carleton identified the wishes of all French Canadians with those of the *noblesse.*
They did not want trial by jury, he said, because "they think it very
strange that the English residing in Canada should prefer to have
matters of law decided by tailors and shoemakers." [5] "Assemblies,"
he claimed, "had drawn upon the other colonies so much distress,
had occasioned such riots and confusion" that the Canadians "wished
never to have one of any kind whatever." [6] French civil law should
be restored, he said, because most of his subjects had not "the least
idea" of what English law was all about. He was followed by a
seigneur, Michel Chartier de Lotbinière, who insisted that if there
was to be an assembly — something that he and others of his class
did not favor — it must include its rightful proportion of Roman
Catholics.

The bill was opposed by the Whigs, some of whose most celebrated orators spoke against it for reasons ranging from a defense of
civil liberties to fear of a Roman Catholic takeover. Isaac Barré
warned of "a popish army" in Canada — a prospect sure to arouse
old fears in the colonies. Charles Fox and Edmund Burke deplored
the loss of trial by jury, habeas corpus, and an elected assembly.
Burke said, "Give them English liberty, give them an English constitution, and then, whether they speak French or English, whether

they go to mass or attend our own communion, you will render them valuable and useful subjects of Great Britain." John Dunning foresaw friction with the colonies over the disposition of the western lands. By giving the Province of Quebec "this monstrous southern extent, you run it down the back of the planted part of many of our colonies," he warned, "and take away, by one stroke, the charter properties confirmed by an act of parliament on those colonies." [7]

But most members of Commons had wearied of speeches. On June 13, the bill was passed, fifty-six to twenty. Sent to the House of Lords for approval, it was dealt a final broadside by William Pitt, who described it as "a most cruel, oppressive and odious measure" that established "Popery and arbitrary government" in Canada and would "lose the hearts of all his Majesty's American subjects." [8] Only five voted with him. On June 22, the day Parliament adjourned, King George the Third, impervious to shouts of "No Popery!" from a street mob and ignoring a deputation headed by the Lord Mayor of London that sought to remind him of his coronation oath to uphold the Protestant religion, rode to Westminster and gave his approval to the Quebec Act.

Carleton had had his way, but in January Lord Dartmouth sent him a list of private instructions, urging the restoration of both habeas corpus and English civil law in suits involving debts, damages, and business contracts — a measure that would have placated most of the English-speaking merchants. Unhappily, Lord Dartmouth included other instructions that would have denied much of the freedom accorded the Roman Catholic Church: the bishop would be forbidden to correspond with officials in Rome or to perform episcopal acts without a license from the governor, religious orders for men would be forbidden further recruitments, seminaries would be subjected to periodic inspection and to regulations imposed by the governor and council, Catholic missionaries to the Indians would be replaced by Protestants.[9] Carleton, friend of Bishop Briand as well as of the *noblesse*, treated the instructions as optional and chose to pay them no heed at all.

While in England, the governor married Lady Maria Howard, younger daughter of his friend the Earl of Effingham. It is said that he first proposed to her older sister and that when his suit was rejected, Lady Maria led him to expect a more favorable response if the offer was transferred to her. Although petite and of tender years, she possessed an assurance that befitted a governor's wife and, having been brought up and educated at Versailles, a partiality for things French.

Carleton felt sure that the Quebec Act would be welcomed by all but a small fraction of his subjects. He wrote Lord Dartmouth that he found the French Canadians "vying" to show their approval.[10] The day after his arrival, he was asked by General Gage to send the 10th and 52nd Regiments to Boston. Although this would leave him only the understrength 7th and 26th, he gave up both regiments, confident that he could replace them with Canadian militia. The French, he wrote Gage, "have testified to me the strongest marks of joy, and Gratitude, and Fidelity to the King, and to His Government, for the late arrangements at Home in their Favor." [11]

Those whom Carleton talked with, however, were limited largely to the *noblesse*. The *habitants*, who had to supply the rank and file in every Canadian regiment, were alienated by his break with custom in the selection of militia officers. During the French regime, the militia captains, although appointed by the governor, had been chosen from the ranks of the *habitants*, with the approval of their peers. Ignoring tradition, Carleton appointed members of the *noblesse* to the captaincies, a change that brought beating orders nearly to a standstill. Nor were matters eased by the behavior of some of the *seigneurs*, whom Chief Justice Hey accused of giving "very just offense as well to their own people as to the English merchants." [12] Predictably, recruitments lagged. "The disinclination of the lower class of Canadians to engage in so odious a service . . . completely spoiled the project," Francis Masères said.[13] By early February, Carleton had acknowledged that the *habitants* "have in a manner emancipated themselves, and it will require Time, and discreet management likewise, to recall them to their ancient Habits of obedience and Discipline." [14] Hey said that the governor had "taken an ill measure of the influence of the seigneurs and Clergy over the lower order of people, whose resentment breaks out in every shape of contempt or detestation of those whom they used to behold with terrour." [15]

Even as the *habitants* responded haltingly to beating orders, nearly 200 English-speaking Canadians signed petitions for the repeal of the Quebec Act. The list included such unswerving loyalists as Alexander Paterson of Montreal and Malcolm Fraser of Murray Bay. Although the petitions were ignored at Whitehall, the fact that they were sent was significant enough. Lieutenant Colonel Henry Caldwell of Quebec, a firm supporter of the Crown and no critic of Parliament, declared that the act had disrupted the life of the province, turning the French against the English. "It is to be hoped, however," he wrote Lord Dartmouth, "that a future system of Politics for America will admit a Change in our Constitution. What Country is more liable to oppression than that ruled by a Governor with the sanction of a Council which he may garble at his pleasure?" He had written words that might have come more plausibly from the Boston agitators he so despised.[16]

The Quebec Act went into effect on the 1st of May. That morning, in Montreal's Place d'Armes, early risers were shocked at what had happened to the bust of King George the Third. His Majesty's face had been blackened, his neck draped with a rosary of potatoes. A mock cross suspended from the rosary carried the scrawl *Voilà le Pape du Canada ou le sot Anglois.* As all of Montreal streamed into the Place d'Armes, charges bred countercharges. An irate *seigneur* grabbed a British merchant by the nose and was knocked senseless in return. Someone who blamed it on the Jews was flattened by a Jewish tradesman. Francis Masères accused unidentified conspirators of stage-managing the incident to cast suspicion on the British merchants. Rewards were posted for the arrest of the perpetrators, but no one was caught and the city seethed.

The Quebec Act enabled non-English people to become part of the empire without losing their identity, their religion, or their voice in government — a historic achievement, greatly to Carleton's credit. But it alienated the English-speaking merchants, most of whom could have been placated had the governor heeded Lord Dartmouth's instructions to permit habeas corpus and a measure of English civil law. Fortunately for him, only a few would contemplate a break with the mother country.

3

In the American colonies political leaders, ministers of the Gospel, and plain citizens inveighed against the Quebec Act, bracketing it with a series of punitive measures imposed during a showdown with Britain over taxes and duties decreed by Parliament without the colonists' consent. In themselves, the levies were neither exorbitant nor unreasonable. What irked the colonists was their being denied a voice in the tax-levying process: taxation without representation, a mounting issue even though duties were eventually removed from everything but tea. When a throng of patriots donned Indian war paint and dumped the contents of three British tea ships into Boston Harbor, Parliament retaliated. The port of Boston was closed, the provincial charter was annulled, town meetings were forbidden except for the election of officers. Parliament authorized the quartering of British troops in the city and permitted soldiers and Crown officials charged with murder to stand trial in England or another colony rather than face local juries. The colonists dubbed these measures the Intolerable Acts and ranked the Quebec Act with them, although its intent had been not to punish the colonies, but to win the support of French Canada. Indeed, its authors had stated specifically that "nothing herein contained relative to the boundary of the Province of Quebec shall in any wise affect the boundaries of any other colonies."

Nevertheless, there was hardly an American colony that was not incensed by the Quebec Act. Several took issue with the designation of the western hinterland as a monopoly of the Canadian fur trade. Land speculators and homesteaders would no more tolerate being pinned against the Atlantic seaboard than Boston patriots would tolerate a tax on tea. While the Quebec Bill was still under debate, the first pioneers were filtering across the Alleghenies. Others followed in a stream that would swell to 25,000 before the Revolution ended. They were the vanguard of an army of homesteaders that no act of Parliament could halt and that would one day wrest all the western lands from the fur trade and its Indian dependents.

New England was less concerned with the stirrings of expansionism than with defending its own frontiers against another descent by French and Indian war parties. Memories were still fresh of the bloody raids that had terrorized the back country throughout the long contest with France — of war whoops assaulting the stillness of night, of villages aflame, of tomahawk and scalping knife, of Indian captivities. Only yesterday, men had gone to the fields in armed companies, guns had been stacked in church to be grabbed up on the instant, and the parson had held forth with a musket beside him in the pulpit. In more remote villages in Massachusetts and New Hampshire, many still mourned lost friends and brothers, and some nursed memories of their own children finished off with the tomahawk. Moreover, with an alien Church on the north and an Indian reserve on the west, New Englanders wondered if a government without an assembly and without trial by jury or habeas corpus was a portent of what Britain had in mind for all her colonies, and if a hierarchical Church given privileged status by Parliament would one day seek to snuff out their own stubbornly held Protestantism.

Early in September, a gathering of delegates from the towns in Suffolk County, Massachusetts, met under the leadership of Dr. Joseph Warren to pass a series of resolves relative to the Intolerable Acts. Among their targets was the Quebec Act, which they considered a threat to "the protestant religion and . . . the civil rights and liberties of all America." They deplored the establishment of Roman Catholicism in Canada, the denial of trial by jury and habeas corpus. Their resolves were endorsed by the Continental Congress, which accused Parliament of creating a "tyranny" in Canada, "to the great danger, from so total a dissimilarity of Religion, Law and government, of the neighbouring British colonies." [17] A few days later, Congress put an embargo on trade with Britain.

The religious issue was foremost in people's thinking. Virginia warned of a French and Indian attack motivated by religious fanaticism, South Carolina of a war between French Catholics and English Protestants, Georgia of a plot by the king's ministers to browbeat his "ancient, Protestant and loyal subjects." [18] New England meetinghouses rocked with fulminations against the Quebec Act and the

Catholic Church. Although the Protestant clergy had lost much of their earlier clout, their influence was still formidable. The Pope was villified as "a false prophet," the Church as the "great whore of Babylon." One divine warned of "the flood of the dragon that has poured forth to the northward in the Quebec Bill for the establishment of popery." Another — the Reverend Samuel Langdon, President of Harvard College — blamed the act on the "popish schemes of men who would gladly restore the Stuarts and inaugurate a new era of despotism." [19]

Nor were New England laity any less agitated. In a paper on canon and feudal law, John Adams had described Catholicism as "the greatest system of tyranny devised since the promulgation of Christianity." [20] One day in Philadelphia he was led by "curiosity" to venture inside a "Romish chapel," where he observed "the poor wretches fingering their beads, chanting Latin not a word of which they understood," and concluded that the spectacle had "everything which can charm and bewitch the simple and ignorant." So insidious seemed its hold on "eye, ear and imagination" that this stalwart Puritan marveled that Martin Luther "ever broke the spell." [21] When word of the Quebec Act reached Boston, Abigail Adams wrote her husband that "all the church people here have hung their heads and will not converse upon politicks, tho ever so much provoked by the opposite party." [22] Agitators bent on a break with England warned that dark schemes were afoot to deprive the colonists of their cherished Protestantism. It was too much for General Gage, who wrote Lord Dartmouth that "the Quebec Bill has been made use of to persuade them that their religion is to be changed and they cannot be made to believe to the contrary." [23]

Leaders outside New England expressed similar fears. "Does not your blood run cold," wrote Alexander Hamilton, "to think an English Parliament should pass an act for the establishment of arbitrary power and popery in such an extensive country? If they had had any regard to the freedom and happiness of mankind, they would never have done it. If they had been friends to the protestant cause, they would never have provided such a nursery for its great enemy." Hamilton predicted that the "nursery" would attract "none but papists" and would one day teem with "droves of emigrants from all the Roman Catholic states in Europe." He warned against "the deceitful wiles of those who would persuade us that we have nothing to fear from the operation of the Quebec Act." [24]

John Jay was even more indignant. One of a committee assigned to prepare an Address to the People of Great Britain, he could not contain his distaste for the Quebec Act. When the first draft of the address, written by another member, proved too tepid, Jay submitted one of his own composition. Although eloquent in his defense of the colonists' rights, he denounced the British government for making peace with "a religion that has deluged your island in blood, and dispersed impiety, persecution, murder and rebellion through every part of the World." [25] That freedom of religion had been safeguarded in the Quebec Act seems to have found no favor either with Jay or with the Continental Congress, which approved what he had written.

At the same time, an Address to the Inhabitants of the Province of Quebec was drawn up by a committee composed of John Dickinson, Thomas Cushing, and Richard Henry Lee. It was written by Dickinson, a Quaker and political moderate who still hoped for a reconciliation with the mother country. After reminding the Canadians that the Quebec Act denied them trial by jury, habeas corpus, and an elected assembly, he warned that an arbitrary governor and council might at any time recruit them for an invasion of the colonies, "taking that freedom from *us* which they have treacherously denied to *you*." Quoting from "the immortal Montesquieu" and citing the example of the Swiss cantons, where Roman Catholics and Protestants were "living in the utmost concord and peace with one another," he pictured a similar accommodation in the New World as the American colonies and Canada, exposed to "the transcendent nature of freedom," surmounted "such low-minded infirmities" as religious fanaticism and intolerance. He called on the Canadians to send delegates to Congress, advising them not to forget that they were "a small people compared to those who with open arms invite you into a fellowship" and that "a moment's reflection should convince you which will be most for your interest and happiness, to have all the rest of North America your inalterable friends, or your inveterate enemies." [26] Congress, in giving its ap-

proval to what both Jay and Dickinson had written, apparently was
not bothered by the discrepancies. Two thousand copies of the
Address to the Inhabitants of the Province of Quebec were sent to
Thomas Walker, to be circulated throughout the parishes.

The *Quebec Gazette,* the only newspaper in Canada and a mouth-
piece for the government, ignored the address. Nor was the governor perturbed. He knew that most of the *habitants* were illiterate,
that their knowledge of representative government was limited, and
that neither habeas corpus nor trial by jury was part of their tradition. Their familiarity with "the immortal Montesquieu" was mini-
mal, nor could most of them have cared less about church relations
in the Swiss cantons. Although the invitation to send delegates to
the Continental Congress may have flattered some, it baffled many
others.

In putting its imprimatur on what both Jay and Dickinson had
written, Congress yielded Carleton his most telling point. He obtained a copy of Jay's address and ordered it posted side by side
with Dickinson's for all to see — in public squares, in marketplaces,
on church doors. Meetings were called at which both were read,
so that everyone would know that the Church that Dickinson would
accommodate had been accused of murder and treason by John Jay.
The governor had a strong case but, alas, he did not have time to
make his point in every hamlet in the province. Some of the
habitants — more, surely, than he expected — listened to what the
colonists were saying.

That autumn, some merchants sent 1000 bushels of wheat to be-
leaguered Boston, and sympathizers in Montreal made a cash dona-
tion. Both gestures encouraged patriots to seek closer ties with
friends in Canada. In February, the Massachusetts Provincial Congress directed the Boston Committee of Correspondence to arrange
for sending an emissary to Canada. The committee's choice was a
young Pittsfield lawyer named John Brown, who had volunteered
for the assignment. A graduate of Yale and a relative by marriage
of Benedict Arnold's, he had served on the Pittsfield Committee of
Safety and shown himself a zealous patriot. Before Brown left
Boston, Samuel Adams gave him a letter to the Canadians, inviting
them to throw in their lot with the colonies and send delegates to
Congress.[27]

Brown went first to Albany, where he waited two weeks for the spring breakup on Lake Champlain. Early in March, he set forth with two guides — Winthrop Hoyt, who had once been a captive of the Caughnawagas, and Peleg Sunderland, who had connections with the St. François and could speak their language. Both tribes were based near Montreal. Finding parts of the lake frozen, the three travelers had to abandon their boat and continue to Canada on foot. Brown wrote that "a great part of the country for twenty miles each side of the lake" was completely under water. After making long detours around swollen streams and a drowned shoreline, they reached the British outpost of St. Jean, a fort on the Richelieu River marking the outer rim of Montreal's defenses.

In Montreal, Brown was taken in hand by Thomas Walker, who introduced him to a gathering of merchants in a local coffee house. He began by reading them Adams' letter. A motion was made to send two delegates to the Continental Congress, but when Brown conceded that the merchants would have to comply with Congress's trade embargo, the motion lapsed, the meeting became rancorous, and Isaac Todd, a merchant hitherto friendly to the colonies, accused Brown of threatening an invasion of Canada "if a man of them should dare to take up arms and act against the Bostonians." [28]

Other Americans ranged the province in the guise of traders, distributing copies of Dickinson's address and trying to win over susceptible *habitants*. Their activities failed to disturb the governor, who still hoped for a reconciliation with the colonies. He might have shown greater concern had he seen a paragraph at the close of John Brown's secret report to the Boston Committee of Correspondence. Peleg Sunderland, an associate of Ethan Allen's and one of the half-dozen leaders of the Green Mountain Boys, saw that the New Hampshire Grants, which constituted what is now the State of Vermont, would be the first line of defense in case of a British attack from Canada. He and the other Green Mountain Boys were also aware that there was a way to safeguard their frontier and halt an invading army near its Canadian base. As he and Winthrop Hoyt angled their skiff through the ice floes, he must have mentioned this to John Brown and told how it could be brought off.

"One thing I must mention, to be kept a profound secret," Brown wrote the committee. "The Fort at Ticonderoga must be seized as soon as possible, should hostilities be committed by the King's Troops. The people on New Hampshire Grants have engaged to do this business, and, in my opinion, they are the most proper persons for this job. This will effectively curb this Province, and all the troops that may be sent here." [29]

III

Target on the Lake

1

ONE DAY in late April, two Connecticut officers, Colonel Samuel Parsons of New London and Captain Benedict Arnold of New Haven, met on a road near Hartford. Parsons was on a recruiting assignment. Arnold was taking his command, the Governor's 2nd Company of Guards (known as the Footguards), to join the army in Cambridge. As the two conversed, Parsons bemoaned the lack of artillery among the American troops. Arnold reminded him that there were guns to be had at Fort Ticonderoga. Although neither may have mentioned it to the other, each had the same idea. Presently, they parted company and went their ways.

Arnold was thirty-four, short, swarthy, and hard-muscled. Born in Norwich, Connecticut, to a pious mother and alcoholic father, he had won repute as a village daredevil. Once when delivering corn to a gristmill, he had grabbed the mill wheel and traveled with it beneath the churning waters, to emerge triumphantly on the other side. In celebrating a victory during the French and Indian War, his face had been scorched and his hair singed when he rammed a flaming torch down the powder-filled barrel of a cannon on the village green.

After his parents died, Arnold moved to New Haven with his sister Hannah and opened an apothecary shop, where he dealt in books, jewelry, and clocks, spices and teas, as well as pills and potions. Soon he invested in a small fleet of merchantmen, buying horses in Canada and selling them in the West Indies in return for rum, sugar, and molasses. In Quebec City, he became known as a horse trader — a reputation that would one day prompt Carleton to dub him a "horse jockey" when the two confronted each other as commanders of opposing armies. To circumvent Britain's trade and navigation laws, he turned to smuggling, keeping his crews under such tight rein that when an underling was suspected of publicizing his activities, he had him bound to a post and given forty lashes.

Arnold prospered; he married Margaret Mansfield, daughter of the high sheriff, and acquired a house on one of New Haven's most prestigious streets. Margaret, who seems to have been a dutiful and self-effacing wife, bore him three sons. He was often in Canada, where he made friends with Thomas Walker in Montreal and John Dyer Mercier in Quebec. Back home, he became a leader of the more strident patriots, harassing loyalists and urging armed resistance. Among his henchmen were sailors and dockhands, some of the less affluent merchants, and several Yale students. When the Governor's 2nd Company of Guards was formed, he was chosen captain.

On learning of the battle at Lexington and Concord, Arnold rallied his Footguards and demanded powder and shot from the town fathers. His request was refused because, the fathers told him, his application had not been duly authorized. When he threatened to smash down the powderhouse door, they sent Colonel David Wooster to acquaint him with proper protocol. Wooster was highly esteemed in New Haven, a veteran of the French and Indian War, now sixty-four years old and of venerable mien, but Arnold was unimpressed. He told Wooster that none but Almighty God would deny him the ammunition. Wooster retreated to where the town fathers had gathered. After a short interval, the keys to the powderhouse were handed over.

No one could fail to see the iron in Arnold's makeup. Already he gave promise of becoming a noteworthy field officer, capable of rousing men to surmount danger and great hardship. But he had drives that troubled those who knew him — towering pride, unchecked ambition, an impatience with human foibles. He bore scars from a war with private demons that left him short-tempered and combative — an enigma even to his sister Hannah, who knew him best.

In Cambridge, Arnold sought out Joseph Warren, who introduced him to the Committee of Correspondence. Taking note of the dearth of artillery in the patriot army, he reminded Warren and his colleagues that there were guns to be had at Fort Ticonderoga, and offered to go after them if the committee would issue him a Massachusetts commission and supply him with horses, ammunition, and cash. The committeemen took to the proposal, appointing him a colonel in the Massachusetts militia and authorizing him to recruit 400 men in western New England. When he left Cambridge, still in the scarlet coat and white breeches of the Footguards and attended by a valet, he assumed that he had the field to himself. At Stockbridge, however, he learned that others had had the same idea.

On reaching Hartford, Colonel Parsons had assembled several trustworthy associates and told them of his conversation with Arnold. All favored an attempt on Fort Ticonderoga. Heman Allen, Ethan's brother and a Connecticut resident, was hustled off to Bennington to enlist the Green Mountain Boys. Withdrawing £300 from the colonial treasury, Parsons and his friends assigned command of the expedition to Captain Edward Mott, also of Connecticut, and dispatched two of their number, Noah Phelps and Bernard Romans, to drum up recruits in central and western Connecticut. By the time Mott reached the Berkshires, he had a task force of sixteen men. In Pittsfield he was joined by James Easton, an innkeeper and militia captain, and by the ubiquitous John Brown. He picked up thirty-nine additional recruits in Jericho and Williamstown before crossing into the New Hampshire Grants and conferring with Ethan Allen and his colleagues at the Catamount Tavern in Bennington. Ethan needed no persuasion. He agreed to call out the Green Mountain Boys and rendezvous at Castleton.

The name of Ethan Allen was written large in the chronicles of the New Hampshire Grants. He had come from the hill country of western Connecticut and, having raised a little army of frontiers-men, had held off the New York speculators, surveyors, and sheriffs laying claim to land occupied by settlers whose titles were issued by the governor of New Hampshire. The contest had continued for several years, with much name-calling, some bloodshed, but no fatalities, and Ethan had finally won it by dint of sheer cunning and a towering audacity. He was uncouth, irreverent, impudent, with a flamboyance that delighted his homespun followers but incensed New Yorkers.

Ethan had chosen his lieutenants wisely. Foremost was Seth Warner, also from Connecticut. He was tall for those times and hard and supple as hickory. Shy by nature and short on words, he possessed a gentleness that even the Green Mountain Boys learned to respect. He was the antithesis of Ethan, and most men liked him better. Next in line was Remember Baker, cousin to both Ethan and Seth, who had left Connecticut to fight in the French and Indian War and had moved to the Grants when the war was over. He was towheaded and freckled, and was one of Ethan's more irrepressible cohorts. Close behind him in the hierarchy were Robert Cochran, Gideon Warren, and the same Peleg Sunderland who had guided John Brown to Montreal.

On May 7, 130 Green Mountain Boys gathered in Castleton, armed with firelocks, pistols, swords, and clubs. Only Ethan was in uniform, sporting yellow breeches and a green jacket embellished with gold epaulets. The others wore homespun or buckskins. Many had been alerted by a Rutland blacksmith named Gershom Beach, who was said to have traveled sixty miles on foot to ferret them out. As they milled through Castleton brandishing their assorted weapons, Ethan informed them that Noah Phelps had crossed the lake, entered the fort on the pretext of seeking a shave, and found that no one in the garrison had the slightest idea of what was brewing.

Captain Mott was chosen chairman of the War Committee, and, to no one's surprise, Ethan was named field commander. Hand's Cove, a secluded inlet on Lake Champlain, was designated the point of embarkation. Captain Samuel Herrick of Bennington was detached with thirty men to seize a schooner belonging to Philip

Skene, a loyalist living at the head of the lake, and Captain Asa Douglas was sent to the west shore to locate small craft for ferrying the troops. With this nod to logistics, Ethan left for Hand's Cove. Captain Mott and the War Committee were about to follow when Benedict Arnold, resplendent in his Footguards' uniform and attended by his valet, arrived to lay claim to the command. Mott told him that the men wished to serve under their own officers and would not take kindly to a stranger.[1] Next day at Hand's Cove, Arnold showed his Massachusetts commission to Ethan. Surprisingly, Ethan wavered, uneasy perhaps about his own credentials, but his troops declared that unless he remained their leader, they would shoulder their muskets and go home. Ethan offered to allow Arnold to march beside him but give no orders. Arnold agreed, no doubt grudgingly.

Midnight passed without a sign of a boat. Ethan was about to postpone the crossing when a scow took shape offshore, manned by two teen-age boys. The pair had overheard Captain Douglas discussing his need for boats and remembered that one of Philip Skene's scows was anchored in the neighborhood. By inveigling a crewman to take them to Hand's Cove on a fictitious hunting trip, they succeeded in delivering the scow to Ethan and his troops. Presently, Douglas brought in a second craft. Together, they would accommodate only about a third of Ethan's command, but he could wait no longer. Eighty-three men were ferried to the New York shore. The rest remained at Hand's Cove with Seth Warner.

Both forts were undermanned — two officers and forty-two rank and file at Ticonderoga, a sergeant and eight men at Crown Point. Carleton had reinforced the Ticonderoga garrison with thirty-six regulars, but half the men were "old, wore out and unserviceable" according to one of their officers, Lieutenant Jocelyn Feltham.[2] There were also two dozen women and children at the fort, dependents of personnel. The commandant, Captain William Delaplace, was described as a placid sort who spent much of his time in his garden. Carleton had called Gage's attention to the sorry condition of both forts, but nothing had been done to update them. The walls of Fort Ticonderoga were breached, the barracks crumbling and springing leaks. The Crown Point bastion, which Lord Jeffrey

Amherst had built fifteen years before, had been gutted by fire and was now choked with rubble. But no matter how undermanned and dilapidated both forts might have been, they possessed artillery and men trained to use it. To take them with nothing but small arms, as Ethan proposed to do, would require nerve and no small degree of luck.

By early dawn, Ethan, with Arnold on his left, led his men through an unguarded breach in the south curtain wall and crossed to a wicket gate that opened into the fort. A sentry spied them and snapped his fusee. Happily, the gun misfired, and the sentry fled down the hallway and took cover in a bombproof. As the men flooded into the parade and let forth three mighty whoops, Ethan downed a second sentry with the flat of his sword, sparing him on condition that he divulge the whereabouts of the commandant. Thoroughly cowed, the man indicated a stairway to the second floor of the western barracks.

With Arnold beside him, Ethan mounted the stairway and in the plain English of a Green Mountain Boy ordered the commandant to present himself. A door inched open, and Lieutenant Feltham, wearing vest and jacket but not his breeches, which he held over one arm, inquired with noteworthy aplomb by whose authority Ethan had invaded the fort. Ethan is reputed to have said "In the name of the Great Jehovah and the Continental Congress!" Feltham played for time, asking more questions in the hope that his men might yet redeem themselves, but Ethan was short of patience. Suspecting by now that Feltham was merely a subordinate, he was about to go in quest of the real commandant when Captain Delaplace, properly attired, came forth to present his sword and order his garrison to ground arms. In no more than ten minutes, and without loss of life or limb, Fort Ticonderoga had been taken.

Later that morning, Seth Warner and the rest of the troops were ferried from Hand's Cove, arriving at the height of what would become a legendary debauch. Ethan had discovered ninety gallons of rum and was distributing it to all and sundry, including several Indians and local residents who had come to share in the festivities. In his own words, "The sun seemed to rise that morning with a superior lustre, and Ticonderoga and its dependencies smiled on its conquerors, who tossed about the flowing bowl, and wished success to Congress, and the liberty and freedom of America." ³ Only Benedict Arnold, who had a more refined sense of military etiquette, frowned on the goings-on, but his efforts to curb them induced some of the more obstreperous celebrants to fire several potshots in his direction. Before the festivities waned, he had found the company of the captured British officers more to his liking than that of his own countrymen. To strip him of all semblance of authority, past or present, and to regularize Ethan's credentials, Captain Mott prepared an ex post facto commission authorizing Ethan to "take possession of Ticonderoga and its dependencies" and to be in sole command until instructions were forthcoming from the Continental Congress or the Province of Connecticut.⁴

Seth Warner and Peleg Sunderland were ordered to occupy Crown Point with a small detachment. En route, they met Remember Baker, who was crossing from the eastern shore too late to join in the celebration but was towing two bateaux that he had intercepted on their way to alert the enemy at St. Jean. Crown Point's token garrison speedily surrendered, turning over artillery that would one day help drive the British out of Boston. Ethan and his men were now in possession of the entire defense system on the lakes. They were given a further assist when Captain Herrick arrived with Philip Skene's schooner, skippered by a young New Haven Footguard, Eleazer Oswald, who was an associate of Arnold's and who had joined Herrick with fifty men. Although too late to ferry troops from Hand's Cove, the schooner was admirably suited to a new venture made to order for Arnold.

Ethan and the War Committee had learned that a British sloop rode at anchor at St. Jean, twenty miles down the Richelieu in Canada. As long as she flew the king's colors, she could dispute their hold on Lake Champlain. They agreed that a detachment aboard Skene's schooner must be sent to Canada to seize her — a violation of the frontier, to be sure, but no deterrent to men who had already taken Fort Ticonderoga. Few in their command, however, knew how to handle a schooner. The Green Mountain Boys were landlubbers to a man. Nor had most of the Massachusetts and Connecticut recruits any acquaintance with wind and water. The one bona fide sailor in the lot was Benedict Arnold, who, as a shipowner, had sailed the seas and handled heavy craft. The command was his by default.

Christening the schooner *Liberty* and fitting her out with carriage and swivel guns, Arnold set sail with a crew of fifty and two spare bateaux. The next day, Ethan Allen, not to be outdone, followed with nearly 100 Green Mountain Boys in four bateaux — but without provisions enough for all his men. Beating upwind, *Liberty* stood off Split Rock at nightfall. The next day brought her within thirty miles of St. Jean, where a calm required Arnold to take to the bateaux with a task force of thirty-five. Hiding his boats in an inlet, he caught the garrison off guard, made prisoners of a dozen or so British regulars, seized the sloop, and destroyed nine smaller craft, so that there was not "a single bateau for the King's Troops, Canadians or Indians to cross the Lake in." [5] When he had left, one Moses Hazen, an American living in St. Jean, hurried to Montreal to alert the high command.*

On the upper Richelieu, Arnold met Ethan and the Green Mountain Boys, weak with hunger and bone-weary after rowing long hours in a calm. The sight of the captured sloop was too much for Ethan. As he dined with Arnold, toasting "loyal Congress healths," he declared that he would continue to St. Jean and not return home empty-handed. Arnold supplied him with provisions, but he thought the plan "a wild, impracticable scheme" and considered Ethan and his men "100 mad fellows." [6]

Near St. Jean, Ethan was met by Joseph Bindon, a friend of the colonies, who warned him that a detachment of redcoats was on its way from Montreal. For an instant, Ethan considered waiting in ambush for the enemy, but on second thought he crossed the Richelieu and bivouacked. At daybreak he was roused by the rattle of grapeshot. Lined up on the opposite shore were 200 British regulars under the command of Major Charles Preston of the 26th. Ethan herded his men into the bateaux and shoved off, leaving behind three who were slow of foot. By dint of strong rowing he

---

* Hazen had been a ranger in the French and Indian War and was wounded in the battle of Ste. Foye in 1760.

pulled swiftly out of musket range, but his reputation was so tarnished that even the glory of having captured Fort Ticonderoga lost some of its luster.

2

John Brown carried the news to Congress, but not all the delegates took kindly to what he told them. After hearing him out, Congress ordered the captured ordnance safeguarded at Fort George, from where it could be returned "when the restoration of the former harmony between Great Britain and these colonies so ardently wished for by the latter shall render it prudent and consistent with the overruling law of self-preservation." [7] This met with a storm of protest. Ethan Allen warned that several thousand settlers in the New Hampshire Grants had been placed in great jeopardy. Benedict Arnold said that 500 frontier families were now at the mercy of the enemy.[8] New Hampshire and Massachusetts deplored Congress's action, and when the Connecticut Assembly, at the request of New York, sent troops to garrison the forts, it instructed the commander, Colonel Benjamin Hinman, to "keep those important posts." [9] Congress soon had a change of heart. The forts were not disarmed, nor was there further talk of returning the ordnance to the Crown.

Allen and Arnold now called for an invasion of Canada. Ethan sent a delegation of Stockbridge Indians across the border to invite Canadian tribesmen to help "fight the King's troops." [10] "Should the colonies forthwith send an army of two or three thousand men and attack Montreal," he wrote Congress, "we should have little to fear from the Canadians and Indians and would easily make a conquest of that place, and set up a standard of liberty in the extensive Province of Quebeck, whose limit was enlarged to subvert the liberties of America." [11] Arnold submitted plans that would pit 1700 men against the king's troops at St. Jean, Chambly, and Montreal, with a reserve of 300 to keep watch on the supply lines. He volunteered to command the expedition himself.[12]

Arnold's proposal was regarded favorably by some in Congress, but his bid for the command gained scant support. Two who would become his implacable enemies, John Brown and James Easton, had been discrediting him with Congress and the Massachusetts legislature. Brown, a relative by marriage, seems to have nursed a family grudge. Easton, whom Arnold despised, sided with his fellow townsman. In Philadelphia, Brown had downgraded Arnold's part in the capture of the forts. Reporting to the Massachusetts Congress, Easton had given the credit to Ethan Allen and himself without mention of Arnold. A widely circulated rebuttal, carrying the pseudonym "Veritas" and presumably originating with Arnold, branded Easton a liar and accused him of hiding in a shed at the time of the early morning attack.[13]

Nor did the matter end with name-calling. After the St. Jean fiasco, Ethan Allen promised to relinquish the command, but while Arnold was absent on a reconnoiter, he reversed himself. When Arnold returned, he had a heated exchange with Ethan and his followers, during the course of which he challenged Easton to a duel. When his challenge was sidestepped, he proceeded to kick Easton around the room in the presence of fellow officers, none of whom was tempted to intervene. Only when a committee from Massachusetts came to Ticonderoga with orders to place Arnold under Colonel Hinman and, if necessary, relieve him of his duties, did he relinquish his claim to the command. Nor had his humiliation ended. After he tendered his resignation, his troops were assigned to Brown and Easton.

Arnold took leave of his associates with few farewells. While tarrying in Albany to prepare his report to Congress, he learned that his wife, Margaret, had died and that he was needed by his sister Hannah and his three small sons. He left for home griefstricken and embittered, but there were those at Ticonderoga who rallied to his support. A complaint signed by several local residents charged that his enemies' "envy or self-interested views" had led them to "misrepresent his conduct and give a blamable aspect to actions which, when fairly examined, will be found to merit the highest approbation of his constituents and the publick."[14] And Barnabas Deane of Connecticut, on hand during the dispute, wrote to his brother Silas: "Colonel Arnold has been greatly abused and misrepresented by designing persons, some of which were from Connecticut. Had it not been for him everything here would have been in the utmost confusion and disorder; people would have been plundered of their private property, and no man's person would be safe that was not of the Green Mountain party." [15]

Nor did Ethan fare much better. He had gone to Philadelphia with Seth Warner to ask Congress to incorporate the Green Mountain Boys as a regular unit in the Continental Army. When Congress acceded to his request, he drew up a list of officers with himself at their head, but, alas, the choice was not his to make. It was the prerogative of the committees of safety in the towns on the west side of the mountains in the New Hampshire Grants. When they met in early summer, they showed an independence that he had not anticipated. Jealous of their right to name whomever they wished, and probably irked by Ethan's meddling, they chose Seth Warner to command the Green Mountain Boys and gave Ethan no rank whatever.

Ethan blamed the outcome on the seniority of "the old farmers" who made up the committees of safety. He was probably right. They were set enough in their ways to want a regimental commander with whom they could be comfortable. Ethan had done well by them in their quarrel with the Province of New York, and he had shone at Fort Ticonderoga, but there were disturbing things about him — his glory-hunting, his penchant for taking chances, his impatience with authority, his habit of tilting with time-honored traditions like man's belief in God. Warner, by contrast, was steady. He bridled his emotions. He was deliberate and soft-spoken, slow to get excited, sensibly low key, sparing with words — qualities that were understood and admired in the Grants. The farmers who gathered in Dorset chose one of their own kind, but their action failed to cool Ethan's patriotism and ardor. Shrugging off what had happened, he offered his services to the army, not as the field officer he had hoped to be, but as an unattached volunteer. There was nothing small about him.

Congress chose Philip Schuyler to head the Northern Department of the Continental Army. Unlike Allen and Arnold, he had not called for an invasion of Canada, nor had he sought the command.

Scion of an old Dutch family that had molded much of New York's early history, he was Albany's foremost citizen and he looked it, with a mane of auburn hair accenting unmistakably patrician features. His taste in clothes was impeccable, and at his town house on the edge of Albany he was host to some of the colony's most festive gatherings. He had married Catherine van Rensselaer, also of genteel antecedents, thereby uniting two of the Hudson Valley's more imposing manorial families. She bore him fourteen children, eight of whom survived childhood.

At the beginning of the Revolution, Schuyler was identified with the moderates, who nursed a hope that Britain and the colonies might resolve their differences. But if he was slow to recognize the dimensions of the quarrel, he was never in doubt that Britain's tyranny had to be resisted. After the bloodshed at Lexington and Concord, he asked a friend who was leaving for England to impress on everyone he met that the colonists would stop at nothing in the defense of their rights. He was forty-two when Congress commissioned him a major general. His gifts were essentially administrative, and he would prove to be better at supplying an army than leading it in battle; he lacked the flair for leadership that made Arnold a born field officer and because of chronic gout and asthma was in no shape for a bruising military campaign. Moreover, as a New Yorker he was suspect in New England, especially in the New Hampshire Grants, where distrust of New York could reach monumental heights.

Many in Congress had come to feel that the colonies should invade Canada for their own protection. Whereas in May they had had qualms about using the guns taken at Fort Ticonderoga, a growing number of delegates now inclined toward an invasion of Canada as the only way to prevent a southward thrust by British troops. The change was a measure of the swift course the Revolution was taking. Samuel Adams believed that an invasion was imperative, to deny Britain access to Lake Champlain.[16] John Adams wrote a colleague: "Whether we should march into Canada with an Army Sufficient to break the Power of Governor Carleton, to overawe the Indians, and to protect the French, has been the great Question. It seems to be the general Conclusion that it is best to go, if we can be assured that the Canadians will be pleased with it and join." [17] Growing numbers of delegates favored taking the initiative, to forestall an advance down the Hudson Valley that would split the colonies and isolate New England.

The Canadians were courted assiduously. Ethan Allen and Benedict Arnold suspended their quarrel long enough to sign a joint appeal advising them to "let old England and the Colonies fight it out" and to "stand by and see what our arm of flesh can do." [18] The New York Provincial Congress assured them that the raid on St. Jean had been a precautionary measure to "prevent hostile incursions upon us by the Troops in your Province." [19] General Schuyler urged Colonel Hinman, the commandant at Fort Ticonderoga, to "take every opportunity of giving the Canadians and Indians the strongest assurances of our friendly sentiments towards them; and if they should unfortunately have entertained any that are unfavourable from Mr. Allen's excursion into their country, try and eradicate them by assurances that what he did was without any orders." [20] Late in May, Congress sent a letter to "the oppressed inhabitants of Canada," composed by none other than John Jay. This time he professed concern for the Church's welfare, warning Canadians that their clergy were "exposed to expulsion, banishment and ruin" under Carleton's arbitrary government and that they themselves could be sent to war by "an avaricious governor and rapacious council." [21]

Reports from Canada were encouraging. American agents were well received in the parishes. Carleton wrote Lord Dartmouth that the *habitants* were being "poisoned by the same Hypocrisy and Lies practiced with so much Success in the other Provinces, which their Emissaries and Friends here have spread abroad with great Art and Diligence." [22] Thomas Walker assured his friends in Massachusetts that "the bulk of the people, both English and Canadians . . . wish well to your cause" and that "few in this colony dare vent their griefs but groan in silence and dream of lettres de cachet, confiscations, and imprisonments, offering up their fervent prayers to the throne of grace, to prosper your righteous cause, which alone will free us from those jealous fears and apprehensions that rob us of our peace." [23]

On June 27, Congress acted. General Schuyler was instructed to repair to Fort Ticonderoga and, after sounding out the Canadians and Indians, seize all enemy craft on Lake Champlain and, should it "not be disagreeable to the Canadians," take St. Jean, Montreal, and any other posts whose capture might "promote the peace and security of these colonies." [24] Schuyler had neither the troops nor the supplies to act speedily. Returns submitted by his officers showed that he had only 1352 men. He had to build and equip an army before he could penetrate a country shielded by long miles of lake and forest, and he had to win allies in Canada. Before leaving for Ticonderoga, he shared some of his thoughts with David Wooster, now a brigadier general in the Continental Army:

America has recourse to arms merely for her safety and defence, and in resisting oppression she will not oppress [Schuyler wrote]. She wages no war of ambition, content if she can only retain the fair inheritance of English law and English liberty. Such being the purity of her intentions, no stain must be suffered to disgrace her arms. We are soldiers ambitious only to aid in restoring the violated rights of citizens, and these secured, we are to return instantly to the business and employments of civilized life... Let us act as becomes the virtuous citizen, who seeks for the aid of righteous heaven and the just applause of an impartial world. Liberty, Safety and Peace are our objects — the establishment of the Constitution and not the lust of dominion... These are principles I wish deeply implanted in the heart of every soldier I have the honor to command. They will lead us to glory — they will merit the esteem of our countrymen.[25]

Not all who enrolled in Schuyler's army shared his idealism. He was indeed "the virtuous citizen" who had relinquished, most reluctantly, "the business and employments of civilized life."

3

Although the colonists lived in dread of an attack from Canada, Guy Carleton was so short of men that he had only about 600 regulars to defend the entire St. Lawrence Valley. Even his strongholds invited attack. His engineer, Captain John Marr, found the defenses at Quebec in a state of advanced neglect: the counterscarp could easily be breached, the battlements were short of functioning ordnance. The wall at Montreal was tumbling down; St. Jean was weakly fortified; Chambly was vulnerable to light artillery. Ordered to strengthen St. Jean, Marr built two sod redoubts to enclose a stone house and barracks block, linked the redoubts with a palisaded communications line, and, where the fort did not front on the Richelieu, shielded it with a moat and picket stockade.

Major Charles Preston was assigned to St. Jean with 474 rank and file from the 7th and 26th, thirty-eight cannoneers from the Royal Artillery, ninety French volunteers, a regiment of Royal Highland Emigrants raised among loyal Scots in the province, and, for scouting purposes, an Indian detail led by François Thomas Verneuil de Lorimier, a veteran of the French and Indian War, and Gilbert Tice, an officer of the Indian Department. Captain William Hunter of brigantine *Gaspé* was given orders to build a schooner and a row-galley for service on Lake Champlain. Chambly, designated as a supply base, was assigned to Major Joseph Stopford, with part of the 7th Foot and half a dozen artillerymen. Carleton kept fewer than 100 regulars in Montreal. To guard the approaches to the province he stationed twenty-four regulars on the Chaudière south of Quebec, thirty-two near the mouth of the St. François, thirteen at Lachine Rapids west of Montreal, and another contingent still farther west at Oswegatchie.

"The consternation in the Towns and Country was great and universal," Carleton wrote Lord Dartmouth. "Every Individual seemed to feel our present impotent situation, for tho' in no Danger of internal Commotions, we are equally unprepared for Attack or Defense; not six hundred Rank & File fit for duty upon the whole Extent of this great River, not an armed Vessel, no place of Strength..."[26] He bemoaned the failure of the *habitants* to join their *seigneurs* at St. Jean. "The little Force we have in the Province was immediately set in motion, and ordered to assemble at or near St. John's," he wrote. "The noblesse of this neighbourhood were called upon to collect their Inhabitants, in order to defend themselves, the Savages of those Parts likewise had the same orders;

but tho' the gentlemen testified great zeal, neither their Entreaties nor their Example could prevail upon the People." [27]

With most of his regulars assigned to the forts, Carleton had to depend on citizen soldiers for the defense of Montreal and Quebec. On July 9, he proclaimed martial law, calling out the militia and accusing the Americans of "invading this province with arms in a traitorous and hostile manner." [28] But enlistments lagged. The *habitants*, already angered by his failure to name men from their own ranks as militia captains, were further incensed when three of his appointees staffed their commands with friends and relatives, all members of the *noblesse*. Many *habitants* openly defied their *seigneurs* and even took issue with their priests.

When the young Sieur de La Corne struck a family retainer for refusing to enlist and then threatened to bring his *habitants* to heel with a corps of British regulars, between 300 and 400 angry Canadians assembled near Terrebonne, prepared to resist the king's troops with guns and pitchforks. Only the intervention of one of Carleton's aides could persuade them to put aside their weapons. [29] The *habitants* at St. Cuthbert, furious over their *seigneur*'s order to enroll a whole company of militia instead of their rightful quota of fifteen, took an oath never to bear arms against the colonists. [30] Two members of the *noblesse*, Charles de Lanaudière and Godefroi de Tonnancourt, were halted near Berthier with a squad of recruits and held captive until the village *curé* could arrange for their release. [31]

The dispute divided congregations, turned laity against clergy, and called forth many stern rebukes from Church officials. Abbé Etienne Montgolfier, Vicar General of Montreal, deprived two recalcitrant congregations of their clergy, only to rescind his order when the faithful rang the church bells and threatened to conduct services themselves. [32] While prayers were being offered for the king's troops at a church in Trois Rivières, part of the congregation was suspected of praying secretly for the colonists. [33] In several parishes militia captains appointed by the governor were refused recognition, and on Ile d'Orléans blood was nearly shed when opponents of recruitment would have kidnaped three of Carleton's agents had not the bishop coadjutor, Monseigneur Louis-Philippe d'Esgly, personally intervened. Prompted by the governor, Bishop Briand urged his flock to "bear with joy all that which will be commanded of you by a charitable Governor who has nothing but your interests and happiness at heart" [34] — only to find his call to arms lampooned in an irreverent bit of doggerel:

> *At his command to engage in this crusade,*
> *Let us take arms, my dear friends.*
> *A march to Boston is but a pleasant walk,*
> *And these rebels will soon be subdued . . .*
> *Let us then, my friends, like true and obedient sons*
> *of the Church, begin our march,*
> *And cheerfully go and get our throats cut.*[35]

By no means all the *habitants* took issue with their bishop and the governor. Although the great majority chose to remain neutral, some offered their services to the Crown. Resistance was greater in the vicinity of Montreal than at Trois Rivières and Quebec, but in all three districts militia companies were enrolled. At Montreal, the governor appointed Dufy-Desauniers colonel, Neveu-Sevestre lieutenant colonel, and Saint-Georges Lecompte Dupré major; and at Quebec, Noël Voyer colonel, Jean Baptiste Dumont lieutenant colonel, and Jean Baptiste Lecompte Dupré major.

If the *habitants* were a disappointment to the governor, he rated some of the British merchants in Montreal such indifferent patriots that he threatened to burn the city and retire to Quebec. Although few could bring themselves to join Thomas Walker's coterie, several declined commissions or declared that they would not enlist until the city was attacked. However, by early July a militia company had been raised. It included some who had not been happy with government policy, such as Isaac Todd, one of the merchants who had met with John Brown on his secret visit, and Alexander Paterson, who had signed a petition for the repeal of the Quebec Act. In Quebec, Lieutenant Colonel Henry Caldwell drilled the British militia to the skirl of bagpipes. He, too, had had his disagreements with the governor, but he would not let them cool his patriotism or deter him from drumming up recruits. Seventeen companies of militia were enrolled at Quebec, eleven of them French. They were issued green coats and buff vests and breeches, part of a consignment intended for the 6000 militiamen whom Carleton had hoped to recruit among the *habitants*. In winter they would change to the Canadian cold-weather attire of leggings, wool caps, and blanket coats.

The governor had a strong right arm in Lieutenant Colonel Allan Maclean, a native of the Isle of Mull, off Scotland's west coast. Most of Maclean's adult life had been spent in the British army. He had campaigned in Holland, been captured by the French, served with the 77th Highlanders in the French and Indian War, and fought in the West Indies until his corps was reduced in 1763 and he had gone on half-pay. At the outbreak of the Revolution, he had proposed organizing the many loyal Scots in the colonies as a unit in His Majesty's army. The king's ministers took to the idea, and he was sent to America to raise the regiment that would be known as His Majesty's 84th, or the Royal Highland Emigrants.

Promising his recruits 200 acres of land free of quit rent for twenty years, Maclean canvassed the Mohawk Valley, sometimes in disguise, and sent recruiting officers as far afield as North Carolina, where there were other loyal Scots. Many answered his call. When he learned that Carleton was in need of troops, he crossed into Canada and raised a second regiment of Scots, some of them former members of Highland regiments that had helped wrest Canada from France. General Gage ordered them attired in the uniform of the Black Watch, a directive that must have warmed their Scottish hearts, but the order was sidetracked and to their chagrin they were issued the green and buff of the Quebec militia. Maclean had stalwart lieutenants in Major John Nairne and Captain Malcolm Fraser, both of whom, after distinguished military service, had been awarded *seigneuries* on the St. Lawrence.

Had he chosen, Carleton could have availed himself of massive Indian support. Colonel Guy Johnson and his cousin Sir John Johnson spoke for the Iroquois Confederacy. Guy was the nephew and Sir John the son of the late Sir William Johnson, who had built a fiefdom on the Mohawk. After his uncle's death, Guy Johnson had become Superintendent of Indian Affairs, assisted by Daniel

Claus, one of Sir William's most trusted retainers, and by Joseph Brant (Thayendanegea, to his fellow tribesmen), a Mohawk whose sister had been Sir William's consort. They maintained close ties with the six tribes of the Confederacy: the Mohawks, Cayugas, and Onondagas, the Senecas, Oneidas, and the Tuscaroras, who had joined the Confederacy in 1712. But Guy Johnson's hold was weakening. Harassed by local patriots, he turned his home into a fortress. His communications with the tribes were intercepted. Gunpowder he ordered never turned up. He was accused of inciting Indians against whites. By the summer of 1775 he had had enough. Accompanied by Claus and Brant, he left for Montreal with a large contingent of loyalists and Mohawks, tarrying at Oswego to meet with the Hurons and Iroquois and win their pledge not to take up the hatchet against Britain.

Johnson assigned Daniel Claus to confer with the Caughnawagas at their headquarters near Montreal. Claus told the tribesmen that the colonists had made "slaves and servants" of Indians, had taken their lands "in a fraudulent manner," and were now mounting an "unwarrantable and rebellious invasion of Canada, a country not in the least concerned in the dispute." [36] So telling was his presentation that he had to dissuade the Caughnawagas from making an immediate descent on the New England frontiers.

Claus invited the Caughnawagas to a conclave of tribesmen that took place in Montreal on July 26. In a massive show of loyalty, 1664 Indians offered their services to the Crown, but, as Guy Johnson put it, Carleton "did not think it prudent to let them go beyond the 45th degree latitude, or over the Province line." Johnson urged the governor to follow General Gage's advice and make unrestricted use of the Indians, reminding him that they "could not be managed as other people, it being necessary at times to keep up their spirits and encourage them." But Carleton insisted that the Indians stay within the borders of Canada and "be amused in the best manner that could be found." The tribes were thanked for their support, and about forty Indians were assigned to Lorimier for duty at St. Jean. Some of the chiefs warned that, with nothing to do, their people would be plied with liquor and robbed of their belongings by unscrupulous whites. "The ax would cut them if

they continued long without using it," they said.[37] By the middle
of August many Indians had drifted homeward. Late in the fall
Guy Johnson himself lost heart and sailed for England.

Carleton's refusal to make full use of the Indians baffled the
king's ministers and the military. General Gage reminded him that
the colonists did not scruple to enroll Indian recruits. "I would
repay them in their own way," he said.[38] But Carleton would have
none of it. "I would not even suffer a Savage to pass the Frontier,"
he was to explain later, "though often urged to let them loose on
the Rebel Provinces, lest cruelties might have been committed, &
for fear the innocent might have suffered with the Guilty." [39] He
had his own opinion of the indiscriminate slaughter that character-
ized border raids, and neither the king's ministers nor his military
colleagues could change it.

One August day, gunfire erupted close to the New York border.
François de Lorimier, with five Caughnawaga scouts, had spied an
empty boat tied in a clump of alders near the head of the Richelieu. Taking it in tow, he was hailed from shore by a party of
rebels, who laid claim to the boat. When Lorimier demurred, the
rebel leader, a rangy towhead, took cover behind a tree and opened
fire. Lorimier returned the fire, and in the course of a short exchange two of his tribesmen were wounded. When the rebels vanished, he and his Caughnawagas paddled furiously toward St. Jean.

Next morning Lorimier returned with a detail of Indians and
found the rebel leader's body. In his clothing they discovered
papers showing that he had been in correspondence with Thomas
Walker and a Caughnawaga chief. Lorimier pocketed the papers,
and his Indians hacked off the dead man's head. A chance shot had
ended the life of Remember Baker, pre-eminent among the Green
Mountain Boys and now the first casualty of the campaign for
Canada.

When General Schuyler heard what had happened, he sent an
apology to the Iroquois. Baker had been under strict orders not
to fire on the Indians. His exchange with Lorimier's Caughnawagas
could have set off a chain reaction on both sides of the border.
Happily, the Iroquois agreed to "pull the hatchet out of the head
of the deceased, dig up a pine tree, and then throw the hatchet in

the hole" — their way of promising to let the matter drop.[40] But it had been a near thing. Of all the Six Nations, only the Oneidas and Tuscaroras could be counted on as friends. Late in August, Schuyler met with spokesmen for the Iroquois in the old Dutch church in Albany. About 700 tribesmen turned up, attired in laced hats, ruffled shirts, and blankets trimmed with wampum. After a protracted powwow they agreed to "keep the hatchet buried deep." [41]

Schuyler was especially worried about the Canadian tribes, who he heard had "accepted the hatchet offered them by General Carleton," but emissaries to the Caughnawagas and St. François brought back encouraging reports.[42] The delegation of Stockbridge Indians sent to parley with the Caughnawagas returned with a pledge of friendship that Ethan Allen ascribed to his show of force at Fort Ticonderoga and Crown Point. "The thing that so unites the temper of the Indians to us is our taking the sovereignty of Lake Champlain," he said. "They have wit enough to make a good bargain and stand by the strongest side." [43] One Garret Roseboom, an emissary sent out by the Albany Committee of Safety, was told that the Caughnawagas would remain neutral, and James Dean, representing Eleazer Wheelock, founder of Dartmouth College, was given a pledge of neutrality by the St. François, who had sons in the Dartmouth student body. But Dean's report was guarded. "As the fickle disposition of the Indians is so well known," he cautioned, "it will doubtless be judged a prudent measure to provide against the worst." [44]

The colonists' most dependable Indian allies were the Stockbridge of western Massachusetts. Their relations with the white man had been summed up by one of their chiefs in a speech to the Massachusetts Provincial Congress. "Brothers," he said, "you remember when you first came over the great waters, I was great and you was little — very small. I then took you in for a friend and kept you under my arms, so that no one might injure you. Since then we have been friends. There has never been any quarrel between us, but now our conditions are changed. You have become great and tall, you reach to the clouds and you are seeing all around the world, and I am very small, very little, I am not so high as your

heel. Now you take care of me and I look to you for protection."[45]
The Stockbridge volunteered as Minute Men, took part in the siege
of Boston, and served through most of the Revolution. Unlike
General Carleton, the colonists had no qualms about using them.

IIII

"If Job Had Been a General"

1

WHAT HE FOUND at Fort Ticonderoga was enough to daunt even as strong-willed a Dutchman as Philip Schuyler. Colonel Hinman's command was down to 1300 men. Many recruits had gone home, and others threatened to follow unless given a commander of their choice. Orders were openly flouted. The sloop that Arnold had brought in triumph from St. Jean idled at anchor without a crew. The garrison was rife with sectional jealousies that pitted men from one colony against those from another. While Allen and Arnold quarreled, no one had known who was giving orders, and Colonel Hinman seemed to regard himself as a mere caretaker until someone else took over.

Schuyler left Albany in mid-July. Traveling by bateau, he reached the northern tip of Lake George at ten one night. A blockhouse manned by 100 recruits kept watch at the portage to Lake Champlain, but he found everyone asleep except two nodding sentries. "With a penknife only I could have cut off both guards," he wrote Washington, "and then have set fire to the blockhouse, destroyed the stores, and starved the people there." [1]

In Hinman's command Schuyler found the nucleus of an army. He was promised additional Connecticut troops, reinforcements from New York, and a regiment of Green Mountain Boys. Resolved to instill the mettle that would enable his men to stand up to British regulars, he made sentries stay awake, put an end to idleness, forbade drunkenness, encouraged a proper respect for rank, and preached discipline and obedience. He made enemies by the score, alienating most of the New Englanders with his Dutch tenacity and patrician reserve, and was dubbed a martinet, a toplofty Yorker, even an undercover Tory. When he took over the command, he wrote Washington that he would have "an Augean stable to cleanse." [2] Augean it surely was, but he was determined to clean it out.

Schuyler called on Congress for tents, uniforms, guns, flints, provisions, and rum, even for cash to pay his troops. To build a fleet of bateaux for transporting his army, he wooed carpenters from the seacoast with wages that were the envy of his underpaid rank and file. By the end of July, he had his carpenters but was still short of tools, nails, sail cloth and rope, pitch and oakum — everything needed to build boats. He contracted with mills in New York and Pennsylvania for gunpowder, but they could meet only a fraction of his needs. The New York Committee of Safety wrote Congress: "For God's sake send us money, send us arms, send us ammunition ... If Ticonderoga is taken from us fear, which made the savages our friends, will render them our enemies. Ravages on our own frontiers will foster dissensions among us ruinous to our cause." [3]

Supplies were brought by bateau up the Hudson to Fort Edward, then hauled by wagon to waiting bateaux at Lake George or taken to Fort Ann, where they were floated down Wood Creek into the south arm of Lake Champlain. It was a slow business, and there was pilfering by teamsters and bateau crews. As the summer lengthened, provisions became scarce. Moreover, the number of men unfit for duty multiplied until nearly a hundred lay ill in the crowded, verminous barracks. Schuyler persuaded his family physician, Dr. Samuel Stringer, to serve as medical chief. He goaded Congress into setting aside a hospital at Fort George, where the sick could be quarantined and more adequately cared for. But he was deeply discouraged. In early August he unburdened himself to Washington. He had not received promised reinforcements. His men were short of food. He could not get proper returns out of his officers, and he complained that "the people here ... do not know how to obey." [4] By late summer, however, he could see a change. Congress had appropriated $100,000 toward the campaign and would allow him twice that amount to draw on as needed. By working from dawn to dark, with "barely time to eat," his carpenters had turned out two sixty-foot row-galleys and a fleet of bateaux. His supply of gunpowder had grown, although not as swiftly as he would have liked. And the men were beginning to behave like soldiers. [5]

Actually, not a day should have been lost. The enemy were laying the keels of ships that could seize control of Lake Champlain. Friends in Canada were growing impatient, and every lost day increased the likelihood of a winter campaign. More than anyone else, Schuyler was blamed for the delays. Although hot-tempered, he was a patrician unschooled in knocking heads together. Arnold, who knew how to bend men to his will, would have done it differently, routing out incompetents, brooking no idlers. He would not have waited all summer for tents, as Schuyler did, and when the commissary claimed that he could not supply oars because he lacked the funds to pay for them, Arnold would have galloped off to break an oar, if necessary, over the commissary's head. Yet it is doubtful if even a man with Arnold's drive could have done much better. Inevitably, there were delays, costly mistakes, lost opportunities. The colonists, not ready for a war that many thought would last only a few months, were grappling with supply problems that would have taxed the ingenuity of the most practiced commissary.

Late in August, four companies of the 1st New York Regiment reported for duty — the first contingent in four regiments of foot assigned to the campaign. In spite of shortages and spotty enlistments, the province raised, armed, and equipped more than 2000 men during the spring and summer through the efforts of an energetic legislature and a resourceful commissary general, one Peter Curtenius. The ranks of the 1st Regiment, raised in and around New York City, included sailors, artisans, day laborers, and other urban types whose roughshod ways would jolt the sensibilities of farm-bred New Englanders. Farmers and tradesmen predominated in the other three regiments, enrolled throughout the province. Perhaps one in every six were teen-age boys, and there were many blacks.

Although Colonel Alexander MacDougall commanded the 1st New York, his services were required elsewhere, and the regiment was in charge of Lieutenant Colonel Rudolphus Ritzema, who kept a journal of the campaign. The 2nd Regiment was led by Colonel Goose van Schaick, a member of the Albany Committee of Safety; the 3rd by Colonel James Clinton, an organizer of the Ulster Committee of Safety at New Paltz; the 4th by Colonel James Holmes, a Westchester farmer and at one time a delegate to the Provincial Congress. All three were veterans of the French and Indian War. Because of a scarcity of blue wool, only the 1st could be attired in the blue short coat with crimson facing that distinguished New York troops. The 2nd wore light brown faced dark blue; the 3rd, gray faced green; the 4th, brown with scarlet facing or gray faced blue. Officers were identified by a red silk waistband and by a cockade in their tricorns colored to indicate rank. All carried swords, a fusil in a sling, a cartridge pouch on a waist belt, and a sheathed bayonet. Most wore a ruffled shirt with a stock of white linen or black silk. Each private was issued a tricorn, regimental short coat, vest, brown breeches, two shirts, two linen cravats, white wool stockings, and a pair of low shoes. Officers were expected to supply their own apparel, but the province called on patriotic women to outfit the rank and file.

Gunsmiths and powder mills worked overtime to turn out muskets and ammunition. Bounties were offered for privately owned firelocks, new recruits were encouraged to furnish their own weapons, and guns belonging to men invalided home were impressed and redistributed. Eight powder mills were kept busy, prodded by Peter Curtenius and the Provincial Council. The Continental Congress helped when it could, but it also had to supply Washington's army, which was no better situated. Lead was scarce. Some was acquired by melting down window weights, pewter utensils, even fishing sinkers. In spite of heroic efforts, the shortages persisted, and Schuyler's army would cross into Canada low in gunpowder and ammunition.[6]

In mid-August, Schuyler was joined by Brigadier General Richard Montgomery, one of eight brigadiers commissioned that spring. In early middle life, a shade overweight, with thinning brown hair and a complexion pitted by smallpox, he was an adopted New Yorker who had married into a branch of Schuyler's family. Like Carleton, he was an Ulsterman. His father had been a baronet in Donegal, and he had attended Trinity College in Dublin. Recruited at eighteen into the 17th Foot, he had served with Wolfe at Louisburg and with Amherst at the capture of Fort Ticonderoga and Montreal. Advanced to lieutenant at Louisburg and to captain during the campaign for Havana and Martinique, he had seemed destined for preferment. However, shortly before the Revolution he had been passed over for promotion and, selling his commission, had taken passage for New York. His sympathies were with the colonies. He was a friend of Edmund Burke, Charles Fox, and Isaac Barré, and when the Stamp Act was passed he had said that if his regiment was ordered to America to enforce Crown policies, he would resign rather than accompany it. He left home not expecting to return.

In America, Montgomery renewed his friendship with Janet Livingston, daughter of Robert R. Livingston, Hudson Valley squire and staunch patriot, and Margaret Beekman Livingston, whose grandmother was a Schuyler. Montgomery had met Janet during the French and Indian War and was pleased to find her still unattached at the age of thirty. Six months later they were married and moved into a farmhouse near Rhinebeck, New York, while they awaited completion of a more imposing residence on the Hudson. Montgomery was named a delegate to the Provincial Convention, but he soon tired of "long, useless speeches" and let it be known that he would prefer the military.[7] In June 1775, he was appointed brigadier, with instructions to serve as Schuyler's second in command. Janet accompanied him as far as Saratoga, where they were guests at the Schuylers' country house. "You shall never blush for your Montgomery," he told her at their leave-taking. When Schuyler was negotiating with the Iroquois, Montgomery assumed command at the fort. Although he shared his superior's concern over logistical problems and the small number of troops, he hoped to cross into Canada before enemy ships left the stocks. He wrote his father-in-law that even if the campaign failed, it would not be a complete disaster if the Americans retained their hold on Lake Champlain.[8]

While Schuyler was in Albany, he received word from Washington that a parallel thrust was being contemplated by way of the Kennebec and Dead Rivers. The detachment would number between 1000 and 1200 men and would march directly against Quebec. If successful, it should "distract" the enemy, Washington said, and compel General Carleton to "break up and follow this Party to Quebeck, by which he will leave you a free Passage, or . . . suffer that important Place to fall into our hands, an event which would have a decisive Effect and Influence on the Publick Interests." But first the commander-in-chief wanted Schuyler's blessing on the proposal and his assurance that it would not "alarm the Canadians and detach them from that Neutrality which they have hitherto observed."[9] Schuyler gave his wholehearted approval. "Your Excellency will easily conceive that I feel happy to learn your intentions," he wrote, "and only wished that the thought had struck you sooner."[10] Washington chose Benedict Arnold to lead the expedition.

Before leaving for Albany, Schuyler had dispatched John Brown to reconnoiter St. Jean and sound out *habitants* in the vicinity. Brown and his party ranged through the countryside, sleeping in swamps and taking cover in roadside thickets. Twice they were nearly captured — once when they were seen by a suspicious farm boy, again when they escaped through a rear window as an enemy patrol broke into the house where they were hiding.[11] Brown reported a schooner on the ways at St. Jean, pitched and nearly planked. He was told that the *habitants* wanted "nothing more than to see us with an army penetrate their country."[12] His findings were corroborated by James Livingston, a kinsman of Janet Montgomery's who lived near Chambly and who wrote that the *habitants* were awaiting an American advance with "the utmost impatience."[13] Although Schuyler was still in Albany, Montgomery decided to cross the border on his own responsibility and occupy Ile aux Noix, an island in the Richelieu. "I am so much of Brown's

opinion," he wrote Schuyler, "that I think it absolutely necessary
to move down the lake with the utmost dispatch. Should the enemy
get their vessels into the lake 'tis over with us for this summer." [14]
Schuyler was not surprised. He had already written Washington
that his colleague would "probably be off from Ticonderoga so
soon that I shall only be able to join him at Crown Point." [15] He
knew that there could be no further delay, although he would have
preferred a much larger army, heavier artillery, and supplies sufficient for at least three months.

2

Montgomery set sail with twelve hundred men — four companies
of the 1st New York, most of Colonel David Waterbury's 5th
Connecticut, and Colonel Samuel Mott's corps of artillery. He left
the 2nd New York and Hinman's 4th Connecticut to await Schuyler. The troops were still rent by sectional jealousies, and the New
Englanders believed the army should be run like a town meeting,
with the rank and file choosing and monitoring their officers. Some
recruits had malaria, many looked unkempt, but all were in proper
uniforms and were adequately armed.

On the afternoon of August 28, the fleet stood off Fort Ticonderoga, 200 men aboard the two row-galleys, the rest crowded into
bateaux. Schooner *Liberty* and the sloop that Arnold had seized
at St. Jean, christened *Enterprise,* escorted the fleet. At Crown
Point the army was windbound for two days. The men passed
their time fishing, idling, and poking through the shell of Lord
Amherst's gutted fort. "Everything in ruins," Ritzema observed.
"A bad omen for future operations." [16]

With a change of wind the fleet logged thirty miles to Wills-
boro Bay, where the Connecticut troops swarmed ashore with such
exuberance that a disgusted Colonel Ritzema deemed them country
louts, a sorry contrast to his citified New Yorkers. Schuyler caught
up with his army at Isle La Motte. He was in the throes of rheu-
matic gout and looked spent and ashen. Leaving the lake behind,

the fleet funneled into the Richelieu and put in at Ile aux Noix without incident, although the enemy was only twelve miles downstream.

Ile aux Noix had once been a strategic link in the defense of Montreal. During the French and Indian War, it had boasted a star-shaped earthwork, but by 1775 the defenses lay in ruins and the island was occupied by a solitary farmhouse. After debarking his troops, Schuyler wrote a letter to the Canadians, saying that he had come to rescue them from "enslavement" and to "protect them in the full enjoyment of their temporal and spiritual privileges." [17] He commissioned John Brown and Ethan Allen to deliver the letter to James Livingston, the Canadian ally, and have him circulate it among the *habitants.*

On September 6, Schuyler set forth with most of his troops, dropping downstream until he saw the squat earthen redoubts of St. Jean. Next to the redoubts stood the schooner that scouts had described as pitched and nearly planked. A little way above the fort he ordered his troops ashore. He had no more than gotten out of sight of his bateaux when the woods resounded with war whoops and musket fire. In a surprise attack, Lorimier's Indians took aim from behind trees and thickets, killing eight Americans and wounding five before vanishing into the woods. Lorimier did not escape unscathed, however. Several in his command were killed, and his chief lieutenant, Captain Gilbert Tice, was shot in the leg. His Indians were incensed that no one from the garrison had come to their support. When word spread through the tribes that Lorimier had not been reinforced, although outnumbered ten to one, enthusiasm for the British cause waned measurably.[18]

Schuyler started work on a breastwork but, with the fort so close, changed his mind and built a second breastwork farther upstream. That night he received a visit from Moses Hazen, the St. Jean merchant and *seigneur* who had alerted the Montreal garrison after Arnold's raid but subsequently had decided to support his own countrymen in the contest for his adopted homeland. Hazen told him that most of Chambly's regulars were stationed at St. Jean and Chambly, that the schooner had been christened *Royal Savage* and was about to be launched, and that most of the French Canadians would take no part in the campaign, leaving the British and Americans to settle their own quarrel. When Schuyler shared this information with his officers, all agreed that they should return to Ile aux Noix. In explaining the decision to his troops, he said that the foray had accomplished its purpose of alerting their Canadian allies, but not everyone was convinced. When Colonel Ritzema made the day's entry in his journal he qualified what Schuyler had said with a tart "peut-être." [19]

Schuyler would gladly have evacuated Ile aux Noix. "Should we not be able to do anything decisively in Canada," he wrote John Hancock, President of Congress, "I shall judge it best to move from this place, which is a very wet and unhealthy part of the Country, unless I receive your orders to the contrary." [20] His spirits were partially revived by two messages from James Livingston, offering to seize enemy shipping at the mouth of the Richelieu and cut communications between St. Jean and Montreal.[21] Livingston said that he and his Canadians had captured two supply boats and isolated Chambly, that he could enroll as many as 3000 Canadians if given a hard core of American troops, and that he had acquired an ally in Jeremiah Duggan, an erstwhile barber who wanted to align himself with the colonies.[22] Reinforcements were arriving — 300 from Hinman's regiment, 400 from the 2nd New York. Schuyler, whose health had taken a turn for the worse, directed Montgomery to make a second thrust in the direction of the fort with a task force of 800 men.

On the night of the 10th, Montgomery sailed downstream, debarking his troops near Schuyler's second breastwork. He ordered Waterbury to take the lead, detached Ritzema with part of his command to sever communications between the fort and Montreal, and assigned a second detachment to cover Waterbury's left flank. The men were in mortal terror of Lorimier's Indians. They had gone no more than a mile through the woods when someone heard footsteps on their left. Coming to a quick halt, they could hear the snap of twigs, the rattle of dry leaves. Several started to run for the bateaux. Then the whole column fell apart as the troops broke into a headlong stampede. When they reached Schuyler's second breastwork, they were told that what they had heard was not the tread of Indians but the approach of their own flanking party.

Advancing anew, the column broke ranks a second time when enemy bateaux raked the river bank with grapeshot. Only Ritzema and his men held their ground. Attacking Schuyler's first breast-work, which had been occupied by a few Indians, they killed two of the enemy and routed the rest but presently were summoned to headquarters. A scout had reported *Royal Savage* launched and on the prowl. In spite of Montgomery's opposition, all the officers favored an immediate return to Ile aux Noix. The troops re-embarked, outdistancing a few shells that dropped harmlessly into the Richelieu, and hurried upstream. No one laid eyes on *Royal Savage*.[23]

Blame for the retreat focused on the Connecticut troops, although one of their number maintained that "thrue Courage does not consist in running into Danger without any rational or probable Prospect of Success."[24] James van Rensselaer, one of Montgomery's aides, wrote home that if he were to "judge from the behaviour of our troops on the two late attacks" he would "have but little hope of entire success."[25] To add to the army's woes, Schuyler had become so ill that he had to quit Canada. Bedridden and hardly able to put pen to paper, he turned over the command to Montgomery and set sail for Ticonderoga. Near Lake Champlain he met a fleet of ba-teaux bringing Colonel Seth Warner and 170 Green Mountain Boys to Ile aux Noix. Wearing green coats with red facing, blue and white checked shirts, and buckskin vests and breeches, they were part of a battalion authorized by Congress to include seven companies totaling 500 men. They had ridden out heavy weather on the lake. "The waves ran High and Boisterous," Captain John Fassett had noted in his diary. "The wind increased and we were afraid of being lost."[26] Landlubbers all, they were thankful to reach the gentler waters of the Richelieu.

Later, when he recovered his health, Schuyler took charge of supplying the expedition. He wrote Washington that he was afraid the troops would run out of food because of the "scandalous want of subordination and innattention" on the part of their officers. "If Job had been a General in my situation," he told the commander-in-chief, "his memory had not been so famous for patience."[27]

3

Reinforcements were pouring in. Part of the 1st and 3rd New York and 200 from Easton's regiment had reached Ile aux Noix. Near what is now the site of Burlington, three companies of New Hampshire Rangers awaited bateaux to transport them down the lake. Led by Colonel Timothy Bedel of Haverhill, the New Hampshiremen had been joined by the Independent Company of Volunteers, raised in Hanover and including several Dartmouth students. They arrived on the night of the 16th and were taken to their allotted space in the big encampment.

No reinforcements were more welcome than Captain John Lamb's New York Artillery, which, unlike less favored units, had been assigned bateaux immediately on reaching Fort Ticonderoga. Raised by Congress in June, Lamb's unit numbered about 100 officers and men. He had made sure that they would receive proper recognition. When the Provincial Congress had proposed incorporating them into the 1st New York, he had resigned in protest. His men were artillerymen, not to be equated with ordinary foot soldiers, and he returned to his command only when they were given a classification of their own.

John Lamb, a vintner by trade, was a firebrand and tireless agitator. It was said that he "headed mobs, excited sedition, talked treason, abused Loyalists, harangued the populace, and damned the Toreys." [28] After the passage of the Stamp Act, he had helped organize the Sons of Liberty and had berated the provincial legislature for its weak-kneed deference toward the royal governor. On one occasion he had been part of a mob that occupied the New York customs house. On another he had led a raid on the king's armory, taking guns and ammunition that would be used in the siege of Boston and by his own troops in Canada. When he had established his unit as a separate command, he saw to it that his men were outfitted in blue with buff facing, to distinguish them from the infantry. He was a self-taught artilleryman but a proud one.

On the 17th, Montgomery returned to St. Jean, debarking his troops near Schuyler's first breastwork. "We arrived at the Breast work before night and found no Molestation, tho' we expected a battle as much as we expected to get there," Captain Fassett wrote. "The whole army soon came up where we staid that night and it was very cold and they flung Boms among us and we had a very tedious night of it indeed." [29] Next morning Montgomery ordered Colonel Bedel to loop through the woods and occupy the Montreal road north of the fort, taking with him the Green Mountain Boys and part of Hinman's command, in addition to his own New Hampshire Rangers. Gunfire was heard as Bedel was assembling his detachment. Noticing that some of the men showed signs of the same panic that had proved so disastrous in the two earlier thrusts, Montgomery decided to go along, too. With the Green Mountain Boys in the lead, he kept the troops in close formation and forbade them to speak above a whisper. As they neared the Montreal road, he saw the scarlet coats of British regulars showing blood red through the trees. Although the Green Mountain Boys were "not so expert at forming" as he would have liked, he deployed his troops so as to take advantage of the thick cover.[30]

Earlier that morning John Brown had waylaid a wagon train and erected a breastwork on the Montreal road. The gunfire that Montgomery heard had marked a skirmish between Brown's men and a detachment of British regulars and Canadians led by Captain John Strong of the 26th. Brown and his men had been dispersed. When Montgomery arrived, the enemy had occupied the breastwork and were strung out along the road. Still keeping to the woods, he ordered his men to open fire. "The grape shot and musket balls flew very thick," Captain Fassett wrote, but Strong was heavily outnumbered and after a short exchange retreated to the fort — a maneuver that he brought off with a loss of only two men.[31] Subsequently, Montgomery would claim that had he had an unimpeded view of the enemy he could have wiped out Strong's detachment. "The enemy, after an ill-directed fire for some minutes, retired with precipitation, and lucky for them they did," he said, "for had we known their situation, which the thickness of the woods prevented our finding out till it was too late, there would not a man of them returned." [32]

John Brown, Ethan Allen, and their Canadian ally, James Livingston, had been roaming the countryside like "brigands," according to Simon Sanguinet, a Montreal loyalist.[33] They had seized wagons loaded with provisions for St. Jean, overhauled supply boats on the Richelieu, and enrolled recruits. With the help of Jeremiah Duggan and a blacksmith named Loiseau, Livingston had set up field head-quarters at Pointe Olivier, where he was said to have recruited 300 *habitants*. Ethan wrote Montgomery that he could raise "one or two thousand in a week's time" and eventually "three times the number of our Army in Canada." [34] However, some who joined their ranks had second thoughts. At St. Dénis, where many had enlisted, the village fathers asked for a gubernatorial pardon. Two agents sent by Carleton with a proclamation of amnesty were housed in the village rectory. During the night a pro-American mob took them prisoner, manhandling the *curé* and shooting a servant girl who had been watching from an upstairs window.

In spite of protests from Chief Justice Hey and others, Carleton did nothing to curb Brown and Allen. He may have underrated their influence or felt himself too short-handed to act. To add to his troubles, the Indians at St. Jean quit in a body, smarting over the garrison's failure to send them support during their skirmish with Schuyler's troops.

Everything seems to be desperate [Hey wrote the Lord Chancellor], and I cannot but fear that before this reaches your Lordship Canada will be as fully in the Possession of the Rebels as any other Province upon the Continent. I shall stay till every hope is gone, which will I fear be but a short time. The Rebels have succeeded in making Peace with the Savages who have all left the Camp at St. John's. Many of the Canadians in that Neighborhood are in arms against the King's Troops and not one hundred in the Towns of Montreal and Quebec are with us. St. John's and Montreal must soon fall into their hands — and I doubt Quebec will follow too soon. In this situation I hold my-self in readiness to embark for England.[35]

Subsequently, Hey did indeed embark, together with the son of William Pitt, who had been visiting in Canada and was advised to quit the province for his own safety. Nor were they alone. The governor had arranged passage for Lady Maria and the children, who would stay with her family in England until the threat had passed.

Before rejoining Montgomery, Ethan Allen chose to make a side trip to the south shore of the St. Lawrence opposite Montreal. He was accompanied by Jeremiah Duggan and about eighty Canadians. As he looked across at the weakly guarded city, he may have remembered what he had written two months earlier to Governor Trumbull of Connecticut: "Were it not that the Grand Continental Congress had lately incorporated the Green Mountain Boys into a battalion under certain regulations and command, I would forthwith advance with them into Canada and invest Montreal, exclusive of any help from the colonies." [36] However, he would maintain that he had given no further thought to the matter until he met John Brown with a detachment of 200 Americans on the outskirts of La Prairie.

Brown said that he had something he would like to discuss in the utmost confidence. When he and Ethan had repaired to the privacy of a nearby farmhouse, he proposed that they attack the city of Montreal. Ethan needed no persuasion. He listened intently as Brown outlined the plan: Ethan and his troops would cross from Longueuil to a point north of the city, Brown would cross an equal distance to the south, and at daybreak, after an exchange of "three huzzas," they would converge on Montreal. Neither seems to have questioned the soundness of the proposal or to have felt obliged to notify General Montgomery.

Ethan was given thirty Connecticut recruits to reinforce his Canadians, whom he promised fifteen pence a day and a share in the plunder. Rounding up enough canoes and elmwood dugouts to accommodate about a third of his command, he set forth at midnight with the first contingent. A stiff breeze tore spray off the river as he pointed his overloaded canoes north of Montreal, keeping his distance from an anchored brigantine and several smaller craft. Miraculously, he touched shore without incident. The canoes returned for the rest of the troops, all of whom were safely deposited on the north shore. Sentries were posted, roads cordoned off. A few dazed *habitants* were brought in and placed under arrest. At daybreak everyone waited for John Brown's three huzzas, but not a sound came from below the city, even after the sun was "near two hours high." Ethan considered a return to Longueuil but realized that in the broad daylight he would be lucky to manage even a single crossing, which would leave two thirds of his men marooned on the north shore. "This I could not reconcile to my own feelings as a man, much less as an officer," he wrote in his account of what happened. "I therefore concluded to maintain the ground, if possible, and all to fare alike." [37] Somehow one of his prisoners escaped. When told about it, he knew that within an hour all of Montreal would be alerted to his presence.

As soon as the word reached Montreal, a few panicky souls grabbed up their belongings and sought passage to Quebec. But most citizens gathered in the Place d'Armes, where the governor appointed a task force to disperse and capture Ethan's troops. Led by Major John Campbell, who had succeeded Guy Johnson as Superintendent of Indian Affairs, it included twenty departmental officers and half a dozen tribesmen, thirty-four regulars from the 26th, 120 French volunteers, and eighty English Canadians. Among them were Major John Carden, a member of the governor's council, and Alexander Paterson.

Ethan and his men had stationed themselves about a mile from the city. When they caught sight of Campbell's task force, part of their number fled to the river bank and made their escape in the canoes, Jeremiah Duggan among them. Ethan and his remaining troops took cover in farm buildings and behind trees and hedgerows. Many shots were exchanged, most of them wild, as the regulars advanced on Ethan's center and the Canadians and Indians menaced both flanks. "It is rare that so much ammunition was expended, and so little execution done by it," he would remember. However, some bullets took effect. Five of his men were killed and ten wounded. Major Campbell lost one killed and five wounded, including Alexander Paterson, who survived, and Major Carden, who did not.

Ethan's followers were routed out, disarmed, and herded into Montreal. He himself tried to outrun the enemy, pressed by what he described as "vast unequal numbers," but after being "crowded hard" for nearly a mile, he gave himself up to Peter Johnson, a natural son of Sir William Johnson, the Mohawk Valley baronet. He had no more than turned over his sword when an Indian, "part of whose head was shaved, being almost naked and painted, with feathers intermixed with the hair of the other side of his head," threatened him with a musket. Grabbing Peter Johnson as a shield, he dodged and pivoted until the Indian, together with a second tribesman who had joined him, was brought to heel by one of Johnson's officers.

Brigadier General Richard Prescott awaited the prisoners in Montreal. Assigned to Carleton by General Gage after the loss of Fort Ticonderoga, he could wax choleric at the mere sight of rebels. As Ethan and forty of his followers were lined up in the barracks yard, Prescott twitched a cane that he held menacingly behind his back. He asked Ethan if he was the same man who had captured Ticonderoga. When Ethan said that he was, Prescott shook the cane over Ethan's head and called him "many hard names, among which he frequently used the word rebel." Ethan thrust a clenched fist in the brigadier's face and warned that it was "the beetle of mortality for him." Whatever Prescott may have made of the remark, its intent was clear. Signaling his regulars, he ordered them to bayonet Ethan's followers on the spot. Whereupon Ethan stood in the breach, asking that he, not they, be put to death, and baring his chest to the bayonets. It was too much for Prescott, who ordered him thrown in irons and consigned to the hold of brigantine *Gaspé*. "I will not execute you now," he thundered, "but ye shall grace a halter at Tyburn, God damn ye!" [38]

Ethan never graced a halter. In November he was taken to England, where he was interned in Pendennis Castle, but the British had no more idea of what to do with him than the Americans had had. By spring he was back in the colonies, free on parole.

John Brown left no explanation for his failure to cross the St. Lawrence. Perhaps he could not hustle up enough boats. Or perhaps he was deterred by the whitecaps and gusty weather. But if the river gave him pause, it did not discourage Ethan Allen, whose canoes and dugouts kept their part of the bargain by making repeated crossings on a night when small craft had no business being there at all.

4

With Ethan disposed of, the governor ordered a task force of British regulars and Royal Highland Emigrants to arrest Thomas

Walker for high treason. Surrounding Walker's home on the night of October 5, they found him posted on a second-floor landing with a brace of pistols. As they surged toward the stairs, he fired into their midst, wounding two of their number and driving all of them back into the street. Rather than risk a frontal attack, they set fire to the house. Walker lowered his wife from an upstairs window and followed her to the street, where she was kept standing barefoot and in her nightclothes until a black servant woman slipped off her shoes and gave them to her and an officer in the task force wrapped her in his blanket coat. When the house had gone up in flames the two were marched off, and Walker, like Ethan Allen, was clapped into a ship's hold.[39]

Also suspect was Saint-Luc de La Corne, a *seigneur* who had sought an accommodation with Montgomery on condition that the Americans spare his property and that of a few associates. Montgomery had chosen John Brown to deal with him, confiding in a letter to Janet that since La Corne was "cunning as the devil," only a New Englander could outmatch him.[40] La Corne was asked to post a large sum of money as proof of good intent, to provide the Americans with free access to Montreal, and to arrange for the election of delegates to the Continental Congress. But after Ethan Allen's defeat he had a change of heart. Instead of answering Montgomery's letter, he gave it to the governor, who ordered it burned by the public hangman.

Nearly everyone was angry with Ethan Allen. James Livingston wrote Montgomery that Ethan "should never have attempted to attack the Town without my knowledge, or acquainting me with his design, as I had it in my power to furnish him with a number of men." [41] Seth Warner, on patrol between Longueuil and La Prairie with 300 Green Mountain Boys and 2nd New Yorkers, reported "great consternation" among the *habitants*.[42] Montgomery cited Ethan's "imprudence and ambition, which urged him to this affair single handed." Schuyler said he had "dreaded" Ethan's "impatience of subordination" and had allowed him to accompany the army only "after a solemn promise, made to me in the presence of several officers, that he would demean himself properly." [43]

For the first time many French Canadians dared to side openly

with Britain. *Habitants* poured into Montreal from all parts of the
district, even from the south shore, where the enemy kept close
watch on their activities. More than 300 volunteers arrived from
Varennes, where their homes and even their families had been
threatened by the enemy. Others came from St. Ours in spite of
the enemy's threats to burn their crops. Simon Sanguinet estimated
that as many as a thousand *habitants* flocked to Montreal, as well as
a hundred Indians from St. Régis and Lac des Deux Montagnes.[44]
But the governor seemed loath to use them, restricting them to
reconnaissance and even forbidding them to open fire on the enemy.
Like the Indians, the volunteers idled in Montreal. Those who went
home to visit their families often failed to return. Enthusiasm waned
still more when a toplofty *seigneur*, the Sieur de Rigauville, infuriated the citizens of Verchères by threatening to arrest the wife and
children of a man who had refused to enlist. One night de Rigauville was carried off, while in his cups, by an American patrol that
had been alerted by local *habitants*. His behavior reminded Canadians of the more imperious of the *seigneurs* and of the governor's
affinity with the *noblesse*.

Carleton had all but despaired of the *habitants*. He had seen them
resist beating orders, flout their *seigneurs*, even disobey their bishop.
In a letter to Lord Dartmouth he described them as "wretched
People . . . blind to Honor, Duty & their own Interest" and referred
scathingly to their "stupid baseness."[45] They had not knuckled
under, as he thought they should have, to their clergy and the
noblesse. He often must have shared his thoughts with Bishop
Briand, who was appalled by the rebelliousness of his flock. "My
authority is no more respected than yours," the bishop had written
one of his *curés*. "They say of me as they say of you that I am
English . . . It is true, I am English; as you should be, and as they
should be, since that is what they have sworn to be."[46] And to another *curé:* "I preach not war but obedience and respect for authority, and the fidelity they have promised to their oath and their
King."[47] He threatened to withhold the sacraments from disobe-
dient communicants and impose interdicts on rebellious congregations. In Montreal his vicar general, Abbé Montgolfier, ruled that
persons known to have given aid or comfort to the enemy would
be denied Christian burial.

The governor relied increasingly on Colonel Allan Maclean, whom he had stationed at Quebec with some of the Royal Highland Emigrants. He ordered Maclean to reinforce his command with British regulars and French militia and to join him in an attempt to relieve the garrison at St. Jean. Maclean left Quebec in September with 120 Emigrants, sixty fusiliers of the 7th Foot, and a corps of French militia. On his way up the St. Lawrence he continued to enroll recruits, reaching Sorel with about 400 militiamen.

What Carleton most wanted was a reinforcement of British regulars. On September 25, Lord Dartmouth ordered five battalions to Canada, but wintry weather diverted four to the American colonies, and the fifth put in at Halifax. In mid-October, General William Howe, who had replaced Gage in Boston, detached a battalion of marines for Canada. However, he had not reckoned on the hesitance of his vice admiral, who refused to venture into northern waters so late in the year, even though ships were known to have docked safely at Quebec at the end of November. Carleton was left with what few regulars he had, Colonel Maclean's troops, and the untried militia.

IV

Perils in the Wilderness

I

ON REACHING Cambridge, Arnold was summoned to head-quarters by the commander-in-chief. Behind closed doors, Washington asked him to lead the expedition through the Maine woods to Quebec, following a waterway that led, with few interruptions, from the New England seacoast to the banks of the St. Lawrence. It had been traveled by generations of Indians and, in more recent times, by French missionaries, who had planted a mission on the Kennebec. In 1761, General Murray had had his engineer, Lieutenant John Montresor, explore and map the route. Accompanied by a few Indians, Montresor had descended the Kennebec from Moosehead Lake to Fort Halifax, returned by way of the Dead River and Chaudière Pond (Lake Megantic), and followed the Chaudière River to its confluence with the St. Lawrence. Arnold was given a copy of Montresor's journal. Although General Murray had deemed the route "impractical" for the passage of troops, there were those who thought otherwise.[1]

The idea of invading Canada from Maine had surfaced earlier that spring when Colonel Jonathan Brewer of the Massachusetts militia had volunteered to lead 500 men against Quebec. His offer had come while Congress, recently handed Fort Ticonderoga and locked in debate over what to do about it, was in no frame of mind for an even more compromising venture. However, by August fewer delegates seem to have been concerned with the sensibilities of the mother country. With Schuyler's army on the Richelieu, a complementary thrust through the Maine woods made great good sense. Nor was it surprising that Washington picked Arnold for the command; few could equal him in drive and audacity. Arnold, in turn, welcomed the chance to become part of a campaign that he had helped bring about. He was raised to colonel in the Continental Army.

With Washington's approval Arnold got in touch with Reuben Colburn, owner of a shipyard in Gardinerston on the Kennebec, who chanced to be in Cambridge. He asked Colburn about the feasibility and cost of building "two hundred light Battoos Capable of Carrying Six or Seven Men each, with their Provisions & Baggage (say 100 wt. to each man), the Boats to be furnished with four Oars two Paddles & Setting Poles each." He also requested information about the navigability of the Kennebec — the depth and speed of the river at that time of year, the nature of the terrain, "wheather low, Dry land, Hills, or Swamp." [2] When Washington received Schuyler's consent to the plan, he ordered Colburn to go ahead with the bateaux at forty shillings apiece, lay in food supplies, and get together a crew of carpenters to accompany the expedition. He sent word to a Newburyport shipowner, Nathaniel Tracy, that vessels would be needed to convey the troops from the Massachusetts coast to the head of navigation on the Kennebec.

Washington wrote Congress that a Kennebec expedition would "divert Carleton from St. John's, which would leave a free passage to General Schuyler, or, if this did not take effect, Quebeck in its present defenseless state must fall into his hands an easy prey." He believed that Carleton lacked the troops to defend Quebec and Montreal simultaneously and that if the two thrusts were synchronized, the enemy must either abandon Montreal or be defeated piecemeal. The only flaw was the lateness of the season, with its threat of an early winter to the north. Washington estimated the distance from the mouth of the Kennebec to the St. Lawrence at 210 miles "on a straight line." He wrote Congress that, after making "all possible inquiry as to the distance, the safety of the route, and the danger of the season being so far advanced," he had found "nothing in either to deter me from proceeding."[3]

When Washington took command of the Continental Army he had found himself at the head of a tatterdemalion mob. The men dressed sloppily, were insolent toward officers, took grudgingly to drill, and lived in sailcloth tents, board shacks, and brush lean-tos that gave off as rank a smell as their unwashed homespun. Ammunition was scarce, defenses so makeshift that they invited attack. Washington had taken his men severely in hand, teaching them to drill like self-respecting soldiers, arming them adequately, getting them into proper uniforms, and enforcing the rudiments of sanitation. To win greater respect for his officers he had supplied his generals and aides-de-camp with identifying ribbons worn diagonally across the breast, and had furnished other ranks with cockades and shoulder stripes. As discipline caught on, morale had risen, and when Arnold called for "active woodsmen, well acquainted with bateaux" he was besieged with volunteers.[4] On September 5, he formed his troops on Cambridge Common with all ranks filled.

Christopher Greene and Roger Enos commanded the two New England battalions. At thirty-eight, Greene had prospered as a Rhode Island merchant, operating sawmills and forges, and had served as delegate to the provincial legislature. A major in the militia, he was advanced to lieutenant colonel when he enrolled with Arnold. Enos, a veteran of the French and Indian War valued for his military experience, was already a lieutenant colonel in the 2nd Connecticut. At forty-six he was older than most and had acquired a degree of caution befitting his seniority. Timothy Bigelow of Worcester, Massachusetts, was Greene's major. A blacksmith by trade, he had marched to Cambridge at the head of his own militiamen, whom he had honed to so fine an edge that their even ranks won plaudits from the commander-in-chief. Enos' major was Return Jonathan Meigs of Middletown, Connecticut, steady and methodical as his homespun name. He kept a daily journal of his activities and wrote punctually to his wife.

There were ten New England captains, ranging widely in age and station. Henry Dearborn was a young New Hampshire doctor who had fought at Bunker Hill, Samuel Ward the nineteen-year-old son of a Rhode Island governor, Jonas Hubbard a Worcester merchant and farmer. John Topham and Simeon Thayer were both Rhode Islanders, Topham the organizer of a militia company in Newport, Thayer a wig-maker from Providence who had served with Rogers' Rangers. Oliver Hanchet, a captain in the 2nd Connecticut, had been associated with Arnold and seems to have commended himself to his superior. William Goodrich, whose company included several Maine recruits, had formerly served with members of the Stockbridge tribe and was considered well versed in Indian customs and thought patterns. Samuel McCobb, Thomas Williams, and an officer known to us only as Scott were in Enos' command. Three of the captains — Dearborn, Thayer, and Topham — kept diaries. Dearborn brought along his Newfoundland dog, perhaps as a reminder of the life he had left behind.

Three companies of riflemen enrolled, among the ten raised by order of Congress on the frontiers of Pennsylvania, Maryland, and Virginia. They had come long distances to Cambridge. One of the two Pennsylvania units had journeyed 450 miles in twenty-six days, with time out to tar and feather two suspected Tories.[5] The Virginia company had traveled 600 miles in three weeks. The riflemen wore long, leather-fringed hunting shirts, leather pantaloons, moccasins, and wide-brimmed hats bound in rawhide. Canteen, hunting knife, and powder horn dangled from each man's shoulder strap. Some of the rifles the men carried were more than five feet in length. Although they took longer to reload than the New Englanders' smoothbore muskets, they possessed an accuracy no musket could match. The more adept of Morgan's riflemen could hit a target the size of a man's nose at a distance of 150 yards. The British, who learned to dread their uncanny marksmanship, called them "these shirt-tail men, with their cursed, twisted guns," and pronounced them "the most fatal widow-and-orphan makers in the world." [6]

Washington had served with the riflemen in the French and Indian War, and, although he welcomed them to Cambridge, he considered their arrival a somewhat mixed blessing. Hard to discipline, they were soon trading insults and blows with New England troops. On one lamentable occasion a band of Virginians locked horns with some of Colonel John Glover's Marbleheaders, a regiment of Massachusetts salts, in a donnybrook that only the commander-in-chief could quell. Arnold's call for volunteers brought a quick response from the riflemen, who applied in such numbers that lots had to be drawn. Two companies from Pennsylvania were enrolled, and one from Virginia. Captains Matthew Smith and William Hendricks commanded the Pennsylvania units. Smith, given to loud talk and hard drinking, had formerly been one of the Paxton Boys, a frontier gang accused of murdering some defenseless Indians. Hendricks was the opposite of Smith, courtly and soft-spoken, described by a member of his command as "of a mild and beautiful countenance." [7]

The Virginians were led by Daniel Morgan, who had emigrated to the Virginia hinterland from New Jersey after a quarrel with his father and had hired out as a teamster to frontier farmers. A mighty bear of a man, six feet tall, solid muscle at 200 pounds, with a bellow that no one disregarded, he had taken on all comers at backwoods wrestling matches and had won renown for his military exploits. Once he had escaped an Indian war party by clinging, half-conscious, to his mount, his neck grazed by a bullet that had torn through his cheek and deprived him of half his teeth. He had served with Braddock in 1755, but, whereas Washington had accompanied the high command, Morgan had gone as a nineteen-year-old drover, rattling over the Alleghenies with a wagonload of supplies and evacuating some of the wounded after Braddock's defeat.

In 1773, Morgan married Abigail Curry, a purposeful lass who got him to forsake his raffish ways and even accompany her to church on Sunday mornings. It was a spectacular about-face, but one can be sure that past associates, mindful of his fists, refrained from comment. When Congress called for a company of Virginia riflemen to serve in the Revolutionary War, Morgan was named captain. In ten days he enlisted ninety-six men, a majority of them Scotch-Irish, the rest "Dutchmen" descended from Swiss and German settlers. John Humphries was first lieutenant, William Heth second lieutenant, Charles Porterfield ensign.

In Cambridge, Morgan showed fellow patriots the scars he had collected when he was whipped for striking a British officer during the French and Indian War. Sentenced to 500 lashes, he had taken his punishment without a murmur even though the flesh lay on his back in ribbons. Forever after he would maintain that the scars totaled only 499 and would invite all and sundry to inspect his back and see if their count agreed with his. "That is the doing of old King George," he would explain. "While I was in his service, upon a certain occasion, he promised me 500 lashes. But he failed in his promise and gave me but 499, so he has been owing me one ever since. While the drummer was laying the lashes on my back I heard him miscount one. I was counting after him at the time. I did not think it worthwhile to tell him of his mistake and let it go." [8] Such was Daniel Morgan, thirty-nine years old in 1775. With 499 stripes as his credentials, he was well qualified to ride herd on riflemen.

Eleazer Oswald, the New Haven Footguard who had sailed Philip Skene's schooner to Ticonderoga, was Arnold's private secretary. Christian Febiger, a Danish engineer who had migrated to the colonies from Santa Cruz, was brigade major. Dr. Isaac Senter watched over the health of the expedition. Only twenty-two, he had been apprenticed to a physician in Newport, Rhode Island, before enlisting as a surgeon in the Continental Army. Samuel Spring was chaplain. Twenty-nine and a graduate of the College of New Jersey (now Princeton University), he had acquired such a hardshell brand of theology that John Quincy Adams would one day accuse him of having "the zeal and enthusiasms of a bigot." [9] It took a parson with strong convictions to join the Kennebec expedition.

Aaron Burr, unattached to any unit, was also an alumnus of the College of New Jersey. Although ten years younger than Spring, he had known him at college and had himself entertained thoughts of the ministry. He and his friend Matthias Ogden had arrived in Cambridge with a letter from John Hancock, commending them as "gentlemen of reputation" who came "not as spectators but with a view of joining the army." [10] Washington had been too preoccupied to pay them much heed, and after a month of neglect Burr had taken to his bed with a fever. However, when he learned of the march to Quebec, he left his sickbed and, with Ogden, signed up as a volunteer. The wives of Sergeant Joseph Grier and Private James

Warner of the Pennsylvania riflemen accompanied the expedition. Mrs. Grier, a big, sturdy woman, wanted to share the trials and dangers with her spouse. Mrs. Warner may have been worried about her husband's health.

Washington cautioned Arnold to "restrain every officer and soldier from such imprudence and folly" as "ridiculing" the Roman Catholic Church or "affronting its Ministers or votaries." The Canadians must be shown that the troops came "not as robbers, or to make war upon them, but as friends and supporters of their liberties," pledged to "protect and support the free exercise of the religion of the country and the undisturbed enjoyment of the rights of conscience in religious matters." [11] He also sent a letter with Arnold promising to compensate the Canadians for supplies furnished the army and to spare their property. "Let no man desert his habitation," he told them. "Let no one flee as before an enemy. The cause of America and of liberty is the cause of every virtuous American citizen, whatever may be his religion or his descent. The United Colonies know no distinction but such as slavery, corruption, and arbitrary domination may create. Come then, ye generous citizens, range yourselves under the standard of general liberty, against which all the force and artifice of tyranny will never be able to prevail." [12]

2

Washington had written Schuyler that "not a moment's time is to be lost in the preparation for this enterprise." [13] Nevertheless, whole days went by while supplies were being assembled and the men outfitted. One company refused to march until back wages were paid up. It was September 11 before Morgan's riflemen, the first to leave, began the two- to three-day march to Newburyport, point of embarkation for the Kennebec. They bivouacked on the training green in Newbury. The muskets companies followed two days later and were billeted in a Newburyport church, in the town hall, and in two rope walks on the waterfront.

Arnold made the trip in a day, pausing in Salem to order 270 blankets and a supply of ginger. It was after dark when he dismounted in front of Nathaniel Tracy's brick mansion near Newburyport harbor. Tracy, a stout patriot, had assembled eleven sloops and schooners, but headwinds kept the fleet at anchor. While awaiting a change of weather, Arnold ordered out three picket boats to comb the coastal waters for enemy men-of-war. Word of the expedition had already leaked. Some of Gage's officers had wanted to sweep the coast with a fleet carrying 1000 regulars, but he had vetoed the proposal lest it weaken his Boston garrison. The picket boats reported no enemy craft from the Isles of Shoals to the Kennebec.

On Sunday the troops attended divine worship at Old South Church, where they were introduced to Chaplain Spring's nononsense orthodoxy. Next day the wind shifted, and on Tuesday the fleet weighed anchor. "This morning we got under way with a pleasant breeze," wrote Private Abner Stocking of Hanchet's company, "our drums beating, fifes playing and colours flying. Many pretty girls stood upon the shore, I suppose weeping for the departure of their sweethearts." [14] Stocking supposed correctly. Some of his comrades, more enterprising than he, had not wasted their extra days in the windbound seaport.

Private Simon Fobes of Hubbard's company described the eleven sail as "dirty coasters and fish boats." One vessel promptly ran aground and could not be refloated until nightfall. But however nondescript they may have looked while riding their mooring lines, they took zestily to the open sea and, sped northward by a spanking breeze, logged nearly 100 miles before dropping anchor off the mouth of the Kennebec. It was a fearsome journey for the troops, few of whom could cope with the pitch and roll of their briny transports. They were seasick nearly to a man. "Had I been thrown into the sea," Fobes said, "I should hardly have made an effort to have saved myself." [15] Nor were their trials confined to the Atlantic swell. As the fleet followed the sea lanes inland, it was pelted by rain and shrouded in a thick fog. Some of the vessels grounded on mudbanks, two lost their way in the Sheepscot River, several became separated in the welter of small islands. Arnold, whose flagship, *Broad Bay*, dropped anchor off Georgetown on the night of the 20th, left the fleet next morning and started up the Kennebec. That afternoon he caught sight of Reuben Colburn's shipyard near Gardinerston. Colburn's house, set back from the river on a cleared bluff, commanded a meadow that dipped to the shoreline. Upstream were the clustered buildings and gristmills of Gardinerston, but Arnold took notice only of the meadow, where he saw row on row of newly built bateaux.

With the help of Thomas Agry, a local shipwright, Colburn and his crews had turned out 200 bateaux, flat-bottomed, with flaring sides and tapering bow and stern. From eighteen to twenty-five feet long, they were made of pine boards nailed to oaken ribs and weighed about 400 pounds apiece. Each was equipped with two pairs of oars, two paddles, two setting poles for shallow water. At first Arnold was pleased with what he saw, but on closer inspection he was not so sure. Some were smaller than he wished. All were made of green wood and, he wrote Washington, "very badly built." [16] Moreover, there were not as many as he needed, and he ordered an additional twenty.

Two Vassalboro woodsmen, Dennis Getchell and Samuel Berry, whom Colburn had sent upstream to "see what obstacles Colonel Arnold would be likely to meet," were on hand with their report.[17] They had paddled up the Kennebec to the Great Carry and had crossed through the woods to the Dead River. Following the Dead past a long mountain, they had encountered an Indian named Natanis, who had a hunting camp on the river and who told them he was a spy for Carleton. There were other spies at Chaudière Pond, Natanis warned, and there was a squad of redcoats at Sartigan, the first French outpost. Getchell and Berry returned to report the carrying places "pretty passible," the river "pretty Shoal on Account of the Dry Season," the trees blazed by Indians "so as the way is pretty direct." [18] Arnold put no faith in Natanis, dismissing him as a "noted villain" and ordering him killed on sight.[19] He was supplied maps by one Samuel Goodwin, a local surveyor, showing "the River Kennebeck to the several heads thereof, and the several carrying places to Ammeguntick Pond [Lake Megantic] and Chaudière River . . . and the passes and carrying places to Quebeck." [20] He would also have the counsel of four St. François Indians who had been parleying with Washington and had journeyed overland to join the expedition as guides.

When the fleet caught up, a crew of four was assigned to each bateau. The "green pine boards" made the craft "somewhat heavy," according to Dr. Senter, and the men watched anxiously as water seeped through leaky seams. The rest of the army continued to the head of navigation, downstream from its normal location because of low water, and marched to Fort Western, a magazine and barracks built during the French and Indian War and now a trading post operated by Captain James Howard, its former commandant. Captain Howard had done well during his years in the back country, building himself a frontier mansion where he entertained lavishly. "Headquarters were at Esq. Howard's," wrote Dr. Senter, "an exceeding hospitable, opulent, polite family." [21] Aaron Burr, who had hired a carriage at the head of navigation to spare himself the six-mile march, basked in Captain Howard's hospitality, "falling on roast chickens and wallowing . . . in a good feather bed." [22]

At Fort Western, Arnold sent out two scouting parties. One, a detail of nine men led by a Lieutenant Church, known to us only by surname, would reconnoiter the Kennebec and the portage to the Dead. The other, a six-man scout led by Lieutenant Archibald Steele of Smith's Pennsylvania riflemen, would go to the edge of Canada. John Joseph Henry, a sixteen-year-old rifleman who kept a journal of the march, was assigned to Steele, as were guides Jeremiah Getchell, a brother of Dennis, and John Horne, whom Henry described as "an Irishman who had grown grey in this cold climate." [23]

Arnold formed his army into four divisions. He had chosen Colonel Greene to take the lead with a rifle company and two companies of musketmen, but the riflemen refused to march under anyone but Daniel Morgan. Greene was big enough not to dispute their wishes, and Arnold put Morgan in the lead, assigning him all three rifle companies, with orders to "clear the roads over the carrying places." [24] They left on Monday, September 25, followed the next day by Greene and the second division, composed of Hubbard's, Thayer's, and Topham's units. Major Meigs was given command of the third division, made up of Dearborn's, Goodrich's,

Hanchet's, and Ward's companies. They left on Wednesday. The fourth division, led by Colonel Enos, included McCobb's, Scott's, and Williams' companies. McCobb and Scott left on Thursday and Friday, but Enos was delayed by supply problems and fell in with Williams' company at the end of the long column.

Before leaving Fort Western, Arnold dropped an appreciative note to Nathaniel Tracy, put in a good word for the skipper of his flagship, and wrote Washington that, with Quebec only about 180 miles away (300 would have been more nearly correct), his troops should complete the march within three weeks. He also interceded for a slow-witted soldier who had been sentenced to hang for the shooting of a fellow recruit. In returning him to Cambridge, he cited extenuating circumstances and urged clemency. "The criminal appears to be very simple and ignorant," he wrote Washington, "and in the company he belonged to, had the reputation of being a peaceable fellow... I wish he may be found a proper object of mercy." [25] *

Traveling by canoe, Arnold quickly outstripped the bateaux and caught up with Dearborn's and Goodrich's companies at Fort Halifax, an abandoned cluster of two blockhouses and a barracks at the mouth of the Sebasticook. Here Montresor had turned back in his descent of the Kennebec. At Taconic Falls, half a mile upstream, Arnold watched his crews unloading supplies, hoisting the bateaux out of the water with hand spikes, carrying them along a thickly wooded bank, then easing them back into the river and bringing up the supplies. Dr. Senter noticed that several of the boats had sprung leaks. "Water being shoal and rocks plenty," he said, "with a very swift current most of the way, soon ground out many of the bottoms." [26] Arnold hired a team to carry his canoe past five miles of white water, but the bateaux had to be wrestled upstream. The crews inched their heavily loaded craft forward, leaning waist-deep against the current. "You would have taken the men for amphibious animals," Arnold wrote Washington after he had observed their struggles.[27] When Private Caleb Haskell of Ward's company made that day's entry in his journal he noted tersely, "Now we are learning to be soldiers." [28]

* The man was not hanged but died in jail at Cambridge, according to Private Stocking.

Skowhegan Falls, described by Private Stocking as "nearly 100 feet in height and almost perpendicular," cascaded down a towering wall of rock.[29] Arnold and his party carried their canoe up a fissure that angled to the lip, but the crews made a tottery ascent, hoisting bateaux, oars, paddles, setting poles, and all the supplies up the rock face. By the time they reached the top, a cold rain had settled over the Kennebec. Some awoke next morning to find their clothes "frozen a pane of glass thick." [30] Arnold lodged at the home of a Widow Warren near Norridgewock, the last English outpost before the woods swept without interruption to the French settlements on the Chaudière.

At Norridgewock a French priest, Sébastien Râle, had established a mission to the Indians more than fifty years before, only to be shot by English colonists, who sacked his mission and closed his church. Near his grave, which lay hard by the portage trail that skirted Norridgewock Falls, Arnold found Thayer's and Hubbard's men sorting through their food supplies. Casks of peas had split open, beef cured during the summer heat had spoiled, a supply of codfish had putrified. Much of the food had to be jettisoned. What was left consisted chiefly of salt pork and flour, staples that were already in short supply. Some of the bateaux were giving out — green boards had warped, bottoms were scraped thin. Arnold ordered his carpenters to repair and caulk them, but the troops were beginning to curse Colburn's shipwrights, who, according to Private George Morison of the Pennsylvania riflemen, "would fully have experienced the effects of our vengeance" had they come within reach of his company.[31] Many fell ill with dysentery, including Captain Williams of Enos' division. And the rain kept falling. Major Meigs, who had lost his camp kettle, with its cache of irreplaceable sugar and butter, consoled himself by paying a visit at the home of the first child born to white settlers so far up the Kennebec.

Arnold spent a week seeing his troops off and supervising the repair of damaged bateaux. On October 9 he left Norridgewock, portaging across a peninsula at the mouth of Seven Mile Stream (the Carrabasset) to avoid a mile of white water. That night he camped near Carritunk Falls, where he found the riflemen feasting on a moose they had downed and embellishing their pork and dumplings with freshly caught trout. Next morning he had his first glimpse of the mountains to the north, snow-capped and wintry-looking, although still smoldering with autumn color. During a long day's paddle he watched the Kennebec shrink to a shallow, swift-running stream walled in by conifers, and by nightfall he saw a peak shaped like a sugarloaf that marked the start of the Great Carry. Here his army would cross to the Dead River and avoid a wide, unnavigable loop taken by the Dead before its junction with the Kennebec farther upstream. He understood that the twelve-mile portage was made easier by three strategically spaced ponds, big enough to accommodate bateaux.

Arnold put ashore and bivouacked. At the carrying place by early morning, he found the three forward divisions funneling up the portage trail toward the first pond. The bateaux, bottom-sides up, tilted on men's shoulders. Casks of pork and flour were roped to poles and taken shoulder-high by teams of four. Soon after disembarking he was met by Lieutenant Church, who had gone as far as the Dead and who said that the trail, already given a preliminary brushing out, was "capable of being made good." In ascending the portage trail, he must have marveled at his men's spirits. Winded, mud-spattered, and muscle-weary, they acknowledged his greeting cheerfully. At times he heard shouts of laughter. "We were half leg deep in mud," Private Morison would remember, "stumbling over fallen logs, one leg sinking deeper in the mire than the other, then down goes a boat and the carriers with it; a hearty laugh prevails." [32]

At the first pond Arnold found several of the men angling for trout. "Our People caught a prodigious number of fine Salmon trout," he noted, "nothing being more common than a man's taking 8 or 10 Doz. in one hours time, which generally weigh half a pound a piece." [33] The pond, hemmed by conifers, shone in the October sunlight and looked safe to drink from. A short walk took him to the second pond. It was swampy and brackish, but the men sampled it anyway. At the edge of a thickety marsh the portage trail took off for the third pond, nearly a mile and a half away.

Arnold set up headquarters near the first pond. The next day Lieutenant Steele returned from a scout that had taken him to the edge of Canada. One of his men had climbed a tall tree and detected the glitter of Chaudière Pond across fifteen miles of woods. On the return trip Steele had run out of food. His men had succumbed to a creeping fatigue that persisted even after they had shot and divided three moose. When they reached the Great Carry some of them could barely stand. Most had remained at the Dead, husbanding their strength, but Steele and two companions had managed to cross part of the carry and rejoin Morgan's division. He told Arnold that he had located Natanis' hunting camp but found it empty, that the portage through the mountains into Canada was four miles across, and that the Dead was "a fine deep river" with short carries and a bountiful supply of moose. Arnold ordered Steele and Church to return with twenty axmen, clearing the portages as far as Chaudière Pond and continuing downstream until they caught sight of Sartigan, the first French outpost. Steele's famished comrades were brought in by Morgan's men. They had left their camp on the Dead, abandoning their canoes, and had barely made it through a mile-wide swamp. They had been revived with the last measure of rum from Major Febiger's canteen.

The sick now included men who had sampled the brackish water of the second pond. "No sooner had it got down than it was puked up," Dr. Senter said. Dysentery was on the increase. Arnold had Goodrich's men build a log hospital between the first and second ponds. "No sooner finished than filled," Dr. Senter commented.[34] But only one man died — a member of Meigs's division struck by a falling tree.

Although Arnold ordered a storehouse built to cover a possible retreat, he was not downhearted. His men were "very cheerful," he reported, however "much fatigued in Carrying over their Boats, Provisions, etc." He wrote Schuyler that he hoped to join him at Quebec "in a fortnight," and he sent word to Washington that he had food enough to last more than three weeks. He also wrote John Dyer Mercier, the merchant he had befriended while trading in Quebec before the Revolution, inquiring about the size of the enemy garrison, the number of ships at anchor, and the preparedness of the city.[35] He enclosed his letter to Schuyler, requesting Mercier to forward it by courier. Perhaps foolishly, he entrusted the letters to two of the St. François Indians who had joined the expedition as guides. The Indians were accompanied by Private John Hall, a bilingual deserter from the British army who was instructed to return with Mercier's answer. But the letters never reached Mercier. Whether by an unlucky turn of events or through the duplicity of the couriers, they came into the possession of Hector Theophilus Cramahé, lieutenant governor of Quebec.

3

Arnold broke camp on October 16, leaving the more seriously ill in the log hospital. The trail threaded to the third pond through bogs "choaked up with Roots" but he found the pond "very beautiful and noble," with "deep, clear and fine water," safe to drink.[36] As he crossed he could see a "forked mountain" that overlooked the serpentine windings of the Dead. (One day the mountain would be named for Timothy Bigelow, Colonel Greene's blacksmith major.) Food supplies were dwindling, and he put the men on daily rations. He sent a request to Colonel Enos for a yoke of oxen that had been brought along to help at portages. "Hurry as fast as possible," he wrote.[37] His men were in dire need of meat.

After leaving the pond, the portage trail descended two miles to a savannah that Private Henry expected to be "a beautiful plot of firm ground, level as a bowling green," but that quickly turned into a knee-deep quagmire.[38] The men foundered across, drenched with mud, stumbling over submerged roots, bruising their feet on snags. Daniel Morgan, whose division was in the lead, had changed into Indian leggings and breechcloth, heedless of the scratches inflicted by clutching, razor-edged grass. With only a light canoe to carry, Arnold and his party made a fast crossing and came to a brook bordering the far edge of the savannah. Launching their craft, they followed through massed alders to the Dead.

Private Morison described the river as running "so dead and still that it can scarcely be discerned which way it flows."[39] Arnold kept a close check on Montresor's journal, even quoting him verbatim in his own diary. Had it not been for Montresor's guidelines, he might have wondered if the river would ever take leave of the forked mountain that rose above it. As he conformed to the Dead's "extraordinary windings," his canoe pointed east, west, and even south, as much as north.[40] For two hours the forked peak loomed in front of him when it should have been at his back, or swung around to his right when he expected it on his left, but gradually it pulled behind him as the Dead uncoiled into a fixed, northerly course. As he continued upstream he caught sight of Morgan's riflemen brushing out a pathway for the foot troops, and passed Natanis' hunting camp, shut and vacated in its small clearing.

That night Arnold bivouacked at the head of the column with Greene's division. He admitted to a great fatigue that was not eased by what Greene told him. The division had been put on half rations. Captain Thayer reported that he had only a few pounds of flour for his entire company. Captain Topham said the same. Arnold dispatched an order to Enos to send up all the food the rear division could spare, and assigned Major Bigelow twelve bateaux to collect it. While Bigelow was away, the troops rolled cartridges and angled for trout. There were no moose to be seen. Those that Lieutenant Steele had encountered had been frightened off by the thud of feet, the snap of branches, the shouts of bateaux crews. Meigs arrived with the third division to report that Enos had forwarded the oxen and that they had already been butchered. When the meat was distributed, no one relished his portion more than Dr. Senter, who assembled some comrades for a veritable banquet, enhanced by potatoes and carrots he had brought from Fort Western and a reserve of butter he had kept hidden in his medicine chest.

Morgan resumed the lead, followed by Dearborn and Goodrich. A hard rain kept Arnold in camp for a full day, but on the 21st he was off again, passing uprooted trees that had been toppled into the river by gusts that reminded him of a West Indies hurricane. He caught up with Morgan after dark, "very wet and much fatigued." The storm showed no sign of abating. "The wind," Dr. Senter would remember, "increased to an almost hurricane the latter part of this day. The trees tumbling on all quarters . . . rendered our passage not only exceeding difficult, but very dangerous . . . As the wind continued very heavy, the danger of camping among the trees was thought great." [41] Arnold and his party pitched their tent about a mile above Morgan's encampment, drying out what clothes they could before bedding down for a wet night. They could hear the rain gathering in pools outside the tent.

They were awakened before daybreak by water lapping at their feet. Grabbing up their soaked gear, they retreated to higher ground and waited until it was light enough to see. The Dead had risen eight feet during the night. Downstream, a vast lake spread incongruously across the landscape, isolating trees that had stood far back from vanished shorelines, engulfing the acres of tall grass through which the Dead had coiled so interminably before Arnold could put the forked mountain behind him. The Dead was in a tumult. Small tributaries had swollen into rivers.

Morgan's troops, who had dossed down on a rise eight feet above the river, broke camp and struggled upstream, holding their bateaux on course with setting poles, grabbing at half-drowned thickets and toppled trees. Seven bateaux overturned. Although the men reached shore, casks of irreplaceable pork and flour went spinning downstream. The river had risen ten feet at Greene's encampment, twelve where Enos bivouacked. In skirting lagoons that had not existed the day before, Thayer's men lost their way and spent a cold night without food or shelter. Part of Meigs's division mistook a swollen tributary for the Dead and had to be rescued by bateau. "Our provisions began to grow scarce," Private Morison would recall. "Many of the men took sick, and the whole of us much reduced by our fatigues." [42] Dr. Senter saw some of the men eating candles. [43]

After the rain stopped, a chill wind swept the valley. "We have a melancholy prospect before us," Arnold admitted, "but in general good spirits." [44] In his diary, Private Stocking expressed deep apprehension. "This day our afflictions increased," he wrote. "Fear was added to sorrow. We found to our astonishment that our journey was much longer than we expected; what was more alarming, our provisions were growing scant. Some of our men appeared downhearted, but most of them, with Col. Arnold, stood firm and resolute." [45] Even Captain Thayer was worried. "The men are much disheartened and Eagerly wish to return," he wrote. "However, I am certain if their Bellies were full, they would be willing eno' to advance." [46]

Arnold had to decide promptly whether or not to continue the march. If he was going to turn back, he must do so now, while he still had food enough to reach the Kennebec. He called in the officers of the two forward divisions. Morgan came, with Smith and Hendricks, and Meigs with his captains. Arnold asked how their men were faring. When they had made their reports, he acknowledged that he was short of food and that the distance had proved greater than he expected. But something in the way he spoke showed that he had no wish to retreat. Supplies might be low, he said, but more would be available at Sartigan. Although the distance was still great and they were behind schedule, the worst of the march must surely be behind them. Moreover, the men had shown their staying powers and looked fit to continue. After taking the measure of his officers, all of whom seemed to agree with what he said, he outlined a plan for advancing into Canada. He would leave immediately for Sartigan to obtain supplies, detaching Captain Hanchet to hustle them up the Chaudière. Word would be sent to Greene and Enos to bring only as many men as they could feed for fifteen days. The rest of their troops, together with the sick, would return to Cambridge. Reduced in size, the army should be able to reach Sartigan within a fortnight. He asked his officers how they felt about it. All chose to continue.

Arnold sent orders to Greene and Enos to "proceed with as many of the best men . . . as you can furnish with 15 days' provision" and to return the rest to Cambridge, "as it may be the means of preserving the whole detachment and of executing our plan without running any great hazard, as fifteen days will doubtless bring us to Canada." [47] Next morning twenty-six sick men were eased into bateaux and dispatched downstream, where they were joined by an additional forty-eight invalids from Greene's division. Arnold ordered out Hanchet's detachment and left with a small party for Sartigan, traveling all afternoon in a cold rain and bivouacking within twenty miles of Chaudière Pond. When he awoke at daybreak, his tent sagged under two inches of wet snow.

Downstream, Major Bigelow had returned to his bateaux with just two barrels of flour. He had been told by Enos' men that he was fortunate to be allowed even that. A few days later, Enos and some of his officers came to Greene's encampment. Greene suspected that they had more on their minds than a discussion of food supplies. Indeed, Dr. Senter had heard that they were "preaching to their men the doctrine of . . . non-perseverance." [48] Enos was accompanied by Captains Scott, McCobb, and Williams and two junior officers. He asked for a council of war, and Greene called in Major Bigelow and Captains Hubbard, Thayer, and Topham. With Enos presiding, the council wasted no time on preliminaries. Enos and his officers declared that if they abided by Arnold's orders and furnished even as few as thirty men with provisions for fifteen days, there would not be enough food left to enable the rest of the division to reach the first settlements on the Kennebec. They were down to their last barrels of pork and flour, they said, and had decided, to avoid putting further strain on the army's dwindling food supplies, that their entire division should return to Cambridge. They hoped Greene's division would join them.

Greene and his officers listened in disbelief. They reminded Enos of Arnold's orders to join him "with all possible dispatch," orders given on the assumption that only a small number in each division would be sent back. But the more they debated the matter, the less Enos and his colleagues seemed to be listening. A show of hands was taken. The vote was even. Greene and his men were for joining Arnold; Enos' men for turning back. As presiding officer, Enos broke the deadlock by voting to continue, but his officers declared that they would return to Cambridge in any case. Rather than break with his command, he felt obliged to accompany them. He promised Greene four barrels of flour and two of pork, but when Captain Thayer and Matthias Ogden went to collect them, they were told that the fourth division would need all the food it had for the return trip. They would have gone back empty-handed had not Captain Williams allowed them two measly barrels of flour.

Thayer and Ogden stormed into Greene's encampment cursing "the ill-heart'd minds" of their "timorous" comrades-in-arms.[49] Their fury was shared by officers and men up and down the line, many of whom did not hear the news until they had crossed into Canada. The profanity of the riflemen, noteworthy even by army standards, doubtless possessed a scope and inventiveness unmatched in the other divisions, but we may be sure that Private Stocking and his fellow musketmen made a creditable showing as they recalled that Enos' troops "had their path cut and cleared by us — they only followed, while we led." [50] Dearborn's men, in the words of their commander, joined in "a General Prayer that Colo. Enos and all his men might die by the way, or meet with some disaster, Equal to the Cowardly, dastardly and unfriendly Spirit" they had shown in "returning Back without orders." [51] Arnold was within a few miles of the St. Lawrence when he learned that Enos had turned back — "contrary to my expectations," he wrote Montgomery, "he having orders to send back only the sick, and those that could not be furnished with provisions." [52] He was left with only 675 men to storm Quebec.

Enos was brought before a court-martial in Cambridge, but he was fortunate in having members of his own command as witnesses. The court acquitted him with honor. The presiding officer, Brigadier General John Sullivan, ruled that "the return of the division was prudent and reasonable" and that had it remained with Arnold "it would have been the means of causing the whole detachment to have perished in the woods for want of sustenance." Enos' action was described as meriting "applause rather than censure" in a statement signed by twenty-five fellow officers, including such stalwarts as Colonel John Stark, who had led the New Hampshiremen at Bunker Hill, the same Samuel Parsons who had discussed the ordnance at Fort Ticonderoga with Arnold on the road near Hartford, and the same Jonathan Brewer who had anticipated Arnold in offering to lead a march on Quebec through the Maine woods.[53] Their testimony carried weight with the court, but had they consulted some of the men who heard the news on the flooded waters of the Dead or beyond the mountain range in Canada, they would have been reminded that Colonel Greene and his command, in no less a dilemma than the fourth division, did not turn back.

V

A Fort and Town Capitulate

1

"THE PRIVATES are all generals," Montgomery wrote his father-in-law as he struggled with his unruly, dispirited troops. "The sweepings of the York streets," he said of his New Yorkers, who clashed with New England recruits on the smallest pretext.[1] John Brown accused the Province of New York of practically sabotaging the campaign. "New York have acted a droll part," he wrote Governor Trumbull of Connecticut, "and are determined to defeat us if in their power; they have failed in men and supplies."[2] Incessant rains worked on the men's morale. The Reverend Benjamin Trumbull, chaplain to a Connecticut regiment, described the encampment as "near over Shoe" in mud,[3] and Colonel Samuel Mott, also from Connecticut, found that whenever he tried to erect batteries, "the water follows in the ditch when only two feet deep."[4] Montgomery wrote his wife that the troops were like "half-drowned rats crawling thro' a swamp."[5] Men feigned illness in the hope of being invalided home. Indeed, at Fort George, Dr. Stringer suspected some of his patients of swallowing tobacco juice to make themselves sick; others of inflaming their gullets with scalding hot chocolate.

Schuyler wrote Congress that had he not returned to Fort Ticonderoga when he did, "as sure as God Lives the Army would have starved." [6] Within a week he sent off 300 barrels of pork and flour and a big mortar nicknamed "Old Sow," with a supply of thirteen-inch shells. He was thankful when Congress advanced £6364 in hard cash to pay Canadian suppliers, many of whom refused paper money, but he continued to be plagued by shortages in every department and by prickly relations with Brigadier General David Wooster, commander of the 1st Connecticut. Wooster seemed to scorn protocol. He scheduled a court-martial without notifying his superior. His men were reluctant to take orders from anyone but him, nor did he encourage them to the contrary. "Strange language in an army," Schuyler complained to Congress, "but the irresistible force of necessity obliges me to put up with it." [7]

David Wooster was an anachronism in an army of much younger men. Schuyler's senior by twenty-two years, Montgomery's by more than a quarter of a century, he had become a soldier long before the Revolution and had served throughout the French and Indian War. Although a major general in the Connecticut militia, he had been reduced to brigadier when he enrolled in the Continental Army. Silas Deane, who knew him well, called him "an old woman." [8] Schuyler found him inept and disruptive. Although Wooster apologized for the unauthorized court-martial and pledged to be a proper subordinate to Montgomery, his disregard of protocol and offhand familiarity with the rank and file threatened to undercut the discipline that Schuyler had spent weeks trying to instill. Schuyler was thankful when he finally set sail for Canada.

To tighten his hold south of the St. Lawrence, Montgomery stationed Seth Warner opposite Montreal with the Green Mountain Boys and part of the 2nd New York. He posted Timothy Bedel north of St. Jean with 500 men, and ordered Captain William Douglas, a New Haven sailor, to contain *Royal Savage*, assigning him sloop *Enterprise*, schooner *Liberty*, two gondolas, and ten gunboats. Montgomery was weakest in the one category that could have reduced the fort with dispatch: high-powered artillery. He ordered batteries erected within range of the fort, although his guns lacked the fire power to pound it into submission. Braving a barrage of enemy grapeshot, Colonel Mott set up two twelve-pounders and a mortar. "They played very severely on us when we were erecting our batteries," he wrote Governor Trumbull. "I was for three days successively where the shot and shells came, and the grape-shot rattled around me like hail." [9] But his guns were at too great a distance, according to Colonel Ritzema, who doubted if they "annoyed the enemy in the least." [10] James Livingston and a crew of Canadians erected a second battery across the river, but it, too, did only light damage to the stone house and barracks block behind the squat earthen redoubts. Even Old Sow made a disappointing debut. Many of its shells dropped short, prompting Lieutenant John André of the 7th Foot to remark that "the Sow had brought her pigs to a fine market." [11]

Montgomery had begun to sense a change in his Canadian allies. They had become less friendly, less enthusiastic over the new liberty promised them by the colonies. Indians of uncertain loyalty circulated among his troops, and he feared that spies had access to his encampment. Letters from home reflected a growing uneasiness. A New York writer with Tory leanings declared that the sluggish pace of the campaign had "thrown Congresses, Committees & all their Abettors into very great confusion." [12] Congress was worried, and General Washington seemed to be having second thoughts. "Would it not have been practicable," he asked Schuyler, "to pass St. John's, leaving force enough for a blockade, or, if you could not spare the men, passing it wholly, possessing yourselves of Montreal and the surrounding country?" [13] Schuyler pointed out that if an attempt on Montreal failed, the Canadians "would not have hesitated one moment to have acted against us . . . and all our hopes in Canada would have been at an end." [14] Washington let the matter drop, but he was disturbed by the slow progress.

On the chance that he might have to storm the St. Jean defenses, Montgomery proposed erecting a battery 400 yards to the northwest, from where a breach might be opened in the rampart. He had ordered fascines made and a pathway cleared for the artillery, when John Brown advised him that both the officers and men preferred a location across the river near Livingston's battery, within range of the enemy's shipping. Brown hinted that a mutiny could be in the making if the men's wishes were disregarded.

Summoning his officers to a council of war, Montgomery spoke at length on the advantages of the northwest location. But the officers, including Captain Lamb, remained adamant. Nothing would do but the site on the east bank of the Richelieu. Conscious of his "unstable authority over the troops of different colonies," Montgomery yielded to what he called "the general sense of the army," but he felt undercut and humiliated. "Were I not afraid the example would be too generally followed and that the public service might suffer," he wrote Schuyler, "I would not stay an hour at the head of troops whose operations I cannot direct." [15]

Montgomery ordered Colonel James Clinton with part of the 3rd New York to erect the battery. Rowing downstream in full view of the enemy, they made shore safely and built a battery equipped with two twelve-pounders. Then Lamb's men came over and opened fire, giving most of their attention to *Royal Savage*, which had been warped close to shore between the two redoubts. By sundown they had riddled her hull, shattered her sternpost, and set fire to her rigging. Captain Henry Livingston, one of Montgomery's aides, reported that during the night *Royal Savage* had "careen'd so low that the water ran into her port holes." [16]

2

Major Preston had some 450 regulars in his garrison — 183 from the 26th Foot, 229 from the 7th Foot or Royal Fusiliers, and thirty-eight from the Royal Artillery. Preston was no run-of-the-mill career man. Urbanely handsome in the scarlet coat and pale yellow facings of the 26th, he carried out his duties with crisp dispatch and was possessed of an inflexible backbone. Among his officers were Captain Edward Williams of the Royal Artillery, Captain John Strong of the 26th, who had already skirmished with the enemy, Captain William Hunter of *Royal Savage*, and Lieutenant John André of the 7th Foot. André kept a journal of the siege, quite possibly on behalf of Major Preston, to whom it has been ascribed.* Elegant, debonair, prone to dabble in light verse, he had

---

* Preston may have delegated the actual writing of the journal to André while taking full responsibility for its contents, a not uncommon practice. The document appears to be in André's handwriting, although it speaks for Preston.[17]

brought along his paintbox, to indulge a flair for illustration. In the colonies he would win repute as a lady-killer and would one day conspire with Benedict Arnold to deliver West Point to the British.

The French volunteers, about ninety in all, were led by François Marie Picoté de Belestre, a veteran of the French and Indian War. His lieutenants included Major de Longueuil and Captains Lotbinière, de Rouville, and Deschambault, all members of the *noblesse*. Samuel Mackay and David Monin were captains in the contingent of Royal Highland Emigrants. Mackay was a fervent loyalist who had helped rout Ethan Allen at St. Jean and who vowed to "chastise the presumptuous rebels." [18]   There were also eighty women and children in the fort, dependents of personnel, whom Preston had gathered in from a cluster of outbuildings that abutted the redoubts. Although Captain Marr had done much to update the outpost, Preston was unhappy with the cramped accommodations, which required part of his command to sleep on the floor. To add to their misery, some of the men had no blankets — "in a Climate," André wrote, "where the nights of September and October are as cold as those of the two succeeding months in England." [19]

General Prescott had hoped that Preston would keep the enemy off balance with hard-hitting forays, but the major remained warily on the defensive. Cut off by the enemy, he heard nothing from his superiors in Montreal. Couriers, dispatched by night, failed to return. His men were growing edgy, even the regulars. The accidental discharge of a musket occasioned a general alarm. One night his artillerymen opened fire when a sentry's challenge was not returned. "In the morning," André said, "a Horse was found dead; this was the Enemy our out sentry had seen and challeng'd." André asked himself questions about a war that divided friends and neighbors, even families. "Englishmen fighting against Englishmen," he lamented, "French against French, and Indians of the same Tribe against each other." [20]

At first, Montgomery's cannons caused only minor damage: a sergeant of the regulars grazed by a shell, some splinters knocked off *Royal Savage*, grapeshot penetrating a staff room. But presently the shells began to find their target, arcing over the redoubts to blow out windows, level chimneys, and demolish roofs and walls. At night, men, women, and children crowded into the dank cellar of the stone house, but the smell of unwashed bodies drove many back outdoors, to shiver in the autumn cold. One day some of the French volunteers, seen conversing in hushed tones by several in the fort, vanished from their posts. Others vainly implored Major Preston to give them permission to go home. The first casualties were recorded — a private in the 7th Foot, a Royal Highland Emigrant. André, who overheard laughter in an American battery during a lull in the bombardment, acknowledged that the Old Sow had become "a better Joke to them than to us." There were a few hopeful moments — a party of Indians brought word of Ethan Allen's capture; a herd of roaming beef cattle was coralled by Captain Monin and a French volunteer.[21]

With the new battery lobbing shells into the stone house and barracks block, Preston began losing men at the rate of one every other day. Three regulars were killed in quick succession, a carpenter's arm was blown off, a French volunteer lost both legs. "The Situation of the Sick and wounded was a very cruel one," André said. "They were neither out of reach of danger, nor were they shelter'd from the Inclemency of the Weather, or provided with any of those things which might alleviate their Sufferings." A shell tore through the roof of the stone house, demolishing walls, windows, whole rooms.

As the Windows of the house were all broke [André wrote], as many as cou'd find room in the Cellars slept there. The rest unable either to get a place or to bear the heat and disagreeable smell arising from such numbers being crowded together slept above in cold and danger or walk'd about the greatest part of the night . . . Our Shatter'd House together with the ruinous Traverses and mud Ditches, broken platforms, etc., exhibited a very ragged Scene. Within Doors, if that cou'd be called within doors where Doors and Windows were broken in pieces, the Appearance was no better; Heaps of boards, Earth, glass, brick and other Rubbish lay promiscuously scatter'd.[22]

Food was running out, and Preston put the garrison on half rations. Preston had wanted *Royal Savage* to silence the enemy batteries, but Captain Hunter had refused to take her out lest she be raked by a crossfire. Preston made no effort to conceal his disgust. When enemy artillery disabled the schooner, Hunter was blamed for failing to salvage her guns. Stung by the criticism, he reminded Preston in a terse communication that he had been "many Years at Sea" and that it was "notorious to many in the Navy" that he could "Rigg a ship, Navigate and Maneuvre her." [23] But the major was not impressed. He had expected something better of the vessel that had struck such terror in the hearts of Montgomery's jittery recruits.

On October 13, sentries reported men with knapsacks threading through the trees on the east bank of the Richelieu. That night, invisible to lookouts, two bateaux slipped past, each carrying a nine-pounder. With Montgomery's approval, 300 Canadians led by James Livingston and Jeremiah Duggan were converging on Chambly. Duggan had promised them "all the plunder in the garrison." [24]

Livingston had enrolled several hundred Canadians at his headquarters at Pointe Olivier. Governor Tryon of New York was told that *habitants* from "six Parishes on the River Sorel [the Richelieu] amounting to 1500 fit to bear Arms renounced their Allegiance at the instigation of James Livingston and one Du Gand [Duggan]" but that some of the more responsible citizens, "the principal Farmers, the officers of Militia, etc.," had persuaded a number to defect.[25] Although most seem to have been fair-weather allies, there were some who had adopted an American definition of their rights and liberties. Francis Masères credited "the canting Enthusiasts who have come at different times from New England to preach Liberty and independence among them" with having "more influence over their principles, (if you allow them to have any), in this unhappy contest than all the Jesuits in France." [26] In Quebec, an explosive sea captain named Thomas Gamble declared that "the Canadians talk of that damned absurd word liberty" and that "their minds are all poisoned by emissaries from New England and the damned rascals of merchants here and at Montreal." [27]

Livingston and Duggan were joined at Chambly by John Brown and fifty Americans. The fort's commander, the Honorable Joseph Stopford, son of an earl and a major in the 7th Foot, had eighty-one officers and men from his own unit and a bombardier and four other ranks from the Royal Artillery. He had an ample reserve of food for his garrison, and, although the fort was not proof against heavy artillery, he had three mortars, a large supply of muskets, and 124 barrels of gunpowder. What he lacked was Charles Preston's mettle.

By now, Brown and Livingston had between 300 and 400 men. Readying their nine-pounders, they proceeded to bombard the fort, knocking a chunk of masonry from the wall, damaging a chimney, and inflicting a minor wound on a member of the garrison. After two days of this, Stopford surrendered, turning over all of his gunpowder, which he should have thrown into the Richelieu. When Montgomery heard the news, he was elated. Nearly out of ammunition, he had written Janet, "The instant I can with decency slip my neck out of this yoke I will return to my family and farm, and that peace of mind which I can't have in my present situation." [28] But the acquisition of Stopford's gunpowder gave him fresh hope. "We have gotten six tons of powder which, with God's blessing, will finish our business here," he wrote Schuyler.[29] No less discouraged than his colleague, Schuyler had previously written Washington that the army might run out of ammunition within "a very few days." [30]

Preston learned of the surrender when he was asked to grant safe passage to bateaux carrying the wives and children of Stopford's personnel. One of the bateaux put in at the fort to allow the wives of three members of his own garrison to disembark. As the rest of the women and children continued upstream, Stopford and his troops were herded past. One may assume that they were eyed coldly by the men lining Preston's shell-pocked redoubts.

3

At Montreal the *seigneurs* chafed under Carleton's tight restrictions. Still forbidden to engage the enemy, parties of French militia were put to flight by much smaller American patrols. On one lamentable occasion forty Canadians, under orders not to open fire, were routed by a mere handful of Seth Warner's men. Carleton was accused of cowardice, even of seeking an accommodation with the enemy. "Everyone groaned and murmured against such conduct," Sanguinet said.[31]

However, late in October the governor announced that he would cross to Longueuil and join Colonel Maclean's corps in a drive to relieve the St. Jean garrison. Drums beat for volunteers, and about 800 Canadians and eighty Conosadaga Indians enrolled. Carleton assigned them to Saint-Luc de La Corne and François de Lorimier and reinforced their ranks with 130 British regulars. Forty boats were assembled at Ile Ste. Hélène, and on the afternoon of the 30th, a clear, gusty day, the fleet rounded the island's tip.

Seth Warner had quartered his 300 Green Mountain Boys and 2nd New Yorkers in an empty fortress known as Longueuil Castle. He was expecting an attack and the night before had been provided with a four-pound cannon. On the morning of the 30th, a picket boat had hovered offshore. No shots were traded, but Warner kept close watch and when he saw Carleton's fleet he hustled his fourpounder to the water's edge and deployed his men in woods bordering the river.

Crossing to Longueuil, Carleton probed the shoreline for a landing place. His troops fired into the woods where Warner's men were hidden, and an artillery crew opened up with a small fieldpiece in one of the bateaux. "Several Cannon Balls came very near me," Captain Fassett wrote, "and the Musket balls came close to our heads in great plenty." As his men returned the shots from the shelter of stone walls and thickets, Warner spied an enemy canoe nearing a rock-strewn reef only a short way upstream. He ordered Captain Oliver Potter and a detail of Green Mountain Boys to fend it off, but before they came abreast of the canoe two Indians had scrambled ashore. Potter pinned down the remaining occupants on the reef.

As the afternoon waned, Carleton tried repeatedly to force a landing, only to be stopped by a barrage of musket fire. Bateaux sent downstream were kept offshore by Warner's four-pounder. Toward dusk Carleton ordered his fleet to put about. Lorimier, who had maneuvered his craft close to shore, looked back and saw the entire flotilla in retreat. As he joined it, he detected bonfires on Ile Ste. Hélène, lit to signal scattered Indians. He and his fellow *seigneurs* were incredulous and angry at what had happened. They believed that if Carleton had taken greater risks, he could have made shore and dispersed the enemy.[32]

Warner's men quickly accounted for the few Indians and Canadians who had come ashore. Two were ferreted out in the woods. Five were found on the reef — two Indians already dead, another mortally wounded, and two Canadians, one Jean Baptiste Despins and a barber named Lacoste, cowed but unhurt. After cross-examining the prisoners, Warner sent them to Montgomery in custody of Heman Allen, Ethan's brother. His troops had come through the battle all but unscathed. Captain Fassett reported that one of his men had "lost a piece of skin from his arm as big as a York shilling."[33]

At St. Jean, Montgomery had been vindicated in his choice of a northwest battery. His officers had finally acknowledged that it promised to take a greater toll than the guns across the Richelieu. He ordered mortars, a pair of twelve-pounders, and a nine-pounder installed within 250 yards of the fort, supplying them with Stopford's gunpowder.

The garrison was nearly out of food. What was left of the stone house and barracks block gave scant protection from the rains that had turned the enclosure into a quagmire. Everyone was short of sleep; many had fallen ill. Uniforms were caked with mud, and some of the men had wrapped their feet in rags to replace worn-out shoes. On November 1, as the faithful throughout the province observed the Feast of All Saints, Lamb's artillery opened fire from the northwest battery, lobbing shells into the fort for six consecutive hours. Colonel Ritzema said that, by the time Lamb finished, his guns had "knocked every Thing in the Fort to Shatters."[34] Chimneys, walls, and gun platforms lay in heaps. Three men had been killed, five wounded.

At sundown Lacoste, the captured barber, advanced under a flag of truce to acquaint Preston with the defeat at Longueuil and to convey Montgomery's demand for an immediate surrender. Preston had been told that Lacoste was subject to mental quirks and could not be trusted. He still hoped for relief and, to gain time, asked for a delay of four days. Montgomery would not hear of it. "If you will not surrender this day," he replied, "it will be unnecessary to make any further proposals. The Garrison shall be Prisoners of War — they shall not have the honours of War & I cannot ensure the Officers of their baggage." [35] To substantiate Lacoste's testimony, he offered to allow a British officer to interview his other prisoner, Jean Baptiste Despins, who was in custody aboard a schooner.

Preston sent Lieutenant André to question Despins. Captain Williams of the Royal Artillery accompanied him, to request that the Canadian prisoners be permitted to go home and that the regulars be sent back to England. Presently the two returned, André satisfied that Lacoste had told the truth, Williams bringing Montgomery's terms. The garrison would be allowed the honors of war, Montgomery ruled, but all the prisoners, British and Canadian alike, must be interned in the colonies. Officers might keep their side arms, and quartermasters might collect the prisoners' pay and baggage at Montreal. His terms included an expression of regret that the garrison had not stood for "a better cause." To this, Preston took strong exception, vowing that he and his men would "die with their arms in their Hands" rather than "submit to the Indignity of such a Reflection." [36] Montgomery wisely deleted the slur, and his terms were accepted.

On the morning of November 3, a day both wet and blustery, Preston led his command out of the ruined fort. The regulars came first, the 26th Foot in scarlet coats with yellow facing, the fusiliers in scarlet faced blue, the artillery in blue faced red. They were followed by Captain Hunter's pig-tailed sailors, Captains Mackay and Monin at the head of the Royal Highland Emigrants, and Picoté de Belestre with the French volunteers. At the end of the column came the throng of women and children who had shared the siege with the military. Marching to fife and drum and with colors flying, they grounded arms in the presence of Montgomery's motley troops and boarded bateaux for their journey southward. When Preston and his officers reached Fort Ticonderoga, Schuyler was reminded of happier times. Before the war he had met them while traveling in Ireland, and they had shown him "the most polite and friendly attention." [37] He sent word to Governor Trumbull, in whose colony they were first interned, to treat them kindly.

Preston had lost about twenty men during the siege, Montgomery somewhat more. André said that the members of the garrison had "shew'd a cheerfulness under their Fatigues which . . . can but reflect honour upon them," enduring "dangers and hardships which have often been the price of honour to more fortunate troops." He maintained that only a shortage of food and ammunition had compelled them to ground arms. "We left in the Forts about 3 days provision," he said, "scarce any loose powder and three boxes of Ammunition of each gun that was mounted . . . We may thank our Enemy in some sort for leaving us in such light field Works the credit of having been only reduc'd by Famine." [38]

Montgomery ordered *Royal Savage* raised and reconditioned. He detached James Easton with 300 men to intercept the enemy at Sorel. Joined by John Brown, Easton found Maclean's troops anchored offshore aboard schooner *Providence* and snow *Fell*. Maclean had advanced as far as St. Denis, but when informed of Carleton's defeat, he had discharged his militia and returned to the St. Lawrence. After exchanging a few shots with Brown and Easton, both ships sailed away, *Providence* for Montreal with a corps of regulars, *Fell* for Quebec with Maclean and his Royal Highland Emigrants. Brown would claim that before *Fell* made her escape, he and Easton had "plumped her through in many places" and that in routing the two vessels they had "swept land and sea." [39]

On the night of the 3rd, a snow-laden northeaster turned the road to La Prairie into a morass, "sometimes midleg high," Chaplain Trumbull said. "The Roads ever Since Friday have been mud and mire," he wrote. "Scarce a Spot of dry Ground for miles together." [40] For three days the mud-spattered troops slogged into La Prairie, Lamb's company bringing six captured artillery pieces. Most of the time it rained. "In about four days," Colonel Bedel wrote the New Hampshire Committee of Safety, "we shall have either a wooden leg or a golden chain at Montreal." [41]

From La Prairie, Montgomery sent a message to Montreal's citizens, advising them to surrender peaceably or suffer "the dreadful consequences of a bombardment." [42] On the 11th, he crossed to Ile des Soeurs with the 2nd and 4th New York, Waterbury's regiment, and part of Wooster's command. He was met by William

Heywood, a colleague of Thomas Walker's, who told him that the city was weakly defended and that its walls could be breached. Next morning, he received four citizens deputized to discuss terms.

4

With Montgomery at the city gates, a fleet of eleven sail slipped past Ile des Soeurs. Carleton was aboard brigantine *Gaspé* with General Prescott, his aide Charles de Lanaudière, Saint-Luc de La Corne, and several Canadian officers. He had assigned his remaining regulars to ships in the fleet and had brought along Thomas Walker, consigned in irons to a ship's hold. Before leaving Montreal, he had written Lord Dartmouth that the citizens were "greatly frightened, both at the Rebels in open Arms without, & at those Traytors within, who by their Art & insinuation are still more dangerous to the publick safety." [43] He had been slow to leave the city, first spiking the guns and destroying the military stores, and he was lucky to escape capture.

One of the ships quickly ran aground. By the time she was afloat, the wind had changed and the fleet hove to near Sorel. Easton's troops spied the vessels and opened fire, driving them a short way upstream. Presently Ira Allen, another of Ethan's brothers, rowed out to the anchored fleet. He had come, he said, to deliver Easton's ultimatum to the governor. It was terse and unequivocal:

You are very sensible that I am in Possession at this Place, and from the Strength of the United Colonies on both sides, your own situation is Rendered very disagreeable. I am therefore Induced to make you the following Proposal, viz — That if you will Resign your Fleet to me immediately without destroying the Effects on Board, you and your men shall be used with due Civility, together with women and children on Board — to this I expect your direct and Immediate answer. Should you Neglect you will cherefully take the Consequences which will Follow.[44]

Easton had only a few guns at Sorel and none mounted on the north shore of the St. Lawrence, but Carleton had no way of ascertaining the size of the enemy batteries or of recognizing what was a boldfaced bluff. After Allen returned downstream, Carleton called together his officers and ship captains. All agreed that his presence was essential in Quebec and that a way must be found for him to run the rebel blockade. Captain Jean Baptiste Bouchette, a seasoned pilot known as the "Wild Pigeon," offered to attempt it in a whaleboat. Immense risks would be involved, but no alternative was forthcoming. On the night of November 16 the governor, disguised in the wool cap and blanket coat of an *habitant* and accompanied by Charles de Lanaudière, by a young officer named Bouthiller, and by Joseph de Niverville, a sixty-year-old veteran of the French and Indian War, descended the side of brigantine *Gaspé* to Bouchette's whaleboat. It was agreed that orders would be given in a low whisper or, preferably, by signal. At a wave from Bouchette, the craft pulled away on muffled oars.

Luckily, it was a murky night. Bouchette steered for the north shore, where John Brown was stationed, ordering his passengers to prostrate themselves so that, in the glow of enemy campfires, their craft would resemble a drifting log. The sudden barking of a dog made him stiffen, but he breathed more easily when he heard an "All's well!" from one of Brown's sentries. Distrusting even muffled oars, he signaled his passengers to paddle the whaleboat with their hands as he skirted the dark shoreline and edged past silhouetted islands. Only when he was sure that his craft was safely below the blockade did he allow them to resume rowing.

Bouchette put in at Trois Rivières, where the governor heard that rebel soldiers were already at Pointe aux Trembles (Neuville), a few miles above Quebec. Carleton was exhausted. After a hurried meal at the home of Godefroi de Tonnancourt, he fell asleep. He was wakened by the voices of American soldiers demanding quarters at Tonnancourt's house. With his only exit through the front hallway, he elbowed past the soldiers, relying on the creditability of his disguise and the fluency of his French. Both proved convincing. When he reached the street, he rejoined his comrades and continued downstream until he was picked up by snow *Fell* and taken safely to Quebec.[45]

General Prescott retired the fleet to Lavaltrie, where the eleven sail hove to and dropped anchor. On the 19th, John Brown rowed out in the company of Jonas Fay, a Green Mountain Boy. The pair invited Prescott to deputize one of his officers to come ashore and see the American batteries for himself. In agreeing to the proposal, Prescott chose a man so unschooled in Yankee wiles that Brown apparently convinced him that he had a pair of thirty-two-pounders without showing him either. "If you should chance to escape this battery, which is my small battery," Brown warned, "I have a grand battery at the mouth of the Sorel which will infallibly sink all your ships." Prescott believed what the officer told him and, jettisoning his gunpowder, surrendered the eleven sail to Brown and Easton. The following spring Charles Carroll of Maryland, who came to Montreal as part of a congressional commission, was told that when Brown brought off his bluff, he had not mounted a single cannon on the north shore.[46]

Thomas Walker, finally released from irons, gloated over Prescott and his men, who were taken to Montreal and made to ground arms in the presence of a unit composed largely of teen-age boys. Mindful of Prescott's insolence toward Ethan Allen, Montgomery treated the hated brigadier with the "sovereign contempt his inhumanity and barbarity merit." He was astonished that Prescott had surrendered the fleet without testing Easton's batteries. "I blush for His Majesty's troops!" he wrote Janet. "Such an instance of poltroonery I never met with! And all because we had half-a-dozen cannon on the bank of the river to annoy him in his retreat!"[47]

Montgomery gave the citizens of Montreal four hours to submit terms. Twelve spokesmen, equally divided between French and English Canadians, drew up articles requesting the protection of private property, freedom of religion, the right to choose their own judiciary, continued trade with Britain and the Indians, exemption from bearing arms against the mother country, the return of prisoners of war, and a pledge that troops would not be quartered in private homes.[48] Montgomery reminded them that they were not entitled to a formal capitulation because they had "neither the ammunition, artillery, troops, nor provisions . . . to fulfill one article of the treaty." He had no authority to permit trade with Britain, he said, or to return prisoners of war, but he promised to treat the prisoners well and, if possible, to refrain from billeting troops in private homes. He called for "a virtuous Provincial Convention" that would "set the civil and religious rights of this and her sister Colonies on a permanent foundation," elect delegates to the Continental Congress, and declare Canada the fourteenth American colony.[49]

On November 13, Montgomery's army marched through the Récollet Gate to occupy the city. The troops eddied through the streets, thronged the Place d'Armes, idled outside American headquarters at the Château de Ramezay, and eyed the great churches and the imposing stone houses, with their lush lawns and gardens. Except for Quebec, the whole province seemed ready to capitulate. Forty residents of the Montreal suburbs pledged their support. A delegation from Trois Rivières came to intercede for their fellow citizens' lives and property. It was a promising start, and, as if to underscore Montgomery's triumphs, the weather had cleared. "The Streets which had been over Shoe in Mire were so Stiffened that it was tolerably dry and Comfortable Walking," Chaplain Trumbull said.[50]

Nevertheless, in spite of his successes, Montgomery had to contend with infighting and testiness among his officers and an epidemic of homesickness among his men. Seth Warner had quarreled with him, and Colonel Mott accused him of catering to Colonel Donald Campbell, a loud-spoken New Yorker whose fearful cursing was an affront to Mott's New England piety.[51] Captain Lamb complained about his low pay. "Captain Lamb is a restless genius and of bad temper," Montgomery wrote Schuyler. "He is brave, active and intelligent, but very turbulent and troublesome." [52] Home was on everyone's mind. Although their enlistments did not expire until the end of the year, many of the New England troops believed they had done their duty and were entitled to go home immediately. Montgomery urged them to re-enlist until mid-April lest they "lay him under the necessity of abandoning Canada; of undoing in one day what has been the work of months, and of restoring to an enraged and hitherto disappointed enemy the means of carrying a cruel war into the very bowels of their Country." [53] But few heeded his call. "The troops are very impatient," Chaplain Trumbull wrote, "are averse to enlisting and long to be dismissed home." [54]

At St. Jean, Montgomery had promised some of the Connecticut troops an immediate discharge after Montreal was taken. Now they held him to it and were joined by others from New England. "Most of the New England Men embraced the Opportunity," Colonel Ritzema observed, whereas "the Yorkers in general resolved to see an End to the Campaign." [55] Indeed, the Yorkers kept faith with their commander, together with about 200 from Wooster's regiment, but most New Englanders went home. Seth Warner left with nearly all of his command, although Montgomery had not intended his promise to the Connecticut troops to apply to the Green Mountain Boys or any other New Englanders. Bedel and Easton departed, taking the majority of their men. The New Englanders were an independent lot, prone to make up their own minds and act as they saw fit. They had put up with months of hardship. They had been paid low wages, usually long overdue. A captain's pay was only twenty dollars a month, a private's six and two-thirds. With the capture of Montreal, they believed that they had fulfilled their obligations as soldiers and as citizens, and no appeals to patriotism could change their minds.

"They have such an intemperate desire to return home that nothing can equal it," Schuyler wrote Congress. "It might have been expected that men influenced by a sense of liberty would not have required such a promise, and that others, to whom it was not immediately intended, would not have taken advantage of it; but all this flows from the same unhappy source with the other disorders too prevalent in our troops — a want of subordination and discipline, an evil which may prove fatal to us." [56]

The day after Montgomery's plea for re-enlistments, Chaplain Trumbull slogged with others from his regiment into La Prairie. He had had enough of war and was thankful to be leaving Canada. "Perhaps there never was a more ill governed Profane and Wicked army among a People of Such Advantages, on Earth," he said. "There is no Disposition here to religious Duties. We have not had one Day of Thanksgiving or one of publick Prayer ordered for all the victories of this Season. I hate such company and ardently wish for the Return of Seasons of Domestick and publick Worship." [57] Soon he would know the comforts of a warm hearth and his own bed and would look down from his pulpit on a properly respectful congregation.

Although he admitted it only in letters to Philip Schuyler and to Janet, Montgomery was as homesick as his men. He hoped that Schuyler would take his place after Quebec was captured. "Will not your health permit you to reside at Montreal this winter?" he wrote his colleague. "I must go home, if I walk by the side of the lake, this winter." [58] He promised Janet to "return home the instant I have put matters on such a footing as to be able to retire with propriety." [59] But first he must reorganize his command, provide the city with a military government, and, before the start of winter, take Quebec. He put General Wooster in charge at Montreal, commissioned James Livingston to raise a Canadian regiment, and contracted for arms and ammunition with Christophe Pélissier, proprietor of an ironworks at Trois Rivières. He outfitted some of his thinly clad troops with British uniforms left behind by the 7th and 26th and borrowed £5000 from James Price to buy his men winter clothing. He welcomed the services of Moses Hazen, who had been carried off with Thomas Walker aboard a vessel in Carleton's fleet but was now back in Montreal, eager to identify with the Americans.

In a letter to his father-in-law, Montgomery debated how he could take Quebec. A siege would require heavier artillery than he possessed, but if he stormed the city he might take it by surprise. Of course, his task would be hugely simplified if Carleton would elect to join battle outside the walls, as Montcalm had done. "Wolfe's success was a lucky hit, or rather a series of hits," he wrote. "All sober and scientifick calculation was against him, until Montcalm, permitting his courage to get the better of his discretion, gave up the advantages of his fortress and came out to try his strength on the plain." But he acknowledged that Carleton, who had served with Wolfe at Quebec, would not be apt to leave his stronghold for the uncertainties of equal combat, as Montcalm had been forced to do by dwindling food supplies and the vulnerability of his defenses.[60]

His first letter from Arnold, dated November 8 at "St. Mary's, 2½ leagues from Point Levi," informed him of the expedition's safe arrival. "Can only say," Arnold wrote, "that we have hauled our bateaus up over falls, up rapid streams, over carrying places, and marched through morasses, thick woods, and over mountains, about three hundred and twenty miles, many of which we had to pass several times to bring over our baggage." [61]

On November 28, Montgomery ordered his 300 New Yorkers aboard ship and sailed downstream, leaving Wooster in charge at Montreal. He was joined at Sorel by James Livingston, with nearly 200 Canadians, and by John Brown, with 160 diehards from Easton's command. "I live in hopes to see you in six weeks," he wrote Janet.[62]

VI

"Had I Been Ten Days Sooner"

1

ARNOLD AND HIS PARTY awoke to thick snow squalls. As they pushed up the Dead, now shrunken to the size of a mountain stream, snow gathered on their gear and melted on their wet clothing. After two portages they entered a series of ponds (Chain of Ponds) that would take them to the edge of Canada. Although divided by narrows, the ponds formed an attenuated waterway and were walled in by snow-laden hillsides. "The Sea ran so high," Arnold reported, "we were obliged to go on shore several times to Bail our battoes." [1] At the far end of the last pond, the Dead threaded northward through massed alders. Arnold followed it until dark. He estimated that he had traveled fourteen miles through wind and snow.

Next morning he continued upstream, weaving through bogs and alder thickets, until he came to another clutch of ponds and found Steele's blazes marking the four-mile carry across the Height of Land between the watersheds of Maine and the St. Lawrence. Although it was late afternoon, he and his men started up the ridge, groping for purchase in new-fallen snow and meshed undergrowth. The troops would dub this "the terrible carrying place" and would associate it with grim memories. "The boats and carriers often fell down into the snow," Private Morison wrote after his company had made the two-mile ascent. "Some of them were much hurt by reason of their feet sticking fast among stones . . . This day's movement was by far the most oppressive of any we had experienced." [2]

At the top of the ridge Arnold overtook Hanchet's detachment. Descending by early daylight toward Chaudière Pond, he came to a grassy opening that Montresor had described as "a most beautiful meadow," threaded by Seven Mile Stream (today's Arnold River). Here he was met by Lieutenants Steele and Church and by one Jaquin, a woodsman attached to the expedition who had been directed to sound out the *habitants* near Sartigan. Steele briefed Arnold on the perils of the Chaudière. Jaquin reported that the *habitants* seemed friendly and could be trusted.[3] Before continuing to Chaudière Pond, Arnold sent word to his division commanders to jettison their bateaux, except the few they might need for the sick and the men's baggage.

Arnold followed Seven Mile Stream to Chaudière Pond and, keeping to the east shore, put in near an abandoned wigwam to await Hanchet's troops. He spied them at sundown, marooned on a point of land across two miles of water. Instead of bearing east on high ground, they had blundered into the boggy outlet of Seven Mile Stream and become lost. They were brought off by boats in a series of crossings that continued half the night. Hanchet said that they had "waded two miles thro' water to their waists." [4] In the morning Arnold wrote Washington that he had been "much deceived in every account of our route" and had met with "a thousand difficulties I never apprehended." [5] But he still expected to reach Sartigan within three or four days and dispatched Isaac Hull to warn the army to "keep to the east side of the Lake" and avoid the bogs. "By no means keep the brook," he wrote his officers, "which will carry you into a swamp, out of which it will be impossible for you to get." [6] Hull, who had accompanied Dennis Getchell and Samuel Berry on their preliminary scout to the upper Kennebec and the Dead, was thought to have acquired enough feel for the terrain to avoid Hanchet's mistake and guide the army across higher ground to the east shore of Chaudière Pond.

On October 27, Hanchet and most of his command left on foot for Sartigan. Arnold continued by water. In addition to Steele and Church, he took with him five from Hanchet's detachment. He had found a birch canoe near the wigwam. Appropriating it for his own use, he outdistanced the four bateaux and reached the lake's outlet by midmorning. When the rest caught up, he led them down into the Chaudière, where he would have welcomed a guide to steer him along its surging course, known only to Steele and his men, who had seen it from the shore. Speeding past snags and downed trees, he had gone about fifteen miles when he was swept into a swirl of white water. All five of his craft overturned. Two were smashed to bits. Luckily, the men made shore, but guns, ammunition, and supplies sank to the bottom or were carried downstream. A few supplies were recovered, and Arnold had them lashed to his canoe and to the two remaining bateaux. He was about to shove off when someone shouted, "Cataract!" Listening, he could hear the rumble of cascading water. As he and his men cut through the woods, they passed a cataract that would have demolished their boats and drowned them all. He credited their escape to an "interposition of Providence." [7]

Next morning Arnold divided his command, directing some of the men to continue on foot while he and a picked few went by water. He had not gone far when his canoe sprang a leak. He and his men crowded into the two bateaux, traveling until nightfall against an east wind laced with snow. The following day, they encountered a cataract and, two miles below it, yet another portage. While they were unloading the bateaux, they were hailed by two Indians, who introduced themselves as friendly Penobscots and offered assistance. As the Indians lugged baggage up the river bank and helped with the bateaux, Arnold wondered if other tribesmen he met in Canada would be as accommodating. Toward sundown he passed the mouth of the Du Loup, where the Chaudière slowed into a gentler waterway. He sped downstream until he saw the wink of lights. Sartigan, he had been told, contained only a few log huts and a scattering of wigwams.

2

By the time Arnold had left Chaudière Pond, the first division was crossing the Height of Land, with the second and third close behind it. The men were almost out of food. Some in Thayer's command had made soup from shoe leather. Dr. Senter had boiled up a pig's jawbone, "destitute of any covering." [8] When the troops made the ascent, they were so weak from hunger that what Private Morison described as "a dismal portage . . . covered with fallen trees, stones and brush" became a fearsome ordeal.[9] In keeping with Arnold's order, most of the bateaux had been jettisoned. The Pennsylvania riflemen had abandoned all but one, kept for Lieutenant John McClellan, who was down with pneumonia and too weak to walk. Only Daniel Morgan had refused to give up his boats, ordering his men to carry seven of them across the Height of Land. Private Henry saw the Virginians toiling up the ridge with "flesh worn from their shoulders, even to the bone." [10]

Word of Enos' return traveled swiftly through the column, reaching Dearborn's company on the Height of Land and the Virginians as they launched their bateaux in Seven Mile Stream. The curses heaped on Enos mingled with those already lavished on "the terrible carrying place." The last of the food was distributed — four or five pints of flour to each man, scraps of pork for a lucky few. Dr. Senter mixed his flour with water and baked it in ashes, Indian style, to form minute cakes that he dubbed "Lillipu." He noted that some of the men ate their entire portion at a single sitting, "determined (as they expressed it) to have a full meal, letting the morrow look out for itself." [11] When Isaac Hull brought Arnold's warning to keep to the high ground east of Seven Mile Stream, several companies had already left — Morgan's by bateau, four others on foot.

Dearborn had happened on an Indian canoe and had gone ahead to reconnoiter the web of waterways emptying into Chaudière Pond.[12] He found Goodrich's company halted at a branch of Seven Mile Stream. Goodrich had gone in search of a bateau that carried his company's flour supply. He planned to return with it and ferry his men across the rivulet. Presently, Dearborn's own troops came up, soaked and chilled after wading to their waists. By now it was late in the afternoon. Dearborn paddled to Chaudière Pond and, after a lengthy search, found Goodrich and his party on an offshore island, still looking for the bateau. They had waded long distances, sometimes to their armpits, but they had not seen the bateau or located a ford where the troops could cross.

As they conversed, Dearborn and Goodrich spied a campfire on the east shore of the lake. Crowding everyone into the canoe, they paddled toward it. Gradually, the glow from the campfire lit up a wigwam, and as they neared shore a solitary recruit came to the water's edge. He told them that he belonged to Hanchet's detachment but had been dropped for squandering his rations and ordered to await his unit. He had not seen a trace of the missing bateau. After combing the lake further but to no avail, Dearborn and Goodrich waited out the night at the wigwam. Back in the swamp, their troops bedded down so close to the water that had it rained they would have been awash. Private Melvin of Dearborn's company had a few scraps of pork to chew on, but most of the men had nothing to eat and spent the night tending smoky campfires fed by logs cut in knee-deep water.

Smith's riflemen followed the others into the bog. John Shaeffer, a purblind drummer boy, tripped and fell so many times that Private Henry took him in hand and guided him through footing that was risky even for the unhandicapped. Kept off balance by the drum on his shoulder, Shaeffer sloshed through quagmires, groped amid alder thickets, stumbled over roots and tussocks. With Henry's help he kept up with the rest, uttering fewer complaints than many with normal eyesight. When someone stole his rations, Henry and his comrades allowed him a cup of their closely guarded flour.

Henry was in the same group as the wives of Private Warner and Sergeant Grier. They had come to the edge of a flooded swamp when James Warner was reported missing. His wife insisted on going to his assistance, although no one knew how far back he might be. The rest waited an hour before crossing the swamp, which was glazed with ice. Private Henry marveled at Mrs. Grier, who hoisted up her skirts and forged through the waist-deep water, making less fuss than the men. On the far shore they tarried again but there was still no sign of Mrs. Warner. She had found her husband propped against a tree, too weak to rise, and had remained with him until he died. Covering him with leaves, she had shouldered his rifle and followed where the rest had gone. She rejoined them near Seven Mile Stream.[13]

At daybreak, Dearborn and Goodrich returned with the canoe and began ferrying the troops. Many crossings were required, but with the help of the riflemen's bateau they brought everyone to Chaudière Pond. Dearborn had left some pork and flour at the wigwam, but when he returned he was told that Morgan's men had stopped by in their bateaux and appropriated his entire cache.

Greene's three companies, Hendricks' riflemen, and most of Hanchet's command were still encamped when Isaac Hull joined them on the meadow east of Seven Mile Stream. He told them that Arnold had left for Sartigan, that the *habitants* were found to be friendly, and that Schuyler's army had scored a great victory on the Richelieu. The men broke into cheers. As they made ready to follow him over the high ground to Chaudière Pond, some of them finished off their rationed flour, confident that it would soon be replenished.

Somewhere, Isaac Hull went astray. At first he kept to high ground, bearing east of north, but then, all but imperceptibly, he began to slope westward. Within a short time the men were crawling through blowdowns, thrashing amid alders, slogging through swamps glazed with windowpane ice. "We walked in great fear of breaking our bones or dislocating our joints," Private Stocking wrote. "To be disabled from walking in this situation is sure death." [14] Hull turned eastward, following a stream that he hoped would regain high ground, but he came out at an irregularly shaped lake known today as Lac aux Araignées (Spider Lake). In going around it, he led the men to the tips of peninsulas and down long inlets. Some of the recruits, weakened by hunger, dropped far behind. Private Samuel Nichols of Topham's company was not seen again. By nightfall, everyone was cursing Hull. "We find now that the Pilot knows no more the way than the most ignorant of ourselves," Captain Thayer said. [15] Darkness found them at the edge of a vast swamp Private Stocking thought so forbidding that he was sure "no wild animals would inhabit it." [16] Kicking away the snow, the men dossed down in wet clothes. Only Captain Thayer and a few comrades had the makings of a supper in a solitary partridge that Thayer had bagged.

"Never perhaps was there a more forlorn set of human beings collected together in one place," Private Morison said, "every one of us shivering from head to foot, as hungry as wolves, and nothing to eat save the little flour we had left." [17] Hull was as frightened as the men he was supposed to lead. In Dr. Senter's words, they were as lost as though they had been "in the unknown interior of Africa, or the deserts of Arabia." [18] Next day they trudged fifteen miles along the shores of the multipronged lake, not knowing where they were, many too exhausted to care, but at sundown a great cheer went up. Word traveled swiftly through the column. Footprints had been found. They were back on course, close to Chaudière Pond.

With Greene's troops in the lead, they marched to the Chaudière and continued downstream past the same rapids where Arnold's boats had overturned. The shore was lined with debris and wrecked bateaux. Morgan's seven boats, taken at such cost over the Height of Land, had all capsized in the fast water, the crews had struggled for their lives, and one rifleman, Private George Innis, had drowned. Farther downstream were other wrecks. Captain Goodrich had lost his flour supply in the same craft that had eluded him on Chaudière Pond. Lieutenant McClellan, the rifleman with pneumonia, had nearly perished when Smith's bateau overturned. Brought ashore half-drowned, he had been treated by Dr. Senter, who had lost his medicine chest when a boat capsized.

By now the men were eating shoe leather, belts, cartridge pouches, shaving soap, lip salve, pomatum. Some of the riflemen boiled and ate their moccasins. A pair of moosehide breeches was cooked, a stew was made from a desiccated squirrel skin. Captain Dearborn's pet Newfoundland was butchered, and, according to Major Meigs, "even the feet and skin" were devoured.[19]

Many of the men were barefoot, leaving bloodstains on the snow-crusted river bank. Private Stocking saw men reel "like drunken men"; Private Morison saw them collapse on hillsides and roll helplessly to the bottom. "At length the wretches raise themselves up and go in search of their guns, which they find buried in the snow," Morison wrote. "They wade through the mire to the foot of the next steep and gaze up at its summit, contemplating what they must suffer before they reach it. They attempt it, catching at every twig and shrub they can lay hold of — their feet fly out from them — they fall down — to rise no more." [20]

No record exists to tell us how many perished. We know that a man was killed by a falling tree at the Great Carry, that James Warner died near the mouth of Seven Mile Stream, that Samuel Nichols vanished at the spider-shaped lake, that George Innis drowned in the Chaudière. We are told that others died when the long column, in Dr. Senter's words, "scattered up and down the river at the distance of perhaps twenty miles." [21] Some who dropped from exhaustion were abandoned. "We had all along aided our weaker brethren," Private Morison wrote, "but the dreadful moment had now arrived when these friendly offices could no longer be performed. Many of the men began to fall behind, and those in any condition to march were scarcely able to support themselves; so that it was impossible to bring them along; and if we tarried with them, we must all have perished." [22] Private Stocking saw men hunched on the river bank too weak to continue.[23] When Private Fobes escaped from a British prison ship the following spring and retraced the route, he found "human bones and hair" scattered along the Chaudière.

At noontime on November 2, after marching eight miles on an empty stomach, Isaac Senter had "a vision of horned cattle" driven by "animals resembling Plato's two-footed featherless ones." Incredulous, he watched until he was sure that what he saw was a party of *habitants* bringing horses and three head of beef cattle. He muttered a prayer of thanks — a "te deum," as he called it.[24] Shouts of "Provisions ahead!" were relayed up the Chaudière. Some men fainted at the news. Dearborn, Thayer, and Topham, self-contained Yankees given to bridling their emotions, wept openly. Canoes came upstream laden with oatmeal, flour, and mutton. The rescue party, dispatched by Arnold, was led by Lieutenant Church. No time was lost in distributing the food and butchering the cattle. While the troops gorged themselves, some of them devouring the meat raw, the rescue party went in search of stragglers. It was early morning before the last were brought in, to be revived with hot food before a blazing campfire.

Dearborn, who was ill, passed up the food and continued downstream by canoe. He reached Sartigan toward dusk, followed by some of his men and by all of Captain Smith's command. Next morning Ward's troops arrived in a swirling snowstorm, stopping to break into a cheer as they entered the sparse settlement of huts and wigwams. Soon the whole army was there, devouring roast beef, grouse and chicken, potatoes, vegetables, and oven-fresh bread. All the men recovered except Lieutenant McClellan, who died soon after his arrival. The *habitants* gave him a reverent burial, causing Private Henry to remark that "this real catholicism towards the remains of one we loved" left him with "a more extended and paternal view of mankind, unbounded by sect or opinion."[25]

Arnold had gone downstream in search of supplies. He had instructed Meigs to allow each captain twenty or thirty dollars in hard money to pay for food, but prices were high. Dearborn felt that the *habitants*, although "very kind," asked "a very Great price for their Victuals."[26] At the village of Ste. Marie, Arnold wrote a second letter to John Dyer Mercier, advising him that he would soon be at Quebec.[27] He summoned the local Indians to a conference. To his astonishment, Natanis was among them. The elusive tribesman had shadowed the expedition all the way from his hunting camp on the Dead, watching as the white men coped with portages, struggled up the Height of Land, wandered off course at Seven Mile Stream, and nearly starved to death on the Chaudière. No one had caught sight of him or found his footprint. When asked why he had not declared himself, he reminded Arnold that if he had done so, he would have met with certain death. Now he and his fellow braves wanted to hear the white chief speak for himself.

Arnold was at his most persuasive. He told his listeners that "a new king and his wicked great men" had schemed to "take over our lands and money without our consent" and had "sent a great army to Boston and endeavoured to set our brethren against us in Canada." He had come, he said, "by the desire of the French and Indians." When he had defeated the king's troops, he would leave the province to "the peaceable enjoyment of its proper inhabitants." To achieve his goal, he would welcome the Indians as allies and would enroll them in his army at one Portuguese johannes a month.[28] His audience was impressed. Natanis himself enlisted, together with fifty others.

Arnold made his headquarters in the manor house of Gabriel

Taschereau, a *seigneur* who had incurred the wrath of his *habitants* by trying to arrest a man who had resisted beating orders. Arnold found some of the Canadians pleased with Washington's manifesto. In spite of the *curé*'s opposition, it was read to a full congregation at the church in Ste. Marie.

"The people looked on us with amazement," Private Morison said, "and seemed to doubt whether or not we were human beings." Ragged, emaciated, emerging from the woods "more like ghosts than men," Arnold's troops were indeed a "most astonishing sight." [29] The *habitants* housed them, fed them, and cared for their sick. Dearborn, who was running a high fever, was nursed by a French family for more than a month before he rejoined his company at Quebec. Private Henry, ill with a digestive disorder after eating unwisely, was put to bed at no expense in a room where seven members of the same family ate and slept. The men liked this hospitable province, with its tilled fields and whitewashed cottages, its church spires, wayside shrines, and compact little villages, so unlike their own in New England and the Alleghenies. Through English-speaking *habitants* they managed to communicate their needs, and if prices were high, the food and grog were good. Dr. Senter and a group of friends, having found nothing to satisfy their thirst but a quart of New England rum, for which they paid a dollar in hard money, knocked at the house of "a merry old woman," who provided them with rum and sweetbreads and, after they had partaken, danced a jig to "Yankee Doodle." [30]

Below Ste. Marie the road cut through woods to the hamlet of St. Henri, much of it knee-deep in mud. Arnold and the advance companies did not reach St. Henri until nearly midnight on November 6. He had sent Major Meigs and Captains Thayer and Topham to round up canoes. They located twenty, which their men carried over the muddy road. Dr. Senter and Chaplain Spring fared better than most. Hiring a pair of horses, they traveled the twelve miles in comparative comfort, although at time the mounts were mired to their bellies.

Leaving St. Henri, Arnold continued all day in a snowstorm. During the night a courier brought a letter from Montgomery, describing his army's progress. In reply, Arnold told of the obstacles and delays his troops had encountered and said that two transports carrying reinforcements were known to have docked at Quebec.[31] That same night he ordered a detail of riflemen to proceed to the St. Lawrence.

By daybreak the riflemen were opposite Quebec. They could make out the snow-shrouded city on its great cliff and could identify a frigate and a sloop-of-war. Gunboats prowled the river. When Captain Thayer arrived with the first of the musket companies, he found the riflemen cheerful and eager to cross.

3

Hector Theophilus Cramahé ruled a frightened city. French and British militiamen patrolled the streets. Naval personnel from His Majesty's warships and crewmen from merchant vessels had been formed into a battalion of nine companies under Captain John Hamilton of frigate *Lizard*. The *Quebec Gazette* reported that snow *Fell*, "compleatly equipp'd with 16 nine-pounders, besides Swivels, &c, and 100 true tars, on board which Commodore Napier hoisted his flag, hauled out into the Stream and is now moored before the City." [32] Cramahé ordered the gates closed at six every night, forbade strangers to enter the city without first declaring themselves to the captain of the guard, and, in the event of an alarm, arranged to have three shots fired at Cape Diamond, at Drummond's Wharf, and aboard a warship in the harbor.

Cramahé despaired of enlisting many *habitants*. "The Gentry, Clergy and most of the Bourgeoisie ... have shown their best Endeavours to reclaim their infatuated Countrymen," he wrote Lord Dartmouth. "No Means have been left untried to bring the Canadian Peasantry to a Sense of their Duty, and engage them to take up arms in Defense of the Province." [33] But the response was disappointing. Captain Thomas Ainslie of the British militia blamed opponents of the Quebec Act, who, in appealing to the *habitants*, had "meant to stir them up to a General application for a repeal of the act — not to Rebellion." [34] Francis Masères, Carleton's erstwhile attorney general, blamed the Quebec Act itself, which he accused of favoring the *noblesse*, the *habitants'* "ancient oppressors." He criticized the governor for failing to appoint any *habi-tants* to the Provincial Council or to district judgeships.[35]

Rumors of dark goings-on swept the city. Spies were reported on the Chaudière, armed strangers near Pointe Lévis. John McCord, Edward Antill, and Zachary Macaulay were accused of aiding the rebels. John Dyer Mercier was under constant surveillance. Captain Ainslie said that some of the merchants, fearful for their property, talked openly of capitulation. "If we attempt to hold out, our ruin is unavoidable," he quoted them as saying. "Why suffer our property to be destroyed? Let us abandon Quixot schemes of defence & think of terms of surrender." [36] It was too much even for Cramahé, by nature a bureaucrat who shrank from decisive action. He told off Zachary Macaulay, accusing his "dam'd committees" of contributing to the city's plight, and late in October ordered John Dyer Mercier confined to a sloop-of-war.[37]

Cramahé ordered all canoes and small craft removed from the south shore and Ile d'Orléans. On the weekend of November 3, frigate *Lizard* had dropped anchor, bringing arms, specie, and a shipment of green and buff uniforms for the Quebec militia. More than a hundred volunteers arrived from Newfoundland, recruited at St. John's by Captain Malcolm Fraser. On the 8th, members of the Royal Navy had the first brush with the enemy. A landing party from sloop *Hunter* had put in at Caldwell's Mill, a gristmill near Pointe Lévis operated by Lieutenant Colonel Henry Caldwell of the British militia and used as a supply depot. One of their number hopped ashore. Fired on by Morgan's riflemen, who had concealed themselves along the riverbank, he tried to swim to safety but was stopped by bullets that freckled the water within inches of his head. He was spirited to headquarters, where he was found to be the badly frightened teen-age brother of Captain Thomas McKenzie of sloop *Hunter*.

That same day, Colonel Allan Maclean dropped anchor at Trois Rivières on his way downstream from Sorel. His Scots would eventually adopt the green and buff of the Quebec militia, but many were veterans of Highland regiments and still wore kilts. Their lace-trimmed jackets, feathered bonnets, and sporrans far outshone the more prosaic white and scarlet of the British regulars, and made the Quebec militia look drab indeed. Near Quebec, gale winds forced Maclean to continue by land. He reached the city on November 12, ahead of Arnold.

Cramahé had been much criticized. Colonel Caldwell described him as "thoroughly frightened." Lieutenant John Starke of frigate *Lizard* deemed him "a feeble old man." But not everyone agreed. Captain Ainslie spoke well of him and said he was "indefatigable in putting the town in a proper state of defense." [38] More bureaucrat than soldier, Cramahé was happy to entrust military matters to Colonel Maclean, who promptly gave proof of his mettle. On the day of his arrival the explosive Scot stormed into the bishop's chapel, where a group of citizens was debating whether to treat with the enemy, and, ejecting their spokesman from the pulpit, warned that he would tolerate no further talk of capitulation.

Maclean tightened discipline in all ranks. He ordered trenches dug, gun platforms built, artillery mounted, and he ruled that the great bell of the cathedral would no longer summon the faithful to worship but would ring only to warn of danger. He stiffened the backbones of merchants by declaring that no one's property would be safe if the rebels got inside the city. The enemy were thieves and looters, he said, who would plunder everything in sight — shops, warehouses, even private homes. His warnings strengthened resolve and helped unite the city.

Ainslie estimated that when Maclean took over he had a garrison of 1126 men, including 200 Emigrants and fusiliers, 300 British militia, 480 French militia, twenty-four seamen, and ninety additional Emigrants and thirty-two artificers recruited in Newfoundland.[39] He was fortunate in his lieutenants — Colonels Henry Caldwell and Noël Voyer of the Quebec militia, Captain Hamilton and his naval colleagues, Captains John Nairne, Malcolm Fraser, and George Laws of the Royal Highland Emigrants — all men to depend on. "If we fall," he wrote Lord Barrington, "it shall not be our faults." [40]

4

The gale that forced Maclean ashore kept Arnold's canoes beached near the mouth of the Chaudière. They now totaled about forty, including some that had escaped Cramahé's order. While he waited for calmer weather, Arnold had his men build scaling ladders and fashion pikes for clearing the ramparts. One day a man showed up who introduced himself as John Halstead, manager of Colonel Caldwell's gristmill. He said that he had withheld a large quantity of his employer's flour for Arnold's troops. Properly thanked, he was appointed a commissary.

On November 13, the wind dropped, the river looked less threatening, and there was a thick cloud cover. At nine that night, Arnold ordered out the first wave of canoes. Boarding the pilot craft with Daniel Morgan, Isaac Senter, and several riflemen, he led his fleet toward the gap between sloop-of-war *Hunter* and frigate *Lizard*, both athwart his course. Near midstream, he caught sight of an enemy watchboat and signaled his men to stop paddling. The craft vanished, giving no sign of alarm. With *Hunter* on his left and *Lizard* at a safe distance downstream, he took his fleet noiselessly through the gap and touched shore a mile above Wolfe's Cove. Finding the escarpment too steep to scale, he led his men along the shoreline to the cleft where Wolfe's army had made its ascent before funneling onto the Plains of Abraham. While the canoes returned for a second crossing, some of the men broke into a vacant house near the river bank. Chilled to the bone, they built a fire, which was seen by the crew of an enemy watchboat. The craft swung shoreward to investigate. When it ignored his challenge, Arnold ordered his men to fire. The watchboat vanished amid outcries from its crew. Arnold knew that at best he could risk no more than three crossings.

On the third crossing one of the canoes split apart, emptying its occupants into the river. All were picked up except Lieutenant Steele, Arnold's intrepid scout, who swam to a canoe too crowded to take him in. Locking his arms over the stern and instructing the steersman to sit on them lest his grip loosen, he was towed ashore, still conscious but limp with cold. He was hustled into the vacant house, where he was given a brisk rubdown, a change of clothes, no doubt a spot of rum, and a place by the same fire that had caught the attention of the enemy patrol. It was four o'clock. Gusts of wind had torn holes in the cloud cover, letting through bright moonlight. Arnold was fortunate to have managed three crossings. Within a space of seven hours, he had brought 500 men from the south shore. The rest would follow in a day or two, but he would leave Captain Hanchet and a rear guard of sixty at Pointe Lévis.

Arnold led his troops to the top of the escarpment, following the same pathway that Wolfe had taken. The Plains of Abraham lay unguarded in the moonlight. His scouts reported no signs of alarm from the walled city. He called together his officers, to debate whether to storm Quebec that night. Daniel Morgan was for it, but others had their doubts: the army was not at full strength, they said, most of the scaling ladders were still on the south shore, the city would be alerted at any moment by the British ships. Morgan was outvoted. Within a few days, however, he would be proved right. Crucial hours passed before word of Arnold's crossing reached Quebec, and a city gate remained unlocked all night, guarded, Private Henry learned, by "a single cannon under the care of a drowsy watch." [41]

Morgan reconnoitered the suburb of Ste. Foye, occupying a farm owned by Colonel Caldwell. He billeted his men in barns and outbuildings, and Arnold set up headquarters in the farmhouse. "They got there before day," Caldwell later lamented, "seized all my working bullocks, about 20, and 4 or 5 fat ones, with all my horses; and there they lived away on my beef and potatoes about a week." [42] With his men cared for, Morgan assigned Private George Merchant to sentry duty near St. John's Gate, but Merchant, weary after the night's crossing, fell asleep at his post. He awoke to find himself surrounded by an enemy patrol. He was disarmed before he could cock his rifle and was whisked inside the city.

Impressed by the boldness of the enemy, Arnold hoped he could tempt Maclean to risk a sortie. Rousing his men, he formed them in marching order and drew them up in full view of the city. By now the walls swarmed with troops — militiamen in green and buff, kilted Royal Highland Emigrants, naval personnel, a scattering of British regulars. Cramahé must have been among them, thankful for Maclean's timely presence, and surely Maclean himself, taking a long look at the rebels he so despised.

After taunting the enemy, Arnold's men gave three insolent cheers. Shots were exchanged, all wide of the mark. A few riflemen crawled to a vantage point in front of Arnold's lines, but their shots failed to disconcert the men who peered down at them from the ramparts. Major Febiger, intent on having a closer look at the city's defenses, strode within a hundred paces of the walls and returned unscathed. When it became clear that the enemy would not come out on the plain, as Montcalm had done, Arnold ordered his men back to their encampment. At headquarters, he wrote Cramahé a letter, promising to spare private property if the city capitulated.[43] As he wrote, fire broke out in a cluster of houses near St. John's Gate. The sight should have prepared him for the kind of reply he might expect, for Colonel Maclean had ordered the buildings burned to deny cover to enemy snipers.

Arnold chose Matthias Ogden, Aaron Burr's friend, to deliver his letter to Cramahé. Ogden set forth at sundown, accompanied by a drummer and holding aloft a flag of truce. As the two approached St. John's Gate, a shell burst a few feet from where they walked, and they were persuaded to retreat to their own lines. Next morning they tried again but were turned back when a shell came within inches of Ogden's head. Arnold accused Cramahé of firing on a flag of truce "contrary to humanity and the laws of nations," although Cramahé would not have conceded that either the dictates of humanity or the pacts made by civilized nations applied to rebels.[44]

On the 16th, Cramahé called a meeting of his chiefs. Maclean was present, together with two members of the Provincial Council, Captains Hamilton and McKenzie of the Royal Navy, Colonel Caldwell of the British militia, and Captain Laws of the Royal Highland Emigrants. Maclean produced returns, showing that his garrison now totaled 1178 of all ranks and that he had supplies enough to feed Quebec's 5000 citizens until spring. In spite of the enemy, food and firewood were still reaching the city. It was voted unanimously to defend Quebec "to the last extremity." [45]

Meanwhile, in the American camp, Morgan had quarreled bitterly with Arnold, convinced that his riflemen were being kept on shorter rations than the other units. Although matters were resolved in his favor, he moved his command to the meadows bordering the St. Charles and ordered a task force to cross the river in search of beef cattle. His men found the ferry to the east shore so packed with refugees that it had mired in mud. As they joined crew and passengers in an attempt to work the craft loose, their long hunting shirts made choice targets for Maclean's artillery. A thirty-six-pound shell landing in their midst caught Sergeant Robert Dixon in the leg, nearly severing it at the knee. Hurried inside a nearby house, he was found to be beyond help. A member of the household offered him hot tea, but he declined it. "No, madame," he replied, "it is the ruin of my country." [46]

On the 18th, Arnold learned that Maclean was contemplating a sortie with fieldpieces and a large task force. He ordered an inventory of his arms and ammunition, and found to his dismay that nearly 100 firelocks and rifles had been damaged beyond repair and that he had barely enough cartridges to supply his musketmen with five rounds apiece. He was convinced that if he had arrived only a few days earlier, he would have taken Quebec. "Had I been ten days sooner," he wrote Washington, "Quebec must inevitably have fallen into our hands, as there was not a man then to oppose us." [47] At a council of war, all of his officers, even Morgan, agreed that the army should withdraw immediately to Pointe aux Trembles, twenty miles upriver, and await Montgomery. Hanchet was notified to evacuate Pointe Lévis.

By sunrise the troops were filing through closely spaced villages, each with its soaring church spire and its own sweep of the St. Lawrence. The people seemed hospitable — even the priests watched from rectory doorways — but Arnold allowed no one to tarry. Midway to Pointe aux Trembles, he saw two ships speeding downstream and identified one as snow *Fell*. Subsequently, guns were heard from the direction of Quebec. Although Arnold had no way of knowing it, they were saluting General Carleton, who had successfully run the American blockade.

At Pointe aux Trembles the men indulged themselves as few had done since leaving Captain Howard's on the Kennebec, sleeping in soft beds, thawing out in front of hot cookstoves, luxuriating in overheated kitchens. They were served big helpings of roast beef and pork, with potatoes, cabbages, and turnips, until even the most emaciated began to put on weight and lose their scarecrow look. When a snowstorm swept in from the North Atlantic, it could be watched through the windows of a warm house instead of from a brush lean-to on the Chaudière. The village rang with sleigh bells. Roads, packed to the hardness of stone, were lined with fresh-cut saplings, to mark their course when the snow rose higher than a man's waist. Some of the men ventured into the village church, where they breathed the unfamiliar smoke of incense, watched the faithful genuflect and bless themselves, and heard the priest say mass in a tongue they did not understand.

Arnold sent Matthias Ogden to Montreal for all the flannel shirts, wool stockings, caps, and mittens that Price and Heywood, the army's suppliers, could come up with, as well as more ammunition, more rum, more hard money to satisfy the *habitants*. He gave him a letter for Montgomery, stating his opinion that 2000 men would be needed to take Quebec.[48] Soon after Ogden left, lookouts sighted four British ships, including *Fell* and *Hunter*, beating upstream to intercept Montgomery. John Halstead, the erstwhile manager of Caldwell's Mill, was dispatched to warn of their approach, but headwinds slowed the vessels and caused them to turn back off Cap Santé. Arnold chose Aaron Burr to inform Montgomery of the ships' return, introducing him as "a volunteer in the army and son of the former president of New Jersey college."[49] He might have added that Burr's grandfather, the Reverend Jonathan Edwards, had been president of the same institution, as well as the colonies' most celebrated divine. Although Burr compensated for his small stature with the impudence of a gamecock, Montgomery took to him and made him an aide-de-camp.

Carleton's return to Quebec boded ill for the colonies' friends and allies. Three days after his arrival, the governor issued an edict banning all suspected collaborators from the city:

In order to rid the Town of all useless, disloyal and treacherous persons, I have thought fit to issue this Proclamation. And I do hereby strictly order and enjoin all and every person and persons whatsoever, liable to serve in the Militia, and residing at Quebeck, who have refused or declined to enroll their names in the Militia lists, and to take up arms in conjunction with His Majesty's good subjects of this City, and who shall still refuse or decline to do so, as well as those who, having once taken up arms, have afterwards laid them down, and will not take them up again, to quit the Town in four days from the date hereof, together with their wives and children, and to withdraw themselves out of the limits of the District of Quebeck, before the 1st day of December next, under pain of being treated as rebels or spies, if thereafter they shall be found within the said limits.

He refused the outcasts any provisions, reminding them that "the country abounds with the necessaries of life." [50]

The exiles included John McCord and Zachary Macaulay, John Bondfield and John Welles, Udney Hay and Murdoch Stewart, all opponents of the Quebec Act. Edward Antill was among them. A New Jersey native who had settled in Canada, he was suspected of collaborating with the enemy. Some of the outcasts would prove useful to Montgomery. Welles would become his secretary, Hay a quartermaster, Bondfield a commissary, Antill his chief engineer. Others would continue to the colonies. Guy Carleton had had his Walkers, Prices, and Bindons at Montreal. There would be none at Quebec.

In anticipation of Montgomery's arrival, Arnold sent Morgan and the riflemen back to Ste. Foye and ordered Captain Hanchet to transport some of the ordnance by bateau to Sillery. Hanchet flatly refused. He called the assignment too risky, casting doubt on his superior's judgment. Arnold threatened him with arrest. Hanchet had been a favorite of his, chosen to hurry supplies up the Chaudière when the expedition faced disaster and to command the rear guard at Pointe Lévis. But at some point he had turned against his chief. He was not alone — Aaron Burr had taken a dislike to Arnold; Morgan had quarreled with him and nearly come to blows; John Brown and James Easton were his mortal enemies. Arnold's towering ego and savage temper could leave festering wounds. A few, like Daniel Morgan, could face him down. Others, Hanchet among them, nursed their grievances in secret.

Arnold called in Captains Thayer and Topham, both of whom

wanted the assignment. Since only one could have it, they flipped a coin. Thayer won the toss. He assembled a crew and began loading the artillery aboard three bateaux. That night he slept near his boats. In the morning a schooner and two smaller vessels hove in sight, their decks aswarm with American troops.

VII

"Overwhelmed As with
a Whirlwind"

1

"HE IS a genteel appearing man, tall and slender of make, bald on the Top of his head," Captain Thayer wrote after watching General Montgomery debark from the schooner.[1] The urbane New Yorker was of a different cut from the swarthy, stocky colonel who had brought Thayer and his men through flood and snowstorm to the banks of the St. Lawrence. He possessed a grace that Arnold lacked, and he looked like a general — properly remote, yet putting subordinates at ease. "General Montgomery was born to command," Private Morison wrote. "His easy and affable condescension to both officers and men, while it forbids an improper familiarity, creates love and esteem; and exhibits him the gentleman and the soldier. He is tall and very well made; and possesses a captivating address."[2] Although the antithesis of Arnold, he got on well with his colleague and admired the mettle of his troops.[3] "I find Colonel Arnold's corps an exceeding fine one, inured to fatigue, and well accustomed to cannon shot," he wrote Washington. "There is a style of discipline among them, much superior to what I have been used to see in this campaign."[4]

That night, Captain Thayer and his crew left with the ordnance, rowing until daybreak and unloading the guns at Sillery in a heavy snow squall. The troops followed, slogging through the same villages that had watched Arnold's retreat from Quebec. Fresh snow made marching difficult, and the men reached the outskirts of the city footsore and muscle-weary. Montgomery set up headquarters in Holland House, a private residence in Ste. Foye. He stationed his New Yorkers on the Plains of Abraham; Arnold's musket companies in St. Roch, a suburb north of the city; and the riflemen, who had come in advance of the rest, on the meadowlands bordering the St. Charles.

While awaiting Montgomery, some of the riflemen had raided homes in Ste. Foye, helping themselves to food, household goods, and family heirlooms. A band of Pennsylvanians broke into Cramahé's country house, stealing blankets, mattresses, and cutlery. They were followed by some Virginians, who made off with what was left. Next day the Pennsylvanians raided a farmhouse, butchering livestock and carrying off sleighloads of fresh meat. Their depredations underscored Colonel Maclean's warning that no private property would be safe if the rebels got inside the city.[5]

Having deployed his troops, Montgomery wrote an ultimatum to the governor, advising him that the Quebec garrison consisted of "a motley Crew of Sailors, the greatest part our friends, of Citizens who wish to see us within their Walls, and a few of the worst Troops who ever stiled themselves Soldiers." He had difficulty, he said, in restraining his men from "insulting your works, which would afford them the fair opportunity of an ample and just retaliation." He hoped the governor would recognize "the absurdity of resistance" and capitulate.[6]

Montgomery chose a noncombatant to deliver the ultimatum, an old woman not apt to arouse suspicion. As he anticipated, she had no difficulty gaining entrance to the city and reaching headquarters, where she was conducted into the presence of the governor and his aides. As Carleton scanned the ultimatum, logs crackled in the fireplace. When he had finished reading, he ordered a drummer to take the fire tongs, pick up the ultimatum without contaminating himself by touching it, and submit it to the flames. His command obeyed, he consigned Montgomery's emissary to the city jail, to repent her folly until drummed out of town.

Montgomery wrote a message to the Quebec merchants, assuring them that his army had come "with the professed Intention of eradicating Tyranny and giving Liberty and Security to this oppressed Province, Private Property having ever by us been deemed sacred." [7] He ordered copies of the message attached to arrows and shot over the wall by Indians.

Carleton had moved swiftly after debarking from *Fell*. He assigned the regulars, the marines, and the Royal Highland Emigrants to Colonel Maclean, the sailors to Captain Hamilton, the British militia to Colonel Caldwell, the French militia to Colonel Voyer. He ordered blockhouses repaired, gun platforms installed, guns mounted. His engineer, James Thompson, set up barricades at each end of the Lower Town — two at Sault au Matelot on a narrow roadway that an enemy must follow when approaching from the northeast, a third at Près de Ville, where the road paralleling the St. Lawrence threaded past the face of Cape Diamond. At Près de Ville, a log building was loopholed for muskets and armed with four small cannons.

Carleton put little faith in some of his untried troops. He was unsure of his militia. He had heard the *seigneurs* complaining that they should have been given a place in the regular army instead of being enrolled in the less respected militia. He had doubts about the sailors, many of whom had been kidnaped by press gangs and held prisoner by tyrannical sea captains. He feared, too, that there might still be collaborators within the city. "Could the People of the Town, and Seamen, be depended on," he wrote Lord Dartmouth, "I should flatter myself we might hold out till Navigation next Spring . . . but tho' the severe weather is far advanced, we have so many Enemies within, and foolish People, Dupes to those Traitors, with the natural Fears of Men unused to war, I think our Fate extremely doubtful, to say nothing more." [8] Late in November, he dispatched Lieutenant Thomas Pringle of the Royal Navy to London with a request for massive reinforcements and for prefabricated boats that could be shipped in segments and reassembled on arrival. Already he was looking to the time when he could free the city of its besiegers and pursue them to Lake Champlain.

After the failure of his ultimatum, Montgomery ordered the city shelled. Captain Isaiah Wool of Lamb's company erected a five-mortar battery in St. Roch, but two days of fairly sustained shelling failed to disconcert either the garrison or the civilians who thronged the streets. "Before they gave us a sample of their savoir faire in the bombarding way," Captain Ainslie said, "the towns people had conceived that every shell wou'd inevitably kill a dozen or two people, & knock down two or three houses ... but after they saw that their bombettes, as they called them, did no harm, women and children walked the streets laughing at their former fears." [9]

But Ainslie could not dismiss the havoc wrought by the riflemen. Aiming through chinks in a log hut and from the cupola of the Intendant's Palace, they picked off men on the ramparts as if they had been treed bears in the Alleghenies. Their marksmanship took a deadly toll. A sentry was shot through the head; three men were wounded in a single day; a Royal Highland Emigrant was killed. "Skulking riflemen," Ainslie said, as they continued to demonstrate the range and accuracy of their long weapons. "The indignation of our Militia is raised against these fellows who call themselves soldiers. They are worse than Savages, they will ever be held in contempt with men of courage. Lie in wait to shoot a sentry! A deed worthy of Yanky men of war." [10]

Arnold was having further trouble with Hanchet, who refused to occupy an advance post within reach of Carleton's gunners. He again turned to Thayer and Topham. Ever willing to carry out his directives, the pair underwent such a withering barrage that neither they nor their men could show themselves by day. On one occasion a bullet drilled through the bed the two captains shared in their crowded outpost, passing between them as they slept. Indeed, no part of St. Roch was wholly safe. Stray bullets penetrated Private Fobes's quarters; a bomb shook the house where an off-duty guard was stationed. Captain Hubbard, who had been shot at several times, made light of "the rascals" who fired down at them from the walls, but not everyone could share his nonchalance. [11] Montgomery himself was nearly hit when a shell demolished his sleigh and killed his horse while he conferred with aides. Another battery was needed, closer to the city.

Captain Lamb chose a site only 700 yards from St. John's Gate. The frozen ground would not permit earthworks, so he had his men fashion withes into gabions, packing them with snow and wetting them down to form rock-hard walls of ice. Platforms were laid for five cannons and a howitzer. The men worked only by night, in snow and sleet and biting cold. Some, still in their thin summer clothing, nearly froze, but after a few brutal nights the installation was finished.

The battery "seemingly consisted entirely of fascines," Ainslie said, after scrutinizing it from the walls, "and had been hastily thrown up in the darkness . . . like the Bunker's Hill entrenchment." [12] It was partly hidden by a row of houses that frustrated Carleton's gunners. "We sent many balls among them and threw some shells into their midst," Ainslie said, "yet with our glasses we cannot perceive we have done much damage." [13] Carleton ordered the houses demolished, but, instead of tearing them down as he directed, his men set them ablaze. For an instant the flames, whipped to towering heights by a stiff breeze, threatened to leap the walls. Some members of the garrison wished the fire would spread to the adjacent suburbs where the riflemen had found cover. "The militia and sailors murmur much at the governor's not allowing them to burn that hornet's nest, St. Rocks and St. John Suburbs," one officer wrote, "and thereby drive the besiegers at once from the strongholds they possess." [14] But Carleton insisted that none of his subjects' homes be touched except those blocking the line of fire.

With the houses removed, Carleton's artillery blew the installation to bits. Two of Lamb's guns were quickly silenced. Three of his men were killed, several wounded. On the night of the 17th, he ordered the guns removed. By daybreak the battery stood empty, amid tumbled gabions and shards of broken ice. "They have carried away their guns," Ainslie noted, "or have drawn them behind the shattered embrasures." [15]

In a last attempt to persuade Carleton to surrender peaceably, Benedict Arnold, accompanied by a drummer and by one of Montgomery's aides-de-camp, Captain John Macpherson, advanced under a flag of truce. Wrapped in a blanket coat against the chill east wind, he carried a letter from Montgomery promising both Carleton and Cramahé safe conduct to England if they would capitulate. He handed the letter to sentries but was kept outside the gates while he waited for Carleton's answer. After a delay that must have brought his temper to a lively boil, an aide called down to him from the walls. The governor would not treat with rebels. He would neither receive them nor read their communication. If they wished to meet with His Excellency, they must first implore the king's mercy. As Arnold turned to go, John Macpherson shouted that one day Governor Carleton would be made to pay for his rude behavior. It is said that several members of the garrison had to be kept from answering Montgomery's aide-de-camp with musket fire.

Montgomery was being pressed to storm Quebec without further delay. If we are to believe Ainslie, he announced that he would "dine in Quebec or in Hell at Christmas." [16] Many of his men were threatening to go home when their enlistments expired at the end of the year, depriving him of nearly half his army. "The patriotism of the summer of seventy-five seemed almost extinguished in the winter of seventy-six," Private Henry noted.[17] Three of Arnold's captains were pressing for a separate command under John Brown. Montgomery identified the ringleaders in a letter to Washington, but their names were subsequently erased, and we can be sure only of Brown and Hanchet. "The three discontented companies are within a few days of being free from their engagements," he wrote Washington. "I must try every means to prevent their departure, and in this matter I am much embarrassed. Their officers have offered to stay provided they may join some other corps. This is resentment against Arnold, and will hurt him so much that I do not think I can consent to it." [18] Although he risked alienating the officers and triggering a mass exodus of their companies, he ruled that all three units must remain under Arnold. Dr. Senter volunteered to take the place of one of the disaffected captains, but Arnold reminded him that his place was at the hospital. "I am much obliged for your offer," he wrote, "and am glad to see you so spirited, but cannot consent you should take up arms, as you will be wanted in the way of your profession." He advised the young doctor to roll bandages.[19]

Montgomery was under pressure from home as well as from his officers and men. Rumors that he had already taken Quebec swept England and the colonies. *Almon's Remembrancer*, an English periodical, reported the fall of the city, and early in December Colonel William Alexander, an American officer more commonly known as Lord Sterling, wrote John Hancock that Arnold was said to have captured Quebec without losing a man.[20] Congress was impatient. In November a committee had been sent north to assess the progress of the compaign. Composed of three of the colonies' more illustrious citizens, Robert R. Livingston, Robert Treat Paine of Boston, and John Langdon of New Hampshire, it had urged that three regiments be sent to Canada as soon as Lake Champlain was open and that guns and ammunition, blankets, winter clothing, and medical supplies be hurried northward. The three committeemen expressed confidence in Montgomery, who would have liked to confer with them in person had they not turned back at Fort Ticonderoga.[21] Hancock wrote him of Congress's high hopes after the capture of St. Jean and Montreal — "a happy presage of the smiles of Providence on the further designation of the Continental arms in the North," he said, that should "greatly facilitate the entire reduction of the deluded malignants in that Province to Liberty."[22]

Montgomery was prodded, too, by his Canadian allies. He wrote Schuyler that they would "not relish a union with the colonies" until they saw "the whole country in our hands" and that "possession of the town, and that speedily" was essential if he were to retain their support.[23] Everyone expected him to crown his earlier successes with the triumphant storming of Quebec — "exploits so glorious in their execution and so extensive in their consequences," Hancock wrote him, "that the memory of General Montgomery will doubtless be of equal duration with the remembrance of the benefits derived from his command."[24]

Montgomery wrote General Wooster that he would attack when "the first northwester" curtained the city in snow, advancing on both the Lower Town and the Cape Diamond bastion and setting diversionary fires in St. Roch. He had "not much above 800 men fit for duty exclusive of a few raggamuffin Canadians," he said, but with the advantage of surprise he hoped to overwhelm Carleton's thinly stretched garrison. Although he claimed to be "fully convinced of the practicality" of his plan, he told Wooster that "should it not appear in the same advantageous light to the men" he would "not press it upon them." [25]

Indeed, there were those who questioned his strategy. Captain Hubbard, beyond doubt a brave man, was opposed to it. Two other officers agreed with Hubbard. Some of the rank and file were uneasy — Private Stocking considered the proposal "rash and imprudent." [26] But most of the men gave their approval, buoyed by Montgomery's promise that "the Effects of the Governor, Garrison, and of such as have been acting in misleading the Inhabitants and distressing the Friends of Liberty" would be divided among the troops.[27] Apparently his pledge to spare private property did not apply to everyone. "All that get safe into the city will live well," a recruit wrote home, "for they are allowed to plunder and take what they please." [28] On Christmas Day, Montgomery addressed Arnold's troops, promising them that "nothing was wanting to assure victory but the exercise of that valor" that they had "so triumphantly displayed" on their march from Maine. They gave him a round of cheers that could be heard inside the city.[29]

"This is no wall scaling weather," Ainslie observed on the morning of the 26th. "The night was clear and inconceivably cold — it is employment enough to preserve ones nose." [30] But next day snow enveloped the city — not the swirling blizzard that Montgomery hoped for, but a storm that continued all day and was still in progress at nightfall. Ordering ladders readied, pikes issued, and all muskets and rifles checked, he directed his New Yorkers and four of Arnold's companies to attack the Cape Diamond bastion, the other companies to advance under Colonel Greene against the Lower Town. Because some of the men wore British uniforms confiscated in Montreal, he had all his troops attach twigs of hemlock to their hats to distinguish them from the enemy. But soon after midnight the wind shifted, stars broke through, and he called off the attack, reminding his disappointed troops that he was "not only answerable to his country, but likewise to his merciful Creator, for the lives of his fellow soldiers." [31]

Montgomery would soon learn that the sudden clearing had saved him from almost certain defeat. One Joshua Wolf, a clerk of Colonel Caldwell's taken prisoner by the riflemen, had made his escape to the Lower Town and had acquainted Carleton's high command with the plan of attack. His testimony was corroborated by an American deserter, Samuel Singleton, a sergeant in rank. Montgomery changed his strategy and made plans to concentrate on the Lower Town. In spite of the postponement, his troops remained in good spirits, and, as if to give evidence of their zeal, some of Thayer's men knotted ropes around the necks of four shirkers who had failed to show up for drill and led them through the encampment amid a chorus of jeers and taunts.

Carleton slept in his clothes at the Récollet monastery, putting his garrison on a twenty-four-hour alert. "Above a thousand men were ready to oppose the Rebels in case of an attack," Ainslie said. "The rest of the Garrison lay in their cloaths with their arms and accoutrements lying by them." [32] Informants reported an outbreak of smallpox among Montgomery's troops. Ainslie was told that "the small pox does havoc among them — there are 200 now in hospitals, tis a deadly infection in Yanky veins." [33]

Although Ainslie exaggerated, smallpox had erupted in the American encampment and was on the increase. In mid-December, Dr. Senter reported several cases at the General Hospital, where he had enlisted the help of nursing sisters from an adjoining convent. The number grew, not dramatically but steadily. To safeguard men ill from other causes, he transferred the smallpox cases to branch facilities three miles away. Private Caleb Haskell of Ward's Rhode Islanders came down with the disease. He was kept in a quarantined house so packed with patients that many were without beds and where the overworked staff could give no more than cursory attention even to the desperately ill. Several men died for want of medicine and proper care. Haskell was fortunate. He began to mend, but not soon enough to join his company in the assault on Quebec.

Many of the men inoculated themselves. By cutting the flesh under a fingernail with a needle or pocket knife and introducing smallpox discharge into the bloodstream, they contracted the disease in a milder form. The practice had been introduced by Dr. Zabdiel Boylston during the epidemic of 1721 in Boston. Boylston had inoculated two family slaves and his six-year-old son in an experiment that turned out happily in spite of the outcries of shocked colleagues and an incensed public. All three of his patients recovered, and before the outbreak had spent itself 286 persons were inoculated, with only six deaths among them out of a total of 844 in the city. By the time of the Revolution, inoculation was saving thousands of lives, but it spread the disease and was frowned on by some miltary commanders.

At his quarters in the General Hospital, Dr. Senter made an incision in his arm and proceeded to inoculate himself. Apparently, he suffered few ill effects. Two days later he made his offer to take the place of one of Arnold's disgruntled officers but was told that he would be more useful at the hospital.

2

On the night of December 30, General Montgomery paced the floor of Holland House as snow hissed against the windows and swirled through Ste. Foye in blinding gusts. The storm had begun that afternoon, gently at first. At dusk, snow laced with sleet swept inland from the North Atlantic. When the storm threatened to abate, Montgomery wrote another letter to Carleton, offering him safe conduct to New York or any place of his choosing if he would yield Quebec. But the letter was never delivered. After midnight the snow settled into an unmistakable northeaster.

At four that morning Montgomery ordered his troops into formation. In keeping with his revised plan of attack, he would descend to the St. Lawrence with his 300 New Yorkers and march beneath Cape Diamond against the Lower Town. Arnold would approach from St. Roch to storm the Sault au Matelot barricades with some 500 of his own men, fifty artillerymen under Captain Lamb, and about forty Canadians and Indians. Two feints would be made: Livingston's Canadians would advance on St. John's Gate, setting it on fire, and about 100 of John Brown's men would engage the guard at the Cape Diamond bastion and send off rockets to signal Arnold. After joining forces, Montgomery and Arnold would push up the steep roadway to the Upper Town. Montgomery hoped that the Quebec merchants would bring pressure on Carleton for a quick surrender in order to save their dockside properties, but he underrated the enemy, who were prepared to destroy the waterfront, if necessary. "Shells wou'd soon have reduced it to a heap of rubbish," Ainslie said.[34]

Earlier that night, Captain John Macpherson had written his father in Philadelphia. Twenty years old, he was a dutiful son and an enthusiastic patriot. "If you receive this it will be the last this hand will ever write you," he had said. "Orders are given for a general storm of Quebec this night; and Heaven only knows what may be my fate; but whatever it be, I cannot resist the inclination I feel to assure you that I experience no reluctance in this cause, to venture a life which I consider is only lent to be used when my country demands it." [35]

Macpherson's fellow aide-de-camp, Captain Jacob Cheeseman of the 1st New York, had had a premonition of impending death. Dressing himself punctiliously, he had slipped five gold coins into his pocket, to pay for a proper burial.[36]

Montgomery's staff found him edgy and preoccupied. In a letter to Janet, he had written longingly of home. "I wish it were well over with all my heart, and sigh for home like a New Englander," he had said.[37] In writing to Schuyler, he had expressed hope for a happy outcome. "Fortune often baffles the most sanguine expectations of poor mortals," he had told his colleague. "I am not intoxicated with the favours I have received at her hands, but I do think there is a fair prospect of success." [38]

The troops formed at their designated stations — the New Yorkers on the Plains of Abraham, Livingston's Canadians across from St. John's Gate, Brown's men, led by his brother, Captain Jacob Brown, opposite the Cape Diamond bastion. At St. Roch, Arnold's "famine-proof veterans," as Dr. Senter called them, were lined up by company, some with "Liberty or Death" scrawled on the scraps of paper they had pinned to their hats, to distinguish them from the enemy. Dearborn's company had been stationed on the east side of the St. Charles. Word had been sent to them, but they had not shown up. Arnold hoped they would overtake his column in the Lower Town. Captain Smith was absent for reasons that are not clear. One story has it that he was on Ile d'Orléans that night, but Private Henry ascribed his absence to "particular causes," which may imply that Captain Smith was drunk.[39] His place was taken by Lieutenant Steele.

Arnold joined the advance party of thirty men who would spearhead the attack. Next came Captain Lamb and his artillery-men, with a brass six-pounder lashed to a sled, followed by Morgan's Virginians and by the Pennsylvania companies led by Steele and Hendricks. Behind them were the musket companies: Greene and his Rhode Islanders first, Meigs's troops at the rear with the Canadians and Indians. As the men waited in formation, shielding their guns to keep the powder dry, two snow-shrouded rockets arced above Cape Diamond. They were the signals from Captain Brown announcing that Montgomery had left.

That snowy morning Captain Malcolm Fraser, of the Royal Highland Emigrants, was patrolling the city walls. For two weeks, the garrison had been awaiting an attack. Early one morning, a sentry had reported an enemy detachment on the march. Drums had beaten an alarm, bells had tolled, but the sentry was proved wrong — not a rebel was sighted. On the 29th, men on snowshoes were seen reconnoitering near the walls. Their activities were further proof that an attack could be expected on the first dark night.

As Captain Fraser scanned the snow-swept plain, he was sure that he saw the wink of lanterns. He checked with sentries, who said that they too had seen them. Fraser hurried into the city to alert everyone he met. As men and women swarmed into the narrow streets, the great bell of the cathedral began to toll. Off-duty members of the garrison ran to the walls, joined by boys, seminary students, even septuagenarians. All were handed muskets. Fireballs, shot from the walls, lit up hiding places under jutting bastions. Beneath Cape Diamond, at Près de Ville, some fifty sailors and militiamen kept watch in the fortified log house. They were led by Captain Chabot and Lieutenant Picard of the French militia, Captain Adam Barnsfare, master of a merchantman, and a Boston loyalist, John Coffin, who had fled to Quebec in June with his wife and eleven children. They had four cannons, which they aimed toward the barricade, seen dimly from the house.

Montgomery led his column down the pathway to Wolfe's Cove. While he made the descent, Brown's detachment released the rockets and engaged the guard at the Cape Diamond bastion. Livingston's Canadians advanced on St. John's Gate but failed in their efforts to set it afire. Montgomery was accompanied by his three aides, Macpherson, Cheeseman, and Aaron Burr. Close behind them was his deputy quartermaster general, Colonel Donald Campbell, whose expletives had given offense to Samuel Mott and other pious New Englanders during the siege of St. Jean.

Turning downstream, Montgomery's column threaded through slabs of ice heaped on the river bank. Long delays occurred as the men angled their ladders through the chunk ice or made time-consuming detours. Campbell called it "the worst Path I ever traveled, being obliged in several places to scramble up the slant of the Rocks (with 2 foot snow on them & a precipice to the Right) & then descending by pulling the Skirt of our Coats under us & sliding down 15 or 20 foot, & this repeated several times before we got to the first Barrier." [40] As the troops neared Près de Ville, they could hear a church bell above the rattle of sleet. Although few could identify it, it hung in the belfry of Notre Dame des Victoires in the Lower Town and had pealed in times past to warn of danger.

Near the tip of Cape Diamond, the column halted before a barricade of thick posts stretched from the escarpment to the river's edge. Four posts were felled to create a narrow opening. Montgomery stepped through, still accompanied by his three aides, and continued about a hundred yards to a second barrier. Ordering Campbell to hurry along the troops, he grabbed a saw and felled two of the posts himself, close to the cliff where his command would be less likely to cross a line of fire. He edged through, followed by his aides and a few others. Still unchallenged, he advanced toward a two-story log building and unsheathed his sword.

Inside the log house the sailors and militiamen waited with raised muskets. Chabot and Picard warned their citizen soldiers not to open fire until the command was given. Matches were lit for Adam Barnsfare's cannons. After stepping through the barricade, the Americans stopped briefly to confer. Then their commander held his sword aloft and advanced across the opening, followed by his men. They were not fifty yards from the house when Barnsfare spoke the command. Canister and grapeshot, followed by a burst of musket fire, downed most of them. One rose to his feet but dropped after a few steps. Those left standing fled toward the barricade.

Richard Montgomery lay dead on his back with one arm pointed upward. When found after the battle he would still have his arm outstretched above a covering of fresh snow. John Macpherson and Jacob Cheeseman lay beside him. Others were close by. A sergeant, still breathing, was picked up hours later by the enemy, but died, refusing to acknowledge that his chief had been killed. A few escaped, including Aaron Burr.

The command devolved on Colonel Campbell. At the sound of gunfire he had hurried forward, to find fifty or sixty men gathered at the barricade. He shoved past them and located a lieutenant in Cheeseman's company, who told him what had happened. As the two conferred, several shots were fired from the log house. Some of the men tried to retaliate, but their guns failed to discharge. Snow had seeped into the gunpowder. Campbell was joined by some of his fellow officers, all of whom advised against continuing. He nodded agreement. Directing a subordinate to assist the wounded, he gave orders for an immediate retreat, taking command of the rear guard. The long column, turning in its tracks, put the Lower Town behind it. "There was no Confusion or Disorder in the retreat," Campbell would report, "and we got to Head Quarters (just 2 Miles W. From town) as Fatigued as ever troops could be — I never was more so." [41]

Some of those in the log house were close to panic. They had no way of knowing that they had turned back one prong of Montgomery's army and that he lay dead within yards of where they were stationed. Later that morning, when word came that an enemy column had penetrated the Lower Town, several would have thrown down their guns and fled had not John Coffin stopped them at the point of a bayonet.

At the sight of the rockets, Arnold led his column, Indian file, along the shore of the St. Charles, taking advantage of the high bank that concealed him from Carleton's lookouts. He could hear Captain Wool's mortars and hoped they might divert the enemy. Snow blown in from the river had gathered in knee-deep drifts. Leaving the shelter of the river bank, he skirted Palace Gate, still unchallenged, but the troops that followed were sighted by Carleton's gunners. As the Americans ran in single file along the base of the cliff, fireballs lit their pathway and several men were hit. "The enemy was covered by his impregnable defenses," Private Henry would remember. "They were even sightless to us — we could see nothing but the blaze from the muzzles of their muskets." [42] In the rush toward the Lower Town, Lamb's six-pounder had to be jettisoned, its heavily weighted sled nosed into a drift. Lamb and his men continued, armed with muskets.

Arnold threaded through a welter of dockside sheds and warehouses and reached the first barricade near Sault au Matelot, defended by a squad of militiamen with three light cannons. He had hoped to shell the barricade with Lamb's six-pounder while Morgan flanked the enemy by looping across the offshore ice, but, deprived of his fieldpiece, he had to make a frontal attack. While ordering his men forward, he felt a quick stab in his left leg. Blood showed at the top of his boot, and he could feel a warm wetness along his calf and ankle. The bullet, ricocheting off a wall, had plowed obliquely through his flesh and lodged in his Achilles' tendon. He slumped against a wall as Chaplain Spring and a rifleman ran to his assistance. The pain was numbing; he could barely stand. He moved slowly to the rear, where he would join other wounded men at Dr. Senter's hospital. With the chaplain and the rifleman under each arm, he shouted encouragement to his troops as he limped from the scene of battle.

With Arnold invalided, the men turned intuitively to Daniel Morgan. While the enemy were reloading, Morgan led his command in a dash for the barricade. Ladders were set in place. When one of the men held back, Morgan pulled him aside and scaled a ladder himself. Musket fire exploded in his face, knocking him to the street, but he returned to the ladder, followed by Riflemen Charles Porterfield and William Heth. Clearing the barricade, he jumped to a gun platform and rolled under the barrel of a cannon, beyond the reach of bayonets. Then, as his men swarmed after him, he drove the barricade's defenders through an adjacent house and out into the street, capturing all thirty and presently adding to his catch when a large number of frightened citizens flocked from nearby buildings to give themselves up. He had won the barricade and taken more than 100 prisoners, with a loss of one man killed and half a dozen wounded.

Morgan left his men on Sault au Matelot Street, where they were rounding up prisoners and shouting *"Vive la liberté!"* and, accompanied by a French guide, advanced to the second barricade. He found the gate open and unattended. He stepped through and, meeting no one at the barricade or on the street beyond it, climbed the escarpment for a better look at his surroundings. The barricade seemed to be his for the taking, and the way looked clear to the Upper Town. He rejoined his officers and proposed an immediate attack. To his dismay, he found them unwilling to advance until more troops had caught up. They were concerned about their small numbers and expressed fears that the prisoners might overpower their guards and block the line of retreat. Morgan did not press the matter further, but he feared that a great opportunity had been lost.

A short way off reinforcements were searching their way through a dockside jungle of sheds and warehouses. Tripping on hawsers, stumbling over cast-off anchors and abandoned spars, the men probed alleys and byways that took them nowhere. In the heavy snow, even those familiar with the waterfront became confused. A full half-hour was lost before they reached the first barricade. Meanwhile, some of Morgan's men had exchanged their snow-clogged rifles for handsome British muskets surrendered by some of the prisoners — weapons, Private Henry said, that "befitted the hand of a real soldier." [43]

Far to the rear, Dearborn's New Hampshiremen streamed into

St. Roch. A high tide had delayed the courier bringing Arnold's order, and they had not crossed the St. Charles until five o'clock. As they pushed toward the Lower Town they met Arnold on his way to the hospital, supported by Chaplain Spring and the rifleman. He impatiently waved them on. Soon afterward, they lost their way, and at daybreak, blinded by snow, were still groping through a maze of unfamiliar streets and roadways.

At Carleton's order, Colonel Caldwell and a detachment of British militia had gone to investigate the gunfire near the Cape Diamond bastion. Caldwell was not alarmed by Captain Brown's feint, deeming it a minor action, but while returning to headquarters he learned that Arnold had attacked the Sault au Matelot barricade. He sped toward the Lower Town with what troops he had, stopping to ask the officer of the day to allow him thirty Royal Highland Emigrants, led by Captain John Nairne. When he reached the second barricade he was joined by Captain Anderson, a former naval officer, and fifty sailors.

Caldwell found the barricade in a state of wild confusion. Colonel Voyer and Captain Alexandre Dumas were there with some 200 militiamen, but Caldwell noticed that the citizen soldiers were "shy of advancing toward the barrier" and that no one seemed to know what his duties were or where he should be posted. Some British regulars were on hand to reinforce the militia.[44] Given command of the barricade in recognition of his past military service, Caldwell quickly imposed order. He formed the regulars in a double line with fixed bayonets directly behind the twelve-foot barrier and stationed some of the militia in adjoining houses. He mounted artillery on a platform overlooking Sault au Matelot Street, directly behind the regulars.

Morgan's command was filling out. Greene, Hubbard, and Meigs had arrived, and Pennsylvania riflemen had joined his Virginians. He ordered the ladders brought up and, forming his troops, led them around a bend in the narrow street into full view of the barricade. On his approach the door of the barricade flew open. A detachment sallied forth, halting athwart his path while an officer called on him to surrender. Morgan took aim and fired. The officer dropped, and the detachment retreated behind the barricade. Morgan's bullet had struck and killed Captain Anderson, commander of the naval unit.

Morgan and his men forged up the narrow street, shouting, "Quebec is ours!" and aiming at the platform where Caldwell's guns were mounted. Defenseless against snipers in high windows, they challenged the enemy to come out and do battle in the street. Many were hit. Private Fobes's sergeant was shot down as the two advanced together. The man lay on his back, unable to move, and, although under orders not to stop, Fobes turned him over before continuing up the street. Captain Jonas Hubbard, the Worcester farmer who had doubted the wisdom of trying to storm the city, slumped against a wall, urging his men on. He was mortally wounded.

Ladders were propped against the barricade. Morgan clambered to the top but was driven back by musket fire. In spite of repeated attempts, no one could climb over the barricade and descend to the other side alive. Lieutenant John Humphries of the Virginians and Lieutenant Samuel Cooper of Hanchet's company were killed in the street. Others were shot off ladders. Lieutenant Steele lost three fingers, Captain Topham was wounded; Matthias Ogden took a bullet in the shoulder. Grapeshot tore out Captain Lamb's left eye. He was carried to a cooper's shop and stretched unconscious on a pile of shavings.

In an effort to flank the barricade, some of the men broke into an adjacent house, whereupon a brawny French militiaman, Charles Charland, wrested a ladder from Morgan's troops and braced it against the wall. Captain Nairne and François Dambourgès, a French volunteer, climbed to an upstairs window, followed by several Royal Highland Emigrants and militiamen. Clearing the house, room by room, with fixed bayonets, they drove the Americans back into the street. Morgan directed his troops to take cover in houses and continue their fire. In the exchange of bullets, Captain William Hendricks, the soft-spoken rifleman whom Private Henry described as "of a mild and beautiful countenance," was shot dead at an open window.

Recognizing the futility of further attempts on the barricade, Morgan gave orders for a retreat and dispatched Lieutenant Heth to relay this to the men. But Heth found few who were willing to venture into the street again. While he pleaded with them, the chance to retreat was lost.

Carleton, kept posted on developments at Sault au Matelot, ordered Captain George Laws to seal off Morgan's column between the two barricades. With a task force of about 500 Royal Highland Emigrants and sailors, Laws sallied through Palace Gate and encountered Dearborn's troops, still on their way to the Lower Town. Laws shouted a challenge. Dearborn said he was a friend but when asked whose friend he might be declared himself "a friend of liberty." Someone in Laws's command opened fire. "I clapt my piece which was charged with a ball and ten buck shott . . . to give him his due," Dearborn recalled, "but to my great mortification my gun did not go off . . . Neither I nor one in ten of my men could get off our guns, they being so exceeding wet." [45] Short of dry gunpowder and outnumbered, Dearborn surrendered after a brief stand and was taken with his men to the Upper Town.

Captain Laws was in such a hurry to cut off Morgan's troops that when he reached Sault au Matelot he advanced unattended into their midst and informed them that they were his prisoners. When they seemed slow to capitulate to a solitary Royal Highland Emigrant, he told them that he was not alone and that his command would join him "in a twinkling." But for Meigs's intervention, he might have been shot. He was held prisoner until his task force had recaptured the first barricade and bottled up the enemy, in keeping with Carleton's order.[46]

Trapped between the two barricades, Morgan held out until nearly ten o'clock. One in five of his men had been killed or wounded, most were out of gunpowder, and now they were capitulating. Several turned themselves over to Captain Nairne at the house that he and Dambourgès had cleared and occupied. The gate to the barricade was flung open, and great numbers of Americans poured through it to surrender to Colonel Caldwell. At the far end of the street, still others capitulated to Captain Laws. All of Morgan's officers surrendered, including Steele, with his mutilated hand, and Lamb, fearfully disfigured and without an eye. Morgan alone was left. Backed against a wall, he warned his conquerors that if they would take away his sword they must shoot him first. Catching sight of a black-robed figure, he asked if he was a priest. When the man nodded, Morgan handed him the sword. "No scoundrel of these cowards shall take it out of my hands," he said.[47]

Carleton sent a task force to St. Roch to clear the suburb of enemy artillery. His troops were met by Captain Wool and his gun crew at a bend in a crooked street. A member of the task force shouted, "Damn the dogs, we'll take them all!" Wool shouted back, "You lie, you dogs!" and opened up with a six-pounder. Providentially, he was joined at the start of the exchange by troops from the 3rd New York and Livingston's Canadians. The task force withdrew, taking the guns in Wool's abandoned battery.[48] "A glorious day for us," one of Carleton's officers declared, "and as compleat a little victory as ever was gained." [49]

There were those, however, who could not wholly agree, including Colonel Caldwell. "The General did not choose to risk anything further," he wrote General Murray. "His ideas seemed entirely to centre in the preservation of the town, certain of succours arriving in the spring; nor did he seem to carry his views towards the operations of the summer campaign, which might have been much forewarded by the entire route of the enemy." [50] Had Carleton taken the offensive and annihilated what was left of Montgomery's army, as Caldwell wished, a British thrust at Albany might have been made that summer.

Arnold sent word to Wooster that the attempt on Quebec had failed, that Montgomery had been killed, and that the troops were in great jeopardy. When he heard that an enemy task force had penetrated St. Roch, he ordered a musket issued to every patient in the hospital and had his sword and a brace of pistols placed beside him on the bed. He may have relaxed after Captain Wool reported the withdrawal of the task force, but he kept his weapons within reach. "I have no thoughts of leaving this proud town," he wrote his sister Hannah, "until I first enter it in triumph." [51]

Four hundred and twenty-six Americans were taken prisoner, forty-two of them wounded. At least thirty were dead — possibly twice that number, because many lay buried in the snow. A few had escaped across the St. Charles, including most of the Canadians and Indians. Natanis was taken prisoner, but he paid no penalty for having sided with Arnold. Quickly released, he was allowed to return to his trap lines on the Dead.

Carleton lost half a dozen men — five French and British volunteers in addition to Captain Anderson. He was extolled for the cool-headedness he had shown and for his unwavering resolve. Great credit, too, was bestowed on Colonel Maclean. "He had his eye everywhere to prevent the progress of the attackers," Captain Ainslie said. "His activity gave life to all who saw him." There were accolades for Colonel Caldwell, whose men had been on hand "wherever danger made their presence necessary," for the guard at Près de Ville, for Captain Hamilton's sailors, who had behaved "like British tars," and, indeed, for all who had helped save Quebec.[52] Some thought that only divine intervention could account for what had happened. "Let us therefore, with one voice, express our gratitude to the King of kings for our miraculous preservation," one officer urged, "for the Almighty was with us in the day of distress; the Lord of Hosts severely smote our enemy; they were overwhelmed as with a whirlwind, and left us triumphant to gather them up and lead them into captivity; for which blessing, glory, honor and praise be to the Most High." [53] Bishop Briand ordered all his priests to lead the faithful in the Te Deum and to address prayers of thanksgiving to the Blessed Virgin, the Guardian Angels, and to St. Joseph, patron of Quebec.

On New Year's morning, the bodies were dug from the snow at Près de Ville. One wore a fur cap marked with the initials of Richard Montgomery. Close by lay a sword. Fashioned by a master craftsman, it possessed an ivory handle and a silver dog's-head pommel. James Thompson, Carleton's engineer, felt sure that it was Montgomery's. He ordered the body removed to a house on St. Louis Street, where it was recognized by the Widow Prentice, proprietress of an inn Montgomery had patronized while serving with the British army. Her testimony was confirmed by some of the American prisoners who were brought from their place of detention to identify the general. At sundown on January 5, Montgomery was committed to a grave near the St. Louis bastion. Accorded "a genteel coffin" by order of the lieutenant governor, he was placed beside Macpherson and Cheeseman in a plot that would also accommodate some of his rank and file.* Although he did not live to know it, on December 9 he had been advanced to major general.

* In 1811, Montgomery's remains were removed to St. Paul's Church in lower Manhattan.

General Philip Schuyler. Courtesy of
the American Antiquarian Society.

General Richard Montgomery, from the painting
by Charles Willson Peale. Courtesy of
the American Antiquarian Society.

General Benedict Arnold, engraving
from the contemporary portrait
by Pierre Eugene Du Simitière.

Captain Daniel Morgan.

Captain John Lamb. Courtesy of the
Anne S. K. Brown Military Collection,
Brown University

General John Thomas, engraving
from a contemporary portrait.

Dr. Isaac Senter. Courtesy of
John G. Senter.

General John Sullivan. Courtesy
of the Anne S. K. Brown Military
Collection, Brown University.

General David Wooster.
Courtesy of the American
Antiquarian Society.

Fort Ticonderoga as it looks today. Courtesy of the Fort Ticonderoga Museum.

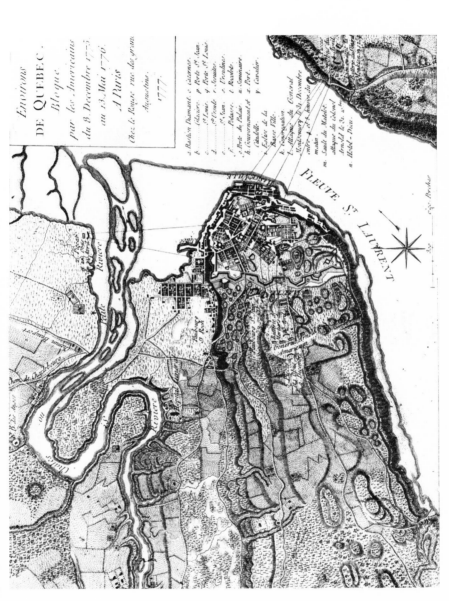

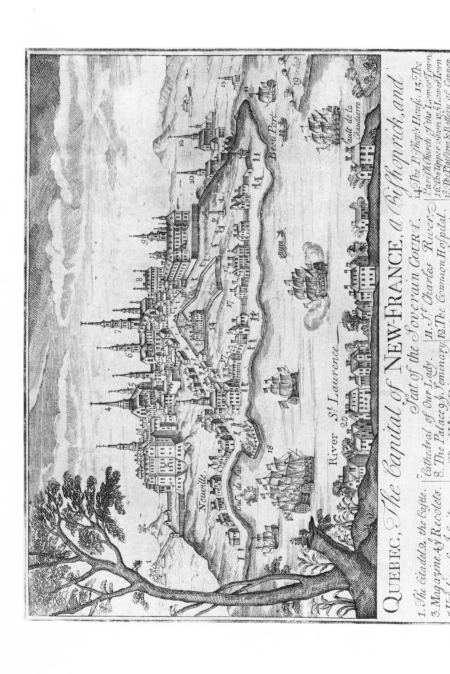

QUEBEC, The Capital of NEW-FRANCE, a Bishoprick, and Seat of the Soveraign COURT.

1. The Citadel. 2. the Castle.
3. Magazine. 4. y.e Recolets.
5. Ursulines. 6. Jesuits. 7.
Cathedral of Our Lady.
8. The Palace & Seminary.
10. The Hôtel Dieu.
11. St Charles River.
12. The Common Hospital.
13. The Hermitage of the Recolets.
14. The Bishop's House. 15. The
Parish Church of the Lower Town.
16. The Upper Town. 17. Lower Town.
18. The Platform & Batery of Cannon.
19. The Isle of Orleans. 20. Front View.

Eighteenth Century Quebec. Courtesy of the American Antiquarian Society.

General Guy Carlton. Courtesy of the
Metropolitan Toronto Library (JRR3315). In the
J. Ross Robertson Collection, Metropolitan
Toronto Central Library.

Colonel Allan Maclean. By permission of the
Lord Maclean and through the courtesy of
the Canadian War Museum. First used by
George F. G. Stanley in *Canada Invaded*.

Monsignor Jean Olivier Briand, Bishop of Quebec. Courtesy of the National Archives of Quebec, Initial Collection.

Abbé Etienne Montgolfier, Vicar-general of Montreal. Courtesy of the Public Archives of Canada, Ottawa (C-12022).

Lieutenant John André. Courtesy of
the Anne S. K. Brown Military
Collection, Brown University.

Charles de Lanaudière. Courtesy of
the Public Archives of Canada,
Ottawa (C-28244).

Major Charles Preston. Courtesy of
the Scottish National Picture Gallery
and by permission of Colonel
R. Campbell-Preston.

Saint-Luc de La Corne. Courtesy of the
Public Archives of Canada, Ottawa
(C-28244) with permission of Alice
Lighthall.

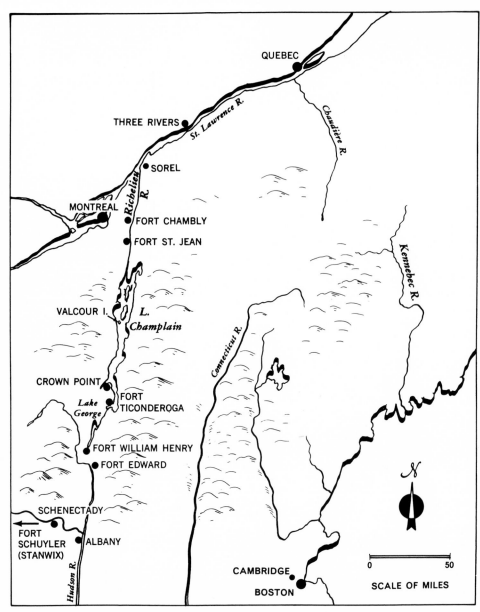

General Montgomery's route to Montreal and Quebec.
From *Canada and the American Revolution, 1774–1783,* by Gustave Lanctot
(Clarke, Irwin & Company, Ltd., Toronto, 1967).

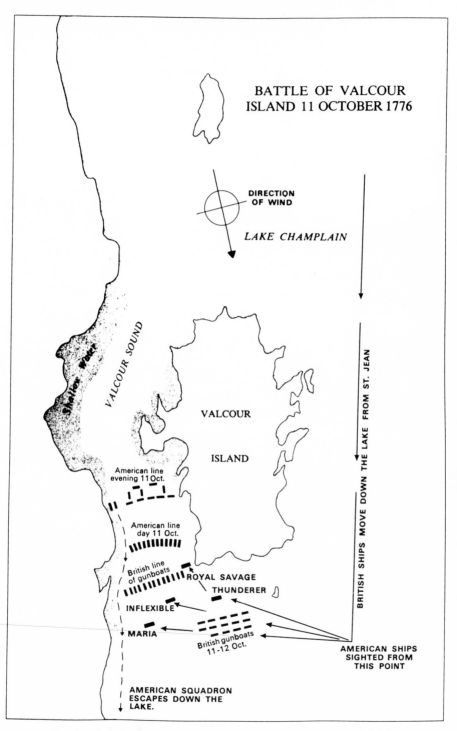

Battle of Valcour Island, 11 October 1776. From *Canada Invaded*,
by George F. G. Stanley (Samuel-Stevens-Hakkurt, Toronto 1973).

Pringle's Squadron on Lake Champlain, by C. Randle. Courtesy of the
Public Archives of Canada, Ottawa (C-13203).

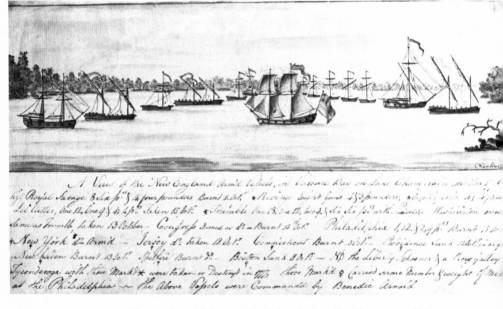

Arnold's vessels at Valcour Island, by C. Randle. Courtesy of the
Public Archives of Canada, Ottawa (C-13202).

VIII

The Unyielding Rock

1

Two days after the defeat, Major Meigs came out on parole to collect the prisoners' baggage. He told Arnold that the men were well treated, that he had dined with Captain Laws, and that Captain McKenzie had given him Montgomery's knee buckles and Macpherson's gold watch.

Arnold was left with about 800 men, including Livingston's Canadians. More than 100 recruits whose enlistments had expired had departed for Montreal without his permission. "I hope you will stop every rascal who has deserted from us and bring him back again," he wrote Wooster.[1] His wound gave him unceasing pain, and he longed to be relieved of the command. "The burden lies very heavy on me, considering my present circumstances," he told Wooster. "I find myself unequal to the task." [2] At first he had wanted Colonel Campbell to act in his stead, but the officers would have none of it. In a letter to Washington he suggested Major General Charles Lee for the command. Lee was a British military man who had served with Braddock and Amherst in the French and Indian War, with Burgoyne on the Continent, and with the Poles in their war against the Turks. A republican in his thinking, he had offered his services to Congress and was considered a great catch.

On his return from Près de Ville, Campbell had dispatched Edward Antill to notify Wooster of Montgomery's death, but in spite of what happened, Wooster was unwilling to leave Montreal. He feared a Canadian uprising and had a garrison of only 600 men. "There is little confidence to be placed in the Canadians," he wrote Schuyler. "They are but a small remove from the savages, and are fond of being of the strongest party . . . The Clergy almost universally refuse absolution to those who are our friends, and preach to the people that it is not now too late to take arms against us; that the Bostonians are but a handful of men; which, you know, is too true."[3] He sent Antill and Moses Hazen to Albany to inform Schuyler of the defeat and to advise him that James Price, who had already advanced £20,000 toward the campaign, could raise nothing more among allies in Montreal. After notifying Schuyler, Antill and Hazen would continue to Philadelphia and break the news to Congress.

A fast trip by sleigh brought Antill and Hazen to the Schuyler mansion on the edge of Albany. Schuyler was dumfounded at what they told him. He was distressed over Montgomery's death, for he had valued him not only as a trusted colleague but as a close and like-minded friend. His grief was compounded by his lack of reinforcements to send north. Recent beating orders had turned up only a few recruits. Among men whose enlistments would soon expire only a fraction seemed willing to re-enlist. Moreover, he was about to leave for Tryon County, where Sir John Johnson had rallied Tories and Indians in the service of the Crown. A woman spy, the wife of a patriot, had reported that Johnson was forming an alliance with the Iroquois and that he had the nucleus of a small army in the many Scottish tenants who had settled on his family acres. Indeed, it was some of these same Scots who had enrolled with Allan Maclean when he was recruiting on the Mohawk. Schuyler called on Seth Warner and on leaders in the Berkshires for two short-term regiments. He promised officers a month's wages in advance, the rank and file a bounty. His appeal brought a swift response. Two weeks later he wrote Washington that "Colonel Warner succeeds fast in sending men to Canada" and that troops from the Berkshires were on the march.[4]

Nor could Washington spare reinforcements. Congress had been unwilling to authorize a forty-dollar bounty for men who re-enlisted for another year and had frowned on enrolling a standing army for the duration of the war, lest it encourage a military dictatorship. As a result, many of his troops who had completed their terms were reluctant to re-enlist. In an attempt to fill his ranks he had appealed to Massachusetts for 5000 short-term militiamen. "Since the Dissolution of the old Army," he wrote Schuyler, "the Progress in raising Recruits for the new, has been so very slow and inconsiderable, that five Thousand Militia have been called in for the Defence of our Lines. A great Part of these are gone Home again, and the rest induced to stay with the utmost Difficulty and Persuasion . . . In short we have not a Man to spare." [5] He called on Massachusetts, Connecticut, and New Hampshire to raise one regiment each to reinforce the army in Canada.

Washington's troubles reflected a lack of resolution in the country at large. Although he and others like him realized that the colonies could gain control of their own destiny only by making an irrevocable break with England, most Americans considered themselves still subjects of the king and thought of the war not as a struggle for independence but as a quarrel with a tyrannical ministry and Parliament. Even as staunch a patriot as Philip Schuyler was quoted as having expressed the hope that "Heaven may speedily reunite us in every bond of affection and interest, and that the British empire may again become the envy and admiration of the universe." [6] The year 1776, a time of conflicting loyalties, opened on an uncertain note, with many citizens still hoping for reconciliation.

These were bleak months for Washington, who had moments when he would have happily quit his post. In a letter to his friend Joseph Reed, he described the "dearth of public spirit" among his troops and the "fertility in all the low arts to obtain advantages of one kind or another." He was heartily sick of uncommitted soldiers and self-serving patriots. "Such a dirty, mercenary spirit pervades the whole," he wrote Reed, "that I should not be at all surprised at any disaster that may happen . . . Could I have foreseen what I have and am likely to experience, no consideration upon earth should have induced me to accept this command." [7] Sectional jealousies persisted in spite of all his efforts to root them out. "Connecticut wants no Massachusetts men in her corps," he wrote. "Massachusetts thinks there is no necessity for a Rhode Islander to be introduced into hers; and New Hampshire says it is very hard, that her valuable and experienced officers, who are willing to serve should be discarded." [8] Some of his men, still billeted in tents, were so short of firewood that they ate their meals uncooked. For lack of muskets many carried spears, and late in December he learned that his powder supply was down to ninety barrels. The siege of Boston had turned into a morale-destroying, seemingly endless stalemate. In January, Colonel Henry Knox and a crew of teamsters crossed the Berkshires with the guns captured at Fort Ticonderoga, and Washington began to have hope again. Arnold wished that some of the guns had been diverted to Quebec.

Congress was as divided as the people. Some delegates continued to defend the king, but when he berated the colonies in an address to Parliament, accusing them of waging a "rebellious war . . . for the purpose of establishing an independent empire," moderates like John Dickinson were irreparably undercut. Although Dickinson managed to have colleagues of his own persuasion named to the committee that would reply to the king's address, his influence was waning. Talk of independence mounted after the publication early in the year of Thomas Paine's *Common Sense*, an attack on the very principle of monarchy. Paine declared that if nature had approved of the institution of kingship, she would not "so frequently turn it into ridicule by giving mankind an ass for a lion." His broadside sold 120,000 copies in the first three months. "Everything that is right or reasonable pleads for separation," Paine said. "The blood of the slain, the weeping voice of nature cries, 'Tis time to part."

A letter from Montgomery, dated December 4, had reached Congress on the same day as the king's address. "The Canadians will be our friends as long as we are able to maintain our ground," he had written, "but they must not be depended upon, especially for defensive operations. The great distance from any support or relief renders it in my opinion absolutely necessary to make the most formidable preparations for the security of this important Province." [9] Congress had assigned the 1st Pennsylvania and the 2nd New Jersey to Canada and had called for a battalion each from New York, Connecticut, and New Hampshire. On January 10, it had advanced Arnold to brigadier.

A week later Edward Antill was ushered into Independence Hall. After describing the defeat, he was questioned for two hours by the stunned delegates. When they finished, they appointed five of their number to probe further into the disaster and return with recommendations. Samuel Adams was among the five. So was Samuel Ward, father of the Rhode Island captain taken prisoner with Arnold's men. They were not out long. They asked that the army in Canada be reinforced "with all possible dispatch," that New Jersey and Pennsylvania be urged to "quicken" their recruiting efforts, and that when the first two companies in each battalion had been raised, they set forth immediately, followed "in the same numbers, with like expedition, by the rest of the corps." [10] Washington would be asked to contribute any units he could spare. In approving the recommendations, Congress requested Moses Hazen to raise a second Canadian regiment organized into four battalions and, it was hoped, numbering 1000 officers and men. Jeremiah Duggan was authorized to enroll a three-company ranger battalion.

Montgomery was extolled as a patriot and martyr. He was praised even in Parliament by Barré, Fox, and Burke. Through the influence of John Dickinson, the Reverend William Smith of Philadelphia was picked to eulogize Montgomery in Congress. Like Dickinson, Smith hoped for a reconciliation with the mother country, and in the course of his oration claimed that Montgomery had never disavowed the king and had hoped the capture of Quebec "might have some influence on Parliament in hastening a reconciliation." In an aside that left no doubt about his sympathies, he accused some of his fellow clergy of inflaming "men's minds to the purpose of wild ambition and mutual destruction." [11] This infuriated delegates like John Adams, who valued the preaching of their clerical allies and bridled at talk of reconciliation. Congress declined to publish Smith's oration or even to thank him for it — a further blow to the moderates.

Congress addressed yet another letter to the Canadians, reminding them that "your liberty, your honor and your happiness are essentially and necessarily connected with the unhappy contest which we have been forced into for the defence of our dearest privileges." It promised that they would not be abandoned to the enemy's "unrelenting fury" and urged them, in spite of "vicissitudes" and "disappointments," to send delegates to Philadelphia.[12]

But the time for letter-writing had passed. In early February a Canadian ally, Prudent Lajeunesse, came to Philadelphia to urge that a congressional delegation be sent to Canada. He was not the first to do so. Montgomery had stressed the need for a delegation. Both Schuyler and Arnold had requested one. But Congress had been slow to act. In a letter to Schuyler, John Hancock had expressed the hope that "your Care and Prudence will render any Delegation from this Body unnecessary, at least for the present." [13] The delegation sent north during the autumn had gone no farther than Fort Ticonderoga. But by midwinter, with Quebec still holding out, Congress took action. On February 15, a commission of three was named, headed by Benjamin Franklin and including two noted Marylanders, Samuel Chase and Charles Carroll of Carrollton.

Nearing seventy, renowned in two hemispheres for his scientific attainments and powers of intellect, Franklin had taken a lively interest in Canada, and seventeen years before, when there had been talk of returning Canada to France, had urged its retention as a British colony. He had served many years as a colonial agent in London, where he was admired for his wit and intellect but less appreciated for his firm espousal of his countrymen's rights. He had worked for the repeal of the Stamp Act and, on his return to Philadelphia in 1775, had been named a delegate to Congress. As head of the commission, he would bring it instant prestige.

Samuel Chase was the youngest of the commissioners. Just half Franklin's age in 1776, he, too, had opposed the Stamp Act. More radical than Franklin, he had joined the Sons of Liberty, raiding Crown properties and once burning a tax collector in effigy. He had served on the Maryland Committee of Correspondence, participated in the first Provincial Convention, and, at the time of his appointment, was a delegate to Congress. Subsequently, he would become a signer of the Declaration of Independence and a justice of the Supreme Court.

The third commissioner had unassailable credentials. Charles Carroll of Carrollton had been educated in France, spoke fluent French, and, as the foremost Roman Catholic layman in the colonies, had taken issue with Britain's policy of taxing Catholics in Maryland for the support of the Anglican Church while denying them their own schools and the right to vote. He preferred to be known as Charles Carroll of Carrollton, his family seat, to distinguish him from other Carrolls with the same Christian name. He was not yet a member of Congress but, like Chase, had served on the Maryland Committee of Correspondence and had been a deputy to the Provincial Convention.

John Adams acknowledged that Carroll's Catholicism, however suspect in Puritan New England, would stand him in good stead with Canadians.

I was introduced to him about Eighteen Months ago in this City and was much pleased with his Conversation [Adams said in a letter to James Warren]. He has a Fortune as I am well informed which is computed to be worth Two Hundred Thousand Pounds Sterling. He is a Native of Maryland, and his Father is still living. He had a liberal Education in France and is well acquainted with the french Nation. He speaks their Language as easily as ours; and what is perhaps of more Consequence than all the rest, he was educated in the Roman Catholic Religion and still continues to worship his Maker according to the Rites of that Church. In the Cause of American Liberty his Zeal Fortitude and Perseverance have been so conspicuous that he is said to be marked out for peculiar Vengeance by the Friends of Administration; But he continues to hazard all, his immense Fortune, the largest in America, and his Life. This Gentleman's Character, if I foresee aright, will hereafter make a greater Figure in America.[14]

Thirty-nine years old in 1776, Charles Carroll of Carrollton would live into his ninety-fifth year and become the last surviving signer of the Declaration of Independence.

"If some Jesuit or Religieuse of any other Order (but he must be a man of liberal sentiments, enlarged mind and a manifest friend of Civil Liberty) could be found and sent to Canada, he would be worth battalions to us," General Lee had written Hancock when he

learned about the commission, adding that "Mr. Carroll has a relative who exactly answers the description."[15] The Reverend John
Carroll, a cousin of Charles Carroll of Carrollton, was a Jesuit, and
Hancock, pleased with General Lee's idea, asked Charles to enlist
his relative as a clerical adviser to the commission. John Adams
hoped that Father Carroll would attract waverers in Bishop Briand's
flock and "bestow Absolution upon such as have been refused it by
the Torified Priests in Canada."[16]

Like his cousin, Father Carroll spoke flawless French. He had
studied for Holy Orders in Europe, had been ordained there, and
had taught at a Jesuit college in Liége. Urbane, erudite, and an
accomplished theologian, he favored a break with England as a
means of safeguarding his Church's freedom. After the Revolution,
he would become the first Archbishop of Baltimore and a towering
influence in American Catholicism.

A French printer, Fleury Mesplet, was to accompany the commission. Although many of the *habitants* were known to be illiterate, Mesplet hoped to issue a pro-American newspaper and change
enough minds to justify his lugging a printing press from Philadelphia to American headquarters in Montreal. For the moment he
would have no competition. The only newspaper in Canada, the
Quebec Gazette, suspended publication during the winter of 1776.

Congress directed a committee headed by John Adams to prepare
instructions for the commissioners. The committee came up with a
preliminary draft, but Congress haggled over it for more than a
month. "A great part of these instructions was opposed by our an-
tagonists with great zeal," Adams said, "but they were supported
on our side with equal ardor, and the acceptance of them afforded
a strong proof of the real determination of a majority of Congress
to go with us to the final consummation of our wishes."[17] Adams
and his supporters succeeded in winning for the commissioners wide
civil and military powers, including a voice in military decision-
making.

The commissioners were urged to do everything they could to
promote a union between the colonies and Canada, promising the
Canadians "the free and undisturbed exercise of their religion" and
"the same general system of mild and equal laws" that existed in the

colonies, "with only such local differences as may be agreeable to each colony respectively." The clergy would be assured "the full, perfect and peaceable possession and enjoyment of all their estates." Trade with the Indians would be resumed, and commerce with foreign countries would be "on an equal footing with, and encouraged and protected in the same manner, as the trade of the United Colonies." In addition, the commissioners would correct administrative abuses, settle disputes between civilians and the military, and monitor the conduct of the campaign.[18]

Both Franklin and the two Carrolls had misgivings about the mission. Franklin was concerned for his very life. He was afraid that, because of his age and state of health, he might not survive the journey. Indeed, later, during a pause at Saratoga, he wrote farewell letters to certain close friends. Carroll was aware that most French Canadians would rate Governor Carleton a much safer ally than the Protestants who thronged Independence Hall. He knew that if the Church in Canada had its way, few of the faithful would take kindly to the commission.

No one, however, had deeper misgivings than Father John Carroll, who questioned the nature of the assignment. The Canadians, he believed, did not share the colonists' grievances. The Quebec Act had met their more urgent needs, General Carleton had shown himself to be their friend, and the Church had been fairly treated by king and parliament. Father Carroll was not sure that he could ask them, in good conscience, to turn on a government that had used them so generously. He was unhappy, too, about forsaking his priestly duties for a venture in secular diplomacy.

In a letter written on the eve of his departure, Father Carroll voiced some of his qualms:

I have observed that when the ministers of Religion leave their duties of their profession to take a busy part in political matters, they generally fall into contempt, & sometimes even bring discredit to the cause in whose service they are engaged. Secondly — From all the information I have been able to collect concerning the State of Canada, it appears to me that the inhabitants of that country are in no wise disposed to molest the united colonies, or prevent their forces from taking & holding possession of the strong places in that province, or to assist in any manner the British arms. Now if it be proposed that the Canadians should concur with the other colonies any farther than by such neutrality, I apprehend it will not be in my power to advise them to it. They have not the same motives for taking up arms against England which render the resistance of the other colonies so justifiable. If an oppressive mode of government has been given them, it was what some of them chose, & the rest have not tried the success of petitions & remonstrances, all of which ought, as I apprehend, to be ineffectual before it can be lawful to have recourse to arms & change of government.[19]

Nevertheless, Father Carroll saw the assignment as a call to duty and agreed to go.

While the commissioners waited for the spring melt on Lake Champlain, reinforcements were already on the march. Wooster had asked Seth Warner to hurry men northward "by tens, twenties, thirties, forties or fifties, as they can be collected."[20] In less than two weeks Warner had sent off his first troops, who traveled down the lake ice in scattered bands, clinging to sleighs "like bees about a hive," sleeping in the open or under brush shelters.[21] "Feb. 22nd 1776 set out for another campaign to Canada," Captain Fassett wrote, "and may God of his infinite mercy preserve me."[22] By early March, 417 Green Mountain Boys had reported to General Wooster — not as many as Schuyler hoped, for he had allowed advance pay for nearly twice that number, but it took stalwarts to leave for Canada in midwinter.

Meshech Weare, Chairman of the New Hampshire Committee of Safety, promised a regiment from his colony's western frontier. Drawn chiefly from the ranks of the same New Hampshire Rangers who had served with Montgomery, it consisted of eight companies, each with ninety officers and men. Colonel Timothy Bedel was in command, with Isaac Butterfield as major. Connecticut Valley suppliers were ordered to furnish moose hide for moccasins, coarse cloth for coats and shirts, shoes, blankets and camp kettles, flints, gunpowder and ammunition. There must be ample rum, and on the march to Lake Champlain each recruit must have a daily allowance of a pound of pork, a pound of beef, and half a pint of peas. In trying to fill the order, the suppliers ran short of cash. As late as March 20, part of the regiment was still east of the Green Mountains.

Reinforcements continued to stream northward from western Massachusetts and the New Hampshire Grants. Among the first to reach Canada were a Berkshire captain and twenty-five recruits, who reported at Trois Rivières on January 25. "His arrival had a very good effect," one of Wooster's men observed, "for on the morning of the same day was found, at the Church door, an anonymous seditious paper, very artfully written, calculated to stimulate the inhabitants to rise and cut us all off." [23] Others followed in small parties. On January 20, the Massachusetts legislature commissioned Colonel Elisha Porter of Hadley to raise a regiment of six companies in Hampshire and Berkshire Counties. For two months he struggled to fill his ranks. His first company left the Connecticut Valley on March 3, although he did not get off the last of his troops until nearly three weeks later. A spring snowstorm overtook Porter and his men in the Berkshires, slowing their advance.

Colonel Charles Burrall of Canaan, Connecticut, was ordered to raise a regiment in the northwest corner of the colony. Lieutenant Colonel Nathaniel Buell of Salisbury was his second in command, and among his officers was Captain John Stevens, who had taken part in the capture of Fort Ticonderoga. The Reverend Ammi Robbins of Norfolk, who kept a diary, was chaplain. Although Colonel Burrall was highly esteemed in the northwestern hill country, enlistments lagged. The legislature earmarked more than 700 pounds of gunpowder for the regiment and allotted $12,500 toward the men's wages, but muskets and blankets remained scarce and it was mid-March before most of the troops reached Albany. Burrall suspected that men who had served with Schuyler were warning prospective recruits that the crusty Dutchman held a grudge against New Englanders.

If Chaplain Robbins shared his fellow New Englanders' low opinion of Schuyler, he had reason to revise it while stationed in Albany. Asked to minister to a man under sentence of death, he turned up for the execution, ready to commit the condemned to his Maker. What followed is described in Robbins' diary: "All the troops drawn up on parade and the prisoner brought out blindfolded to his execution, when the General stepped forth and in a moving and striking speech, pardoned the criminal."[24] It was a side of the oft-maligned New Yorker that probably took Robbins and his fellow New Englanders by surprise.

John Hancock had hoped that the Pennsylvania and New Jersey troops would be on their way before the last of January, but it was a month later before any of the men crossed into Canada.[25] Colonel John Philip De Haas led the 1st Pennsylvania; Colonel Arthur St. Clair, the 2nd. Both encountered unforeseen delays. Their men marched piecemeal as soon as they could be equipped, leaning into gale winds on the lake, bedding down in frozen woods. "Any man would rather work in the mines than undergo the fatigue of the march that our battalion has," declared a sergeant in one of De Haas's companies.[26]

Colonel William Maxwell of the 2nd New Jersey complained that his regiment lacked "a great part of everything but men" and would "make a poor figure" until adequately supplied with guns, bayonets, canteens, camp kettles, and something warmer than uniforms issued for a New Jersey winter. "I am distressed beyond measure to have so fine a parcel of men under my command," he said, "and yet so unfit for doing their country service when it is so much wanted."[27] The province confiscated privately owned firelocks for Maxwell's troops and acquired blankets from patriotic housewives. By early February, he had sent off his first company, many of the men still without canteens or camp kettles. About a week later, Schuyler wrote the commander-in-chief that Maxwell's company and five companies of De Haas's Pennsylvanians had left Albany for Canada. "They are much thinned by sickness and desertion, and came very ill provided," he wrote. "The better half of their arms required repairs, and the whole were to be furnished with shoes, socks, mittens, etc., which causes a considerable detention, and distresses me much, as hardly anything is to be bought in this place."[28] Maxwell's frustrations, however, were no greater than Schuyler's own. Asked by Congress to enroll the 1st New York, he had recruited most of the men in Albany County, but the province could not supply him with nearly enough guns, blankets, or winter uniforms, and equipping the unit turned out to be a time-consuming process.

Early in January, Congress ordered two regiments formed in Canada from troops whose enlistments would expire on April 15. Wooster assigned the New York troops to Colonel John Nicholson, who had been a captain in the 3rd New York, the New Englanders to Colonel Samuel Elmore, a former major in the 4th Connecticut. When the terms expired, however, few men were willing to re-enlist, and neither unit attained full strength. In late January, Wooster sent 120 of his men to Quebec, followed by a second contingent of sixty or seventy. Although fewer than Arnold hoped for, they were greeted exuberantly by his troops.

Arnold's Canadian regiments remained consistently understrength. He had energetic recruiting officers in Maurice Desdevens at Pointe aux Trembles, Philippe Baronnet at Deschambault, Etienne Parent in Beauce, Pierre Hayot at Kamouraska, and Clément Gosselin and Germain Dionne at Ste. Anne de la Pocatière, but they enrolled few of their countrymen. James Livingston's 1st Canadian Regiment, raised by order of Montgomery and authorized by Congress in January, peaked at about 200. Moses Hazen's 2nd Canadian totaled no more than 150 in early March, increasing to perhaps 250 a few weeks later. "Recruiting goes slow in this part of Canada," he wrote Edward Antill, his second in command. "I hope you have better success at and about Quebec. Indeed, my money is now exhausted and am not like to get any more till it arrives from below." Not sure that Antill was exerting himself sufficiently, he urged him to "lay aside the delicate Gentleman and put on the recruiting officer." [29]

Jeremiah Duggan's ranger battalion fared no better. Short of muskets, he asked Maurice Desdevens to requisition a supply from private citizens. "Take such as you find," Desdevens was told, "giving a receipt for the arms they deliver you, and by this receipt you will undertake to return them in good order, or to pay their value at the end of the campaign." [30] The measure may have brought forth muskets, but it did not win Duggan many recruits. Neither St. Roch nor St. Charles contributed a man to his battalion, nor was anyone enrolled from the parishes of Cap Santé, Campanais, and Ste. Anne de la Pérade. Bishop Briand thought that, in all, the invaders might have recruited 500 Canadians.

Meanwhile, Arnold continued the siege with what men he had. He had been given no intimation of when he might be relieved. General Lee, picked tentatively for the command, was still in New York, when Congress changed his orders and sent him to repulse a threatened seaborne attack on Virginia or the Carolinas.

Washington made it clear that he anticipated the capture of Quebec before spring. On January 27, he wrote Arnold:

I need not mention to you the great importance of this place, and the consequent possession of all Canada in the scale of American affairs; you are well apprized of it. To whomsoever it belongs, in their favour, probably, will the balance turn. If it is ours, success, I think, will most certainly crown our virtuous struggles; if it is theirs, the contest, at least, will be doubtful, hazardous and bloody. The glorious work must be accomplished in the course of this Winter, otherwise it will become difficult, most probably impracticable. For Administration knowing that it will be impossible ever to reduce us to a state of slavery and arbitrary rule without it, will certainly send a large reinforcement there in the Spring. I am fully convinced that your exertions will be invariably directed to this grand object; and I already view the approaching day when you and your brave followers will enter this important Fortress with every honour and triumph attendant on victory and conquest. Then will you have added the only link wanting in the great chain of Continental Union, and rendered the freedom of your country secure.

Wishing you a speedy recovery, and the possession of those laurels which your bravery and perseverance justly merit, I am, dear sir, etc.,

GEORGE WASHINGTON[31]

2

At Quebec, the winter was one of the worst in memory. Snow-freighted gales slammed inland from the North Atlantic as streets vanished under mountainous drifts, and snow buried doorways and downstairs windows. "The windows of the second storey serve as doors, by which to pass into the streets," Captain Ainslie said, quoting a French saying that it was cold enough "to split a stone." [32] There was never enough firewood. Foraging parties, flanked by militiamen, prowled the suburbs, dismantling fences and prying boards from vacant houses. Arnold ordered the empty buildings burned. One night fourteen went up in a single blaze, sending skyward sheets of flame that gave the night "an orange tinge," according to Ainslie, and turned snow "a redish yellow." He found "the crakling of burning beams" and "hollow roaring of feirce flames" somehow "pleasingly awful." [33] Carleton stationed Captain Nairne with a detail of soldiers in some of the vacant buildings and, to protect shipping, assigned Captain Laws and an all-night guard to the waterfront. But the rebels still applied the torch, burning houses, sheds, and moored ships — especially on snowy nights.

Although outnumbered two to one, Arnold hung on, trading shots with the enemy and denying them firewood when he could. For a while he expected Carleton to try a sortie. "We are in expectation every night that the enemy will come out upon us," Private Haskell said.[34] But Carleton, even with numerical superiority, chose to remain on the defensive until reinforcements came from Britain. The siege continued in glacial cold, through sleet storms, blizzards, and knife-edged winds. Private Haskell wrote of "cold, uncomfortable weather," days "so cold that a man can scarce get out without freezing," and a snowstorm such as "never was known in New England." [35] Yet the Americans hung on. "This is true bravery," Governor Trumbull said in a letter to Philip Schuyler. "It must convince Lord North that Americans are not all poltroons." [36] Twice in February and again in March, Arnold asked for an exchange of prisoners. He was short of experienced artillerymen and was especially anxious for the return of John Lamb, offering a British officer in his stead. But his emissaries were turned away at the city gates and told not to come back unless they would implore the king's mercy.

By late January, Arnold was greeting the first reinforcements. Wooster sent a detachment from Montreal, followed by the foremost companies of Green Mountain Boys. "Perhaps the promise of

a strong reinforcement may have raised their drooping spirits,"
Ainslie remarked after a shouted welcome was heard in the rebel
encampment one February day.[37] The troops kept coming, all
through the winter and early spring — some of the Pennsylvania
companies at the beginning of March, part of Maxwell's command
a few weeks later, Elisha Porter's regiment in April. Reinforcements totaling 1400 men had passed through Trois Rivières by
March 22, an additional 400 after another month, but so many of
the men contracted smallpox that the number fit for duty was no
greater than what Arnold had reported a few days after the defeat.

"From the 1st of January to the 1st of March, we have never
had more than seven hundred effective men on the ground, and
frequently not more than five hundred," Arnold wrote his friend
Silas Deane. In late March, Dr. Senter reported 400 smallpox patients, many of whom had taken the disease by inoculation. "Orders have been repeatedly given," Arnold said, "and as repeatedly
disobeyed or neglected." [38] Seth Warner was quoted as telling his
men, "If you should take it in the Thigh and Diet for it, it would
be much better for you, and they will not find out." [39] By late
March, 271 Green Mountain Boys had inoculated themselves.
More than half of John Brown's men had done the same. Dr.
Senter's wards became so crowded that even the very ill could not
be given proper care. Indeed, Arnold wrote Silas Deane that most
of the New Englanders had smallpox.

When he left Cambridge, Arnold had been urged by the commander-in-chief to be "particularly careful to pay the full value
for all provisions, or other accommodations, which the Canadians
may provide for you on your march." [40] Only hard money could
satisfy the Canadians, but it was scarce even in the colonies, and,
to meet the shortage, Congress issued bank bills or treasury notes,
promising that they would be redeemed over a four-year period.
It was an easy way to finance the war, but soon the paper money
was bringing only a fraction of its supposed value in hard cash. By
1779, when the practice stopped, $241 million in Continental bills
had been printed, each worth about three cents on the dollar. "Not
worth a Continental" became part of the language.

Arnold could offer his Canadian suppliers and work crews nothing but the paper money that all of them distrusted and that many refused to accept. On March 4, he issued an ultimatum. Whoever accepted the paper currency, he ruled, would "receive the Amount of it in Gold and Silver within the space of three or four Months from the date of this Present" but "Every person who shall refuse to accept it at Par and without Discount, shall be considered an Enemy of the united Colonies and treated as such." [41] Although the ultimatum kept the army in supplies, it made even as firm an ally as Edward Antill "tremble for the consequences." He wrote Hazen that "chagrin and discontent universally appeared in the faces of those who received it [the paper money] ... and with it is gone the affections of the people in general." [42]

More and more Canadians were asking themselves if the troops who had come as "liberators" were not in fact thieves and oppressors. Supplies were paid for in a currency that no one wanted. Paper money handed out to unwilling work crews evoked memories of the *corvées* that had made life miserable for the *habitants* during the French regime. Commerce was at a standstill; the Indian trade choked off. Some may have remembered a letter published in the *Quebec Gazette* back in October. Written in French and translated into halting English, it had been signed CIVIS CANADIENSIS. "These people," it said, "to whom you have done no harm come into your province to take your property with arms in their hands under a pretext of being your well-wishers. Can you think that these people who are without food and ammunition will allow you to enjoy peacefully the fruits of your labours, no; they will take your grain, your cattle and everything you have (of which they have need) and they will pay you with notes; (which they call Province Bills, or Bills of Credit) what will you do with such money? nothing." [43] Moses Hazen reported *habitants* forced to supply the army at bayonet point in return for unsigned, illegible notes that the quartermaster general refused to honor. "It is true they have been promised payment from time to time," he said, "yet they look upon such promises as vague, their labour and property lost, and the Congress and the United Colonies bankrupt." The province, he said, was "left without any other kind of law than that of the arbitrary power of the sword in the hands of several commanding officers." [44]

Stories of American troops stealing from civilians and threatening them with bayonets made the rounds of church and marketplace. Captain William Goforth, stationed at Trois Rivières, reported a priest's house broken into and his watch stolen, an *habitant* run through the neck with a bayonet for demanding payment of a debt, women and children forced at bayonet point to supply horses at no pay. Goforth confiscated a spoon pilfered at Montreal, a bundle of baby clothes stolen by a New Jersey recruit. Such instances of misconduct further tarnished the army's reputation. When an American officer could not pay for the care of his sick at the Ursuline hospital in Trois Rivières and asked Jean Baptiste Badeaux, spokesman for the order, to have patience, Badeaux advised him to feed his men on patience. "We shall see how fat they will get," he added.[45]

Morale dropped as men talked openly of quitting Canada as soon as their enlistments expired. Hazen heard that "neither order nor subordination" existed in several companies and that many of the men were so set on going home that "neither art, craft, nor money" could deter them.[46] When Private Caleb Haskell and some of his fellow recruits refused to take orders because their terms of enlistment were up and they considered themselves "free men," they were threatened with thirty-nine lashes on the bare back. Wisely, they had a change of mind, "finding that arbitrary rule prevailed even among free men," as Haskell said.[47] Nor was Hazen's conduct above reproach. He and Antill engaged in a running quarrel with Jeremiah Duggan, their own countryman and a supposed comrade in arms.

Arnold continued to feud with John Brown. In a letter to John Hancock, he expressed disapproval of a promotion promised Brown by Montgomery and accused both Brown and James Easton of stealing the baggage of officers captured aboard General Prescott's fleet at Lavaltrie. "It would give great disgust to the Army in general if those gentlemen were promoted before those matters were cleared up," he wrote.[48] Easton, then in Massachusetts, claimed that he had been ordered to divide the baggage among his men. Brown denied the charge and demanded a court-martial to clear his name. When Arnold sent him on a particularly dangerous mission, he compared himself to Uriah the Hittite, who had been ordered into battle against overwhelming odds by a malicious King David.[49] The quarrel was discussed freely among the rank and file and helped to lower morale.

In Montreal, General Wooster decreed that persons suspected of "furnishing Supplies and maintaining any correspondence with the Town of Quebec" be regarded as "enemies of public liberty, traitors to their country" and, as such, "punished with severity, made prisoners and even banished from the province."[50] Christophe Pélissier, Wooster's Canadian supplier of arms and ammunition, advised him not to molest the clergy, even though some were known to have offered "publick prayers" that God "exterminate" the enemy, but to crack down on former civil servants, members of the military, and suspected loyalists.[51] Wooster arrested twelve of Montreal's more influential citizens, including Simon Sanguinet, Pierre Panet, Saint-Georges Dupré, and Edward William Gray. He was promptly accused of breaking Montgomery's pledge to abstain from "every act of oppression" and, in the furor that followed, backed down and released all twelve.

Several loyalists were sent into exile, some on shaky evidence. When Judge John Fraser asked what charge had been brought against him, Wooster cited his "breach of promise & insolent letter," declaring that they "justly meritt a sett of Iron ornaments, which you & your associates have very lately been so fond of bestowing on the friends of constitutional liberty." But Judge Fraser was still not sure why he was condemned to exile and, even after reaching Albany, asked to have the matter clarified.[52] Wooster's reputation suffered another setback when he ordered the surrender of two hostages, René Hertel de Rouville and William Gray, after three Montreal suburbs had apologized publicly for the welcome they had given Montgomery when he took the city. Their fellow countrymen refused to surrender either of them, and the order was rescinded.

Wooster courted further trouble by replacing Carleton's militia captains with men friendly to the colonies. "I allow each Parish to choose their own Captains, a circumstance which pleased them much," he wrote Washington, "and there has been but few instances that they have not chosen a zealous friend to our cause." [53] Indeed, the zeal of some candidates seems to have outweighed their scruples, for Captain Goforth reported "bribery and corruption" at Trois Rivières.[54] Most of the former captains complied peaceably, but in Montreal Saint-Georges Dupré, Dufy-Desaunier, Neveu-Sevestre, and Edward William Gray refused to surrender their commissions. Wooster clapped all four in jail, Dupré and Gray for the second time.

Schuyler had allowed a few British officers to return to Canada to locate members of their families — a captain and a lieutenant with dependents at Chambly, an officer sent back at the request of the Province of Connecticut, a widowed commissary in search of his four small children. When Wooster questioned this indulgence, Schuyler was incensed and accused his colleague of "unbecoming subacity." "Resolved, sir," he wrote, "to be treated with the respect due to me as a gentleman, and as an officer entrusted with a command by the honourable Representatives of Thirteen Colonies." He informed Hancock that he had returned the prisoners of war as "an act of humanity." "If they have abused my confidence they are scoundrels," he wrote, "and I will treat them accordingly, without repenting that I gave them the indulgence. If they are not culpable they are injured, and I too." Wooster hurried off his own appeal to Hancock. "I know of no reason under Heaven why he [Schuyler] should treat me thus cavalierly, but merely to indulge his capricious humour," he wrote. "Happy would it be for him, and for our cause, if he could learn to bridle his passions." Their quarrel fed the sectionalism that had already driven a deep wedge between New Englanders and New Yorkers.[55]

Wooster showed none of Montgomery's forbearance toward the Church. He made no peace with the Abbé Montgolfier, whom he deemed a mortal enemy. He erred by forbidding mass on Christmas Eve, an affront sure to offend even the most lukewarm among the faithful. Three Récollet brothers who had communicated with the Quebec garrison were placed under arrest, the first of many clerics to be haled into court. No *curé* was safe from informers within his flock, for every parishioner knew that he could involve his priest in deep trouble by reporting him to Wooster's officers.

Clergy who preached loyalty to the Crown or who denied absolution to collaborators risked immediate arrest. Nor was rank any protection — the Abbé Montgolfier was threatened with exile after a quarrel with James Price, and a complaint was lodged against Bishop Briand's coadjutor, Monseigneur d'Esgly.

At least two clergymen sided with the Americans. In Quebec, the Abbé François Louis de Lotbinière became chaplain to Livingston's regiment. Lotbinière, said to have been promised a bishopric for his services, had been interdicted by Bishop Pontbriand and was at odds with Bishop Briand. Father Floquet, a Jesuit, agreed to serve as chaplain to Hazen's troops. Montgolfier wrote the bishop about him. "The final blow came on the Monday after Easter week," he said. "Three habitants who had shouldered arms for Congress and done sentry duty at the city gates presented themselves for communion at a Mass being said by M. Brassier, who recognized them. He refused them communion on the ground that they were strangers and had no certificate from their priest. They said they were from the parish of P. Floquet, who had heard their confessions, admitted them to his church and given them communion." [56] Montgolfier also had his suspicions about Father Huguet, a missionary to the Caughnawagas, Father Charpentier, a Récollet stationed in Longueuil, and the Abbé La Valinière, *curé* at l'Assomption and a friend of Thomas Walker's.

The Americans had scattered support in the higher echelons of the French community. Pierre Du Calvet, a Montreal jurist and *seigneur*, François Cazeau, a merchant, and Valentin Jautard, a lawyer, were all allies. Jautard, who served as Wooster's French-speaking secretary, had composed the letter welcoming Montgomery on behalf of the three Montreal suburbs. Christophe Pélissier of Trois Rivières, proprietor of the St. Maurice Forges, was a friend. Most collaborators, however, were *habitants*, including some resolute women. Mme. Augustin Chabot was accused of "perverting" the minds of the good folk in St. Pierre d'Orléans, the Widow Gabourie of holding secret gatherings at her home in St. Vallier, the wives of Jean and Joseph Goulet of going from house to house in Pointe aux Trembles to solicit support for the colonies. The wife of Pierre Parent in Ste. Marie de Beauce was said to have preached sedition among the townsfolk and been impertinent to her parish priest.[57]

Although the great majority of French Canadians chose to wait out the war and live with whichever side won it, there were some who urged recourse to arms in support of the Crown. Simon Sanguinet, one of the twelve Montrealers arrested and subsequently released by Wooster, warned his fellow countrymen that if they failed to oust the "brigands" who had invaded their homeland they would end up as slaves, a fate that he described as "only too common" in the colonies. He reminded French Canadians of their forebears, whose military exploits had struck fear throughout New England, and predicted that their "mere appearance" on the battlefield would persuade the "hinquis" (Yankees) to beat a hasty retreat from Canada. "They pillage you and you endure it," he declared. "They wrong you and you are silent. Will you be less spirited than the beasts who, contemplating their wounds, turn on their tormentors?" [58]

While Sanguinet was circulating his appeal, an armed outbreak took place near Quebec. In the dark of early morning Jean Baptiste Chasseur and two companions beached their skiff at the Lower Town, where Chasseur unloaded several turkeys and 200 pounds of flour. His purpose, however, was not to bring supplies but to acquaint the governor with plans to launch an attack on Arnold's guard at Pointe Lévis. Carleton gave his approval to the scheme and commissioned Chasseur to deliver various papers, including a declaration of amnesty for contrite collaborators, to the Sieur Louis Liénard de Beaujeu, *seigneur* on the Ile aux Grues below Quebec and an organizer of the expedition.

Beaujeu was assisted by several of Bishop Briand's clergy. The Abbé Porlier of St. Thomas Montmagny took part in the planning. Deacon Jean Marie Fortin, with the aid of the bishop coadjutor, Monseigneur d'Esgly, recruited volunteers. The Abbé Bailly, from the Quebec Seminary, was named chaplain to the expedition. In all, nearly 300 recruits assembled on the south shore from parishes on both sides of the St. Lawrence. On March 23, Beaujeu set forth from Ste. Anne de la Pocatière, ordering his advance guard of forty-six men, among them the Abbé Bailly, to occupy a house at St. Pierre du Sud and await directives.

Arnold heard what was afoot and dispatched Major Lewis Dubois to the south shore with eighty men, followed by an additional detachment of seventy. Before reaching St. Pierre du Sud, Dubois was joined by about 150 Canadians. Taking Beaujeu's advance guard by surprise, his troops surrounded the house and, in the course of a brief exchange, killed three of the enemy and wounded several others, including the Abbé Bailly. A few of the advance guard made their escape, but the rest surrendered amid the taunts of Dubois's Canadians. "Fathers were seen fighting against their children," Sanguinet said, "and children against their fathers." [59] When Beaujeu learned what had happened, he called off the expedition.[60]

In late March, Carleton's sentries spied an artillery crew starting a new battery at Pointe Lévis. Repeated shelling failed to slow its construction, and on April 2 the enemy opened fire, raining redhot cannonballs on houses and shipping. A few buildings were set ablaze and frigate *Lizard*'s mainmast was hit. Captain Dearborn, held prisoner with his fellow officers on the upper floor of the seminary, saw shells burst in the garden beneath his window and felt them shake the seminary walls.[61] But the damage was slight. Arnold's artillery was no match for the 114 guns defending Quebec, many of them carrying a much heavier load of metal than his twelve-pounders and mortars. "A few small cannon — sixes, twelves, and one twenty-four-pounder, a little ball, and less powder — cannot be expected to effect the reduction of a place so strongly fortified as Quebeck," he wrote Silas Deane. He wished more than ever for another John Lamb. "Only one Artillery officer," he lamented, "and twenty matrosses, very few of whom know their duty; not one artificer for making carcasses, or any kind of fireworks. An able Engineer (a most necessary man in an army) wanting, and no prospect of being supplied with one." [62] He ordered a battery erected on the Plains of Abraham, less than 500 yards from the city walls.

Arnold kept close watch on frigate *Lizard*, already "bending her sails" in the April breeze and threatening to sail upstream and cut his supply lines as soon as the ice went out. He designated two beaten-up tubs as fire ships. Loaded with shells, grenades, and other combustibles, they could be sailed close enough to *Lizard* and the other vessels to drift into their midst. With luck they could set fire to the enemy fleet.

On April 2, Carleton's lookouts saw three rebel officers scanning the city from a distance of less than 500 yards. "One of them wore a large grey periwig, suppos'd to be David Wooster," Ainslie said, "another was dress'd in scarlet said to be Arnold, the third, said those who had good glasses was Edward Antill — they stood pointing to the walls probably planning an attack, which they never intend to make." [63] Antill was correctly identified, the scarlet coat was indeed Arnold's, and the outsized periwig graced the head of David Wooster, who had left Moses Hazen in charge at Montreal and come to Quebec to oversee operations.

Arnold had nearly recovered from his leg wound. He could walk without too painful a limp and could mount a horse. On the day following Wooster's arrival, however, his horse fell on the lame leg, injuring it anew. During a week of convalescence he had time to take stock of his situation. Plainly, he could no longer serve any useful purpose at Quebec, for Wooster paid no heed to his advice and probably still smarted from their encounter at the New Haven powderhouse. He requested an immediate transfer to Montreal, where he would replace Hazen as commander. Wooster gave his consent — readily, no doubt. After reaching Montreal, Arnold wrote Schuyler about his new assignment. "Had I been able to take an active part, I should by no means have left camp," he said, "but as General Wooster did not think it proper to consult me in any of his matters, I was convinced that I should be of more service here than in the camp." [64]

When Arnold left, the encampment still lay under a deep blanket of snow, the new battery remained unfinished, and the hospital teemed with more than 400 smallpox patients. Checking the Richelieu Rapids at Deschambault on his way upriver, he wrote Schuyler that a ten-gun battery should be erected there to keep enemy ships from severing the supply lines. Large reinforcements were needed, he said, and heavier artillery. "If we are not immediately supported with eight or ten thousand men," he warned, "a good train of artillery, well served, and a military chest well furnished, the Ministerial troops, if they attempt it, will regain this country, and we shall be obliged to quit it." [65] The city he had come to conquer had proved as unyielding as the rock on which it stood.

IX

If Not Brothers, "First Cousins"

1

THE QUEBEC GARRISON hoped the enemy would strike again. "From the 31st, things wore another face in town," Colonel Caldwell noted. "The garrison was in high spirits and wished for nothing more than a second attack." [1] When dogs were heard barking in the dead of night, everyone was sure the rebels were on the march. "We look'd for an attack last night, the weather being favourable," Captain Ainslie said. "The Garrison was ready." [2] One day a spy reported 800 scaling ladders in the making. As late as May 2, a foraging party discovered a pile of ladders outside the St. Louis bastion and left them undisturbed, in the hope that the enemy would be "fools enough to use them." [3] But no attack came.

Allan Maclean was everywhere, riding herd on his Emigrants, checking on sentries, ferreting out shirkers, but it was Guy Carleton's unfailing composure that gave heart to both civilians and the military. "If ever Emulation was conspicuous," Ainslie said, "it was under General Carletons influence in the garrison of Quebec." [4] Many who wearied of the long siege were buoyed by the governor's example. "During the winter the General's looks were narrowly watch'd," Ainslie wrote. "The tranquillity which appear'd in his countenance, added to the entire dependence we had on his military skill, dayly reliev'd us from former fears." [5] But in private, Carleton, too, had his dark moments, admitting that it was "a close blockade." [6]

Carleton left nothing to chance. He mounted cannons on the walls, armed ships in the harbor, and spaced artillery along the waterfront. He ordered the ditch paralleling the city wall to be cleared of snow lest the enemy gain access by mounting the great drifts that reached nearly to the embrasures. Streets in the Lower Town were barricaded with chunks of river ice, two blockhouses were built outside the walls, and a sentry box was placed atop a thirty-foot pole to command an unobstructed view of Arnold's encampment. At night, fireballs lit the approaches to the city, probing dark crannies formed by the jut of bastions.

The captured Americans were quartered in church buildings — the officers on an upper floor of the seminary, the rank and file in the Récollet monastery. Bishop Briand stopped by to see them, and solicitous merchants brought them gifts of bread, cheese, and a butt of porter. Housewives distributed sugar, boiled rice, and other delicacies to the sick and wounded, who were cared for by nursing sisters at the Hôtel Dieu. Carleton himself visited the prisoners, making sure that they had sufficient food and firewood. The men appreciated his concern. Private Henry extolled "the virtuous, the amiable and venerable Carlton . . . a genuine representative of the gentility of the Irish nation, which is so deservedly famous for the production of real heroes, patriotic statesmen and a generosity and suavity of manners." Private Morison was no less fulsome. [7] But this did not imply any lessening of their commitment to the Revolution.

One day the provost major came to interview prisoners who had been born in the British Isles. Reminding them that they could be hanged for treason, he promised pardon, full pay, and a free trip home if they would swear allegiance to the king and enroll in the Royal Highland Emigrants. Ninety-four accepted his offer, but some members of the garrison questioned the wisdom of putting trust in turncoats. "Many wagers were laid that the greatest part of them will take the first opportunity to desert," Ainslie said. [8] The doubters were proved right. Two of the enrollees made their escape by leaping from the city wall into a twenty-foot drift; three slid down a thirty-foot snowbank into St. Roch; nine others managed by various means to reach the rebel encampment. Carleton disbanded the enrollees and put them back under lock and key.

In mid-March the enlisted men were transferred to the Dauphin Jail, a stoutly built pile within sight of St. John's Gate. Guards kept a close watch on the jail by day, but at night the men were left pretty much to their own devices, and when one of their number got hold of a master key to the cells, they met together in the small hours and probed the ancient edifice from roof to cellar. From a trap door on the roof they could spy on the guards' quarters across the street, where the entire detail could be seen asleep on the floor with their guns stacked nearby. They could watch the sentries at St. John's Gate and the artillery crews idling on the city walls. When the moon was bright, they could look across the Plains of Abraham to Arnold's encampment.

In the cellar of the jail the men found a heap of rusty scythes and barrel hoops that could be fashioned into weapons. They tested bars on windows and found several so corroded that they could be worked loose. They also discovered a plank door, padlocked on the inside, that led into the street. Picking the lock would be a simple matter. The door was embedded in ice, but they believed they could free it with the hunting knives that some of the riflemen had concealed from their captors.

A plan was agreed upon. The prisoners would form into three units. The largest, led by Sergeant Joseph Ashton of Lamb's company, would include about 150 men and would attack St. John's Gate. A party of twenty-five under Sergeant Thomas Boyd would clear the guardhouse across the street and gather up the guards' muskets, before joining Ashton on the city walls. A third unit, under Private William McCoy, would act as a reserve for both Ashton and Boyd and would set fire to the jail, the guardhouse, and several adjacent buildings. After seizing St. John's Gate, the men would turn the artillery on the city and admit Arnold's troops. This time Quebec would be taken.

Nights were spent turning scythes into swords and barrel hoops into cutlasses. Some of the riflemen lashed their hunting knives to poles to make wicked-looking spears. A small amount of gunpowder was bought from guards with money given the men by solicitous nuns and visitors. To increase the supply, the prisoners devised a scheme for hoodwinking their guards, many of whom were old men and teen-age boys. Fashioning toy fieldpieces out of paper and thread, they promised to fire them off if allowed gunpowder. The guards doubted that the paper guns would function but, intrigued by the possibility, came up with some ammunition. To everyone's delight, the guns performed admirably, giving off a retort like that of a small pistol. Not all the powder, however, was fed into the paper cannons. Some found its way into a cache, where spears, cutlasses, and other weapons were concealed.

John Martin, a private in Lamb's company, volunteered to notify Arnold of the plot. Hiding in the yard one windy night, he slipped into white clothing collected from the prisoners and scaled the prison wall. Near St. John's Gate he leaped from the ramparts, undetected in his camouflage, into a deep snowbank. His safe arrival at Arnold's encampment was signaled by a knot tied in a flag that the men could see from the jail roof.

One night two of the prisoners, without anyone's authorization, tried to loosen the cellar door by chipping away some of the ice in which it was embedded. Guards heard the ring of their hatchets on the hard ice. The two were caught red-handed, and by sunrise the provost marshal and several cohorts had descended on the jail. "We could assure the gentlemen that this effort to escape was without the knowledge of any of us," Private Henry said, claiming that this was not wholly untrue, because the pair had acted on their own.[9] The provost marshal "stormed about some time with his threats and foul language," Private Fobes said, "finding that he could not prevail on any of the prisoners to tell who did it or why it was done." [10] However, as he turned to leave, he was stopped by Private John Hall, the British army deserter whom Arnold had picked to accompany his Indian couriers to Quebec. After a whispered exchange, Hall left with the provost marshal.

"The extent and consequences of this disaster" were apparent to everyone, Private Henry said.[11] Some of the men were taken to headquarters for questioning. Wagons heaped with manacles and leg irons drew up at the jail entrance. All the men were shackled, some in groups of a dozen, to twelve-foot bars. The manacles, however, were too large for several of the prisoners, who were able to work their hands free and who proceeded to liberate their comrades with saws made from notched hunting knives. They took care to cut only the rivets so that whenever a guard appeared the manacles could be slipped back on.

Word that the jail break had been thwarted was greeted jubilantly throughout Quebec. One officer ascribed it to "that All-seeing Providence, which so miraculously saved us on the 31st of December." [12] That same night, hoping to deceive Arnold, Carleton called out his entire garrison, ordering two cannons loaded with blanks and three bonfires built near the Dauphin Jail. At two in the morning the blanks were fired, the bonfires lighted. Church bells were tolled and muskets fired off. Shouts of "Liberty forever!" descended from the ramparts. Nothing was omitted that might tempt Arnold to attack the city. "Had our plan succeeded," a British captain said, "they would have met with such a reception as would have completely put an end to the blockade, as well as to our tedious fatigues." [13] But Arnold would not be outfoxed. Although Carleton kept watch throughout the night, not a rebel approached St. John's Gate or came within reach of the artillery crews who lay in wait on the city wall.

A month later, the officers plotted their escape. Confined to two rooms on an upper floor of the seminary, they had incurred the suspicion of their guards and had quarreled with the head jailer, described by Lieutenant William Heth as a "paltroon" who "would shew more Heroism in a Brothel among discarded Bawds & infirm Bullies than in a Field of Battle." [14] Captain Thayer was chosen to mastermind the escape, assisted by Captain Samuel Lockwood of Waterbury's regiment. Two guards were found who agreed, for a price, to supply the men with clubs and see them past enemy patrols.

At first, the officers planned to knot their blankets together and shinny to the street, but Thayer discovered a garret door that promised a safer escape route. Although nailed shut with thick planks, it could be pried open. Behind it was a window from which a ladder reached to within fourteen feet of the ground. When the men dropped from the ladder to the seminary yard, they would be supplied with clubs and, crossing to a sally port, would jump thirty feet into a snowbank outside the walls.

As the day set for the jail break neared, Thayer decided to try the garret door and make sure that it could be opened without delay. While he worked on some of the planking he was spied by a seminarian, who immediately reported him to the guards. He was seized, cross-examined, and clapped into the hold of an armed schooner. Lockwood and Oliver Hanchet were taken next, to be questioned by Colonel Maclean and others before they, too, were hustled aboard the schooner. The remaining officers were placed under tight guard at the seminary.

The battery on the Plains of Abraham was readied, and a third was begun on the east bank of the St. Charles. Artillery had been brought downstream from St. Jean, and an eighteen-pounder and several twelves had arrived from Fort Ticonderoga. Nothing the Americans possessed, however, could match Carleton's firepower. Gun crews were forced to evacuate their positions repeatedly, sometimes after getting off only a few shots. "They can't stand our fire," Ainslie noted when the batteries habitually fell silent after a spurt of early morning activity. A fellow officer estimated that Carleton's guns "gave them twenty to one." Late in April, Ainslie saw several dead or wounded men being taken from the St. Charles battery. "Their fire is much slacken'd," he said, "ours much increas'd. Their works must be very much destroyed." [15] Actually, the Americans were almost out of ammunition. Men were retrieving British cannonballs and salvaging gunpowder from unexploded shells.

Ainslie and his comrades made light of Wooster's artillery. "Many shots were fired at our shipping today — very little damage done," he noted on April 12.[16] But he was incensed by what he considered indiscriminate shelling. "At the hour of going to mass they fir'd on the Town — a diabolical spirit!" he said. "Mean they to kill helpless women and children? They see plainly that they can make no kind of impression on the Town." [17] Another officer said that

Wooster's "infuriate scheme of destruction . . . had not the least effect." [18] Lieutenant Heth, a witness to the shelling from the upper floor of the seminary, would have agreed. "These Circumstances are far from being agreeable to us," he said, "it appearing as if the Commander without thinks the Garrison may be taken by a blockade & cannonading — which we are convinced will not answer." [19] Nevertheless, churches were hit, houses were set ablaze. Ships were damaged where they stood at anchor, and a sailor was wounded. A bullet ricocheted through a window and killed a boy. For most of a month, the city was kept on edge, although Ainslie would credit the enemy with nothing more than having "kill'd a boy, wounded a Sailor & broke the leg of a Turkey." [20]

Intelligence reaching the blockaded city came from spies and deserters. One informant said that German mercenaries had docked in New York; another, that the rebels had been repulsed in an attempt on Boston with a loss of 4000 men; still another, that 300 New Yorkers had refused to re-enlist and in a show of defiance had shouted, "God save the King!" [21] A man who had visited Wooster's encampment accused the enemy of fathering a rumor that sixty Canadian collaborators had been hanged at Quebec. "The New England gentry shew very little knowledge of the Canadian Habitant in imagining that this story wou'd rouse the Country people to arms," he said. "They cannot more effectually serve us than by propagating such falsehoods." [22]

Late in April, a more dependable informant brought word that General Howe had evacuated Boston. While returning to Canada he had encountered a Mr. Thomas, "formerly an apothecary, now a General," on his way north with twelve hundred men.[23] Although no one in the garrison could have known it, the apothecary-turned-soldier would replace Wooster at Quebec.

Carleton and his aides kept close watch on the St. Lawrence, waiting for the arrival of a British fleet. Much of the river was now open, although no one could be sure of conditions at its mouth, where ice could be a hazard. On the night of May 3, the very day when the first of Thomas' troops were seen filing up the escarpment from Wolfe's Cove, a brigantine hove in view off Ile d'Orléans. Under full sail in brilliant moonlight, she pointed toward the British vessels at anchor between a jetty and the Queen's Wharf. Everyone hurried to the city walls, confident that the siege was nearly over. As men, women, and children crowded the ramparts, many embraced one another and waved to the approaching ship.

One of Lieutenant Pringle's duties when he returned to England had been to arrange a set of signals with British sea captains so that their vessels could be recognized as they neared Quebec. In line with the agreement, Carleton ordered five guns fired and a blue pennant and Union Jack run up at Cape Diamond. He waited for the reply — seven guns and a red pennant and Union Jack at the masthead — but the brigantine gave no sign of recognition. After hailing her three times, he ordered his gunners to open fire. Struck amidships, the brigantine exploded in a burst of arcing shells and grenades. Flames swirled through her hull and climbed in towering sheets through her sails and rigging. Members of her crew were seen pulling away in a small boat. The brigantine was an enemy fire ship, intended to ignite the anchored vessels.

The great bell in the cathedral fairly shook the timbers of its belfry. Drums beat an alert, and every post was manned. "Everybody was cool and wishing the rebels would attack," Ainslie said, but the fire ship failed to achieve her purpose.[24] Drifting downstream with the tide, she burned harmlessly to the water's edge. The rest of the night proved uneventful, with a soft rain toward morning.

2

Lieutenant Pringle had reported to Lord George Germain in late December. Germain was Lord Dartmouth's successor as Secretary of State for the Colonies and was pledged to bring the war to a successful and, it was hoped, brisk conclusion. After scanning Pringle's dispatches, he took measures to send massive support to Carleton. By mid-February a small squadron was being readied, including H.M.S. *Isis*, sloop-of-war *Martin*, frigates *Surprise* and *Triton*, two large transports, and four victualers. The vessels would carry the 29th Regiment of Foot and a marine unit, with provisions to feed 3000 men for three months.

A winter of uncommon rigor delayed the squadron for almost a month. *Isis,* whose master, Captain Charles Douglas, was in command of the fleet, sailed on March 11. *Triton* left with the transports and supply ships on March 16 but suffered a further delay when a victualer caught fire in the English Channel. *Surprise* and *Martin* weighed anchor on March 21. A second, much larger embarkation was scheduled for later in the spring. Led by Lieutenant General John Burgoyne, it would embrace eight British regiments, four artillery companies, and nearly 3000 German mercenaries.

Lieutenant John Enys, a member of the 29th and a dutiful diarist, wrote of a gale in the mid-Atlantic, icebergs crowding in on *Surprise* off Newfoundland, a sudden freeze that turned her rigging to "Ropes of Cristal Near four times their usual diameter." An ice field stretching to the far horizon taxed the ingenuity of Captain Robert Linzee, who ordered thick planking nailed to the frigate's bow. With this as a battering ram, *Surprise* butted through solid ice that on one occasion, Enys said, "closed upon us so firm that we could get Neither backwards or forwards." Linzee managed to inch his ship onward, "Sometimes making Saill and pressing thro the Ice and sometimes laying quite steady in it to all appearances." [25] After a week, *Surprise* broke free of the ice and swept into open water.

Like Linzee, Captain Douglas of *Isis* and Captain Henry Harvey of *Martin* rammed their ships through the ice with a heavy press of sail. Douglas would recall, "We thought it an enterprise worthy of an English ship of the line in our King and country's sacred cause, and an effort due to the gallant defenders of Quebec, to make the attempt of pressing her by force of sail through the thick, broad and closely connected fields of ice, to which we saw no bounds towards the western part of our horizon." By the time *Isis* reached open water, she had left in her wake "bits of the sheathing of the ship's bottom and sometimes pieces of the cutwater." [26]

In the lower St. Lawrence the captains rendezvoused, and Douglas ordered *Surprise* to lead the way to Quebec. By sundown on May 5, she stood off Ile d'Orléans, five miles below the city. Next morning, after learning that Carleton still held Quebec, Linzee brought her from behind the island into full view of the walled city atop its soaring cliff. A blue pennant and Union Jack went up on Cape Diamond and, as *Surprise* tacked shoreward, five shots crossed her bow. Answering with seven shots and with a red pennant and Union Jack at her masthead, she dropped anchor near the mouth of the St. Charles. Captain McKenzie rowed out to escort Linzee to the landing.

Drums beat the glad news. Church bells pealed jubilantly. The ramparts were packed with spectators as McKenzie came ashore with Linzee and the officers of the 29th, including Major Thomas Carleton, the governor's younger brother. "The news soon reached every pillow in town," Ainslie said. "People half dress'd ran down to the Grand battery to feast their eyes with the sight of a ship of war displaying the Union flag." [27] Although there had been a frost that night, no one took notice of the cold or yielded his space overlooking the harbor. After the officers had debarked, the regulars came ashore in small boats. While they were assembling at the landing, resplendent in their scarlet coats, *Isis* and *Martin* rounded Ile d'Orléans and dropped anchor near *Surprise*. More troops debarked, among them a contingent of grenadiers in towering bearskin caps. In all, nearly 200 marines and regulars filed up the roadway to the Upper Town.

Earlier that morning, an informant had come to Palace Gate to report that General Wooster had left for Montreal and that the rebel army was about to evacuate. When the regulars had eaten, Carleton ordered a sortie, assigning the advance guard to Captain John Nairne and allotting him four six-pounders. At noon the troops funneled through St. John's and St. Louis Gates, about 900 strong, halting in full view of the enemy. Carleton ordered out Nairne and the advance guard. He stationed the 29th, the Royal Fusiliers, and the Royal Highland Emigrants on the right; the French militia, the marines, and a detail of artisans at the center; and Colonel Caldwell's British militia on the left. "The little army extended itself quite across the plains, making a noble appearance," one officer said. "We looked formidable to the rebels." [28]

Enemy troops could be seen milling outside their headquarters. Several took cover in a clump of woods. "At first they seem'd as if they would form in a Smal wood at the end of the hights of

Abram," Enys wrote.[29] Carleton waited, his men in formation. Scattered shots could be heard from the direction Nairne had taken. Carleton noted that a hush came over the rebel encampment. No one could be seen at their headquarters or in the copse where some of them had formed. After a further wait, he realized that the enemy had retreated, that the long siege was over. "In ten minutes we were in possession of the Heights of Abraham and took one of their batteries," Colonel Maclean would remember. "This was done by Captain Nairne of my Regiment, who commanded the advanced Guard, the Enemy were struck with such a Pannick that they left their Cannon loaded and their Match lighted, without firing a Gun."

Carleton's troops fanned across the abandoned campsite. Field-pieces, small arms, and bayonets had been left behind; food and clothing were strewn about, even orderly books and official papers. "Among the Artillery we found all ours taken at Saint Johns," Colonel Maclean reported.[30] At Holland House some of his Highlanders helped themselves to General Thomas' midday meal, left cooked but untouched on the dining room table.

With the enemy in full flight, Captain Douglas ordered *Surprise*, *Martin*, and a provincial vessel to sweep the St. Lawrence. At the Richelieu Rapids, the ships fired on Burrall's troops, fresh from the colonies. "This is the most terrible day I ever saw," wrote Chaplain Ammi Robbins. "God of armies, help us. Three ships came near us, firing as they came, and our boats and people in a scattered condition, coming up. Distress and anxiety in every countenance."[31] Raking the river bank, Douglas' vessels cut off the guard at Pointe Lévis, and the men retreated in disorder up the south shore. When a landing party from one of the British ships barred their way, they took cover in the woods, surviving on bread bought from the *habitants* with what hard money they had left. Douglas captured an American schooner without firing a shot and overhauled several bateaux carrying sick men and ammunition. Ainslie heard that, in trying to lighten their loads, the bateaux crews "inhumanly threw out many of their sick men upon the beach," some of whom "expir'd before our parties cou'd get to their relief." He was also told that a few bateaux escaped capture when an ebb tide halted the British ships.[32]

Carleton wrote Lord Germain that "the Plains were soon cleared of those Plunderers" after his troops had "marched out of the Ports of St. Louis and St. John's to see what those mighty Boasters were about." [33] But he was slow to pursue his quarry. Colonel Caldwell advised intercepting the enemy at Cap Rouge, but Carleton was unwilling to jeopardize his men. "Nobody was more ready than he was at all times to expose his person," Caldwell said. "His timidity was only shewn in respect to others, and the safety of the town." [34] Colonel Maclean was less inclined to make allowances. In writing a friend in London he spoke of "our Unactivity and want of Spirit" and said that "timidity in the field . . . is a dangerous matter, for I am convinced few Generals are capable of conducting a defensive War." [35] On May 8, frigate *Niger* and three transports arrived from Halifax with the 47th Foot, followed by *Triton* and a convoy of transports and victualers bringing the remainder of the 29th. But Carleton did not bestir himself until May 22, when he set sail for Trois Rivières with both regiments.

Carleton showed his customary magnanimity toward prisoners of war, sending out patrols to bring in the 200 sick men left behind in the retreat. He ordered his militia officers to "make diligent search for all such distressed persons, and afford them all necessary relief and convey them to the general hospital, where proper care shall be taken of them," and he promised the prisoners that when they recovered they would be given "free liberty to return to their respective provinces." [36] Ainslie was impressed by the governor's "goodness of heart." "His enemies will love him," he said. "Those who have fallen into his hands will bless heaven." [37] But hard-liners like Allan Maclean and Henry Caldwell were less approving. Maclean — "Beloved, Dreaded and Indefatigable," as Lieutenant Pringle described him — urged a swift pursuit of the enemy. "I hope we shall follow the Rebells close at their heels," he wrote General Murray, "and not give them time to recover from the Panick and Consternation that their late Precipitate retreat from Quebec has reduced them to." [38] Caldwell had hoped the prisoners would be treated harshly.[39] He was rebuked by Carleton's brother, who reminded him that they were fellow Britons and should be regarded not as the "murderers and deluded fools" that Caldwell deemed them to be but as misguided "brothers." [40]

Carleton had the men's shackles removed, issued them linen shirts, and supplied them with fresh meat and vegetables. "There was no doubt in any reflective mind among us," Private Henry said, "but that the virtuous and beneficent Carlton, taking into view his perilous predicament, did every thing for us which an honest man and a good Christian could." [41] This show of kindness, however, failed to lessen the men's zeal for their own cause. When Daniel Morgan was offered a colonelcy in the British army if he would change sides, he replied that he took deep offense at offers "which plainly imply that you think me a scoundrel." [42]

Shortly after the American retreat, Carleton agreed to send the prisoners home on parole. Dearborn and Meigs left first, sailing from Quebec on May 17 and proceeding by way of Nova Scotia to the Maine coast, where they were put ashore nearly two months later at the mouth of the Penobscot. Although Dearborn never changed his opinion of king and Parliament, he would remember Carleton as "a very humane tender-hearted man." [43] The rest of the prisoners followed during the summer. "It is the duty of all faithful servants of the crown," Carleton announced, "to rescue from oppression, and restore to liberty, the once happy, free, and loyal people of this continent. All prisoners from the rebellious provinces, who chuse to return home, are to hold themselves in readiness to embark at a short notice. The commissary Mr. Murray shall visit the transports destined for them, and see that wholesome provisions, necessary cloathing, with all possible convenience for their passage, be prepared for these unfortunate men." [44] As a parting gift, he supplied the men with wine and mutton. "Since we have tried in vain to make them acknowledge us as brothers," he has been quoted as saying, "let us send them away disposed to regard us as first cousins." [45]

3

Although a doctor by vocation, John Thomas had had more military experience than any of Washington's native-born officers. He had served with colonial regiments as an assistant surgeon and, ulti-

mately, as a company commander. He had been stationed in Nova
Scotia, where he had been involved in the transfer of hapless Acadians to Cape Breton and Louisiana. He had participated in Lord
Amherst's advance on Montreal. By the time the French and Indian
War was over, he had won repute as a seasoned and competent
officer. An ensign at twenty-two, a captain at thirty-two, and a
colonel at thirty-six, he had taken part in eight campaigns and fought
in several minor engagements. At the outbreak of the Revolution,
he was fifty-one years old, a practicing physician in Kingston, Massachusetts, a family man, and an outspoken patriot. Named a lieutenant general in the Massachusetts militia, he was assigned the
command at Roxbury, a strategic location near the thin neck of the
Boston peninsula. However, when Washington replaced Artemas
Ward as commander, Thomas was on the point of resigning from
the army because Congress had given him a brigadier's commission
lower in seniority than those of two less qualified Massachusetts
officers. Washington, who had a high regard for Thomas, retained
his services by persuading Congress to name him senior brigadier, a
solution made possible when one of the appointees, the elderly Seth
Pomeroy, declined his promotion.

After a winter of skirmishes and artillery duels, Washington
picked Thomas to fortify and occupy Dorchester Heights, an eleva-
tion commanding Boston from the south. On the night of March 4,
Thomas loaded more than 300 ox carts with wooden frames, fascines, and gabions and, hidden by a ground haze, led his troops to
the summit of the heights. By daybreak, the frames had been stuffed
with the fascines and gabions and shielded by an abatis of trees
felled in a nearby orchard. Taken by surprise, General Howe was
deterred from making a frontal assault by an immobilizing storm.
On March 17 he evacuated Boston.

Congress advanced John Thomas to major general and assigned
him to Quebec, where he would replace General Wooster. "The
situation of Canada being, at this juncture, an object of the greatest
importance to the welfare of the United Colonies," John Hancock
wrote him on the day of his promotion, "the Congress have been
anxious to fix upon some General Officer, whose military skill,
courage, and capacity, will probably insure success to the enterprise.

In Major General Thomas they flatter themselves they will not be disappointed." [46] Thomas reached Albany near the end of March, to learn that Lake Champlain was still ice-locked. Two companies of reinforcements waited near Crown Point, five at Fort Edward, eleven at Albany. Thomas found that several regiments were incomplete and advised Hancock that the army would total only about 5000 men.[47] He was still in Albany when the commissioners and Father Carroll came upriver from New York. He accompanied them as far as Saratoga, then left with Schuyler for Fort George, where a spring snowstorm delayed him further. He did not reach Montreal until late April.

In Canada, Thomas was told that he could count on an army of no more than 4000 men, that many whose terms had expired refused to re-enlist, and that some had already started home. Little had been done to repair the city's defenses; no gunboats had been built to patrol the river. The *habitants*, who had seemed friendly to Montgomery, now kept their distance. Thomas wrote a bleak letter to Washington, expressing regret that he could not, "consistently with truth," give "a more pleasing account of the state of affairs in Canada." [48]

By the time the commissioners arrived, Thomas had left for Quebec, but they reiterated the need for reinforcements and hard money. The Canadians, they wrote Hancock, would never make common cause with the colonies until they saw "our credit recovered and a sufficient army arrived to secure possession of the country." [49] At Quebec, Thomas found an army of only nineteen hundred, nearly half of them down with smallpox. Of those fit for duty, about 300 had completed their terms of enlistment and were determined to go home. Some, he wrote Washington, "peremptorily refused duty." [50] At least 200 had inoculated themselves and needed hospitalization. Thomas forbade further inoculation and set an example by refusing it for himself, although he had never had smallpox.

Thomas found his troops so thinly spread that he could rally no more than 300 men in one place at the same time. There were no proper entrenchments nor tools for digging any. Provisions would run out within a week unless he could obtain supplies from the *habitants*, who spurned paper money. A few reinforcements had arrived — Colonel Porter's Massachusetts regiment and most of Colonel Maxwell's 2nd New Jersey. Six companies of the 2nd Pennsylvania were reported a short way upstream. But these were only a start on what was needed. The failure of the fire ship added to his woes, and, as if this were not enough, General Wooster was still in camp, miffed at having been replaced. Rumors of British men-of-war at the mouth of the St. Lawrence had spread through the encampment, but Thomas thought the vessels would be slowed by ice, permitting him time for an orderly retreat. He would be proved wrong, and Dr. Senter would accuse him of "strongly neglecting the reports of the approach of the enemy's fleet, tho' repeatedly attested to by several of the good inhabitants." [51]

On May 5, Thomas called a council of war. Porter and Maxwell were present and the same Donald Campbell who had ordered the retreat at Près de Ville. General Wooster attended, although he was scheduled to leave for Montreal that same day. All agreed that the sick should be removed to Trois Rivières and the artillery to "some tenable place up the river." [52] Thomas heard that British men-of-war were only a few miles below the city.

Next morning, as the sick were being readied for transfer, *Surprise* hove into view, followed by *Isis* and *Martin*. Thomas could assemble only about 250 of his widely dispersed troops before the enemy — "a thousand strong," as he thought, "formed in two divisions, in column six deep" — sallied through the city gates.[53] After conferring with his field officers, he ordered an immediate retreat. "The army was in such a scattered condition," Dr. Senter said, "as rendered it impossible to collect them either for a regular retreat, or bring them into action. In the most irregular, helter skelter manner we raised the siege, leaving every thing. All the camp equipage, ammunition, and even our clothing, except what little we happened to have on us." [54] Colonel Porter covered the withdrawal. "When the enemy were within about 80 rods of us," he said, "we had orders to retreat slowly and in good order which we did, untill we could find a convenient place to defend ourselves. We formed in the first wood we came to and remained till the rear had got up with us. We then had orders to retreat again." [55] Porter was supported by Maxwell's Jerseymen and part of the 2nd Pennsylvania.

Many of the men marched all night. Lowlands flooded by the

spring run-off necessitated long, time-consuming detours. In crossing tributaries, the troops had to depend on what boats they could requisition from the *habitants*. Porter's regiment, joined by several of Dr. Senter's more ambulatory patients, reached Pointe aux Trembles at daybreak, pursued by *Surprise* and *Martin*, whose gun crews raked the shoreline and overtook bateaux carrying the sick. "They still kept in chase of us up the river both by land and water," Dr. Senter said, "and in the most disorderly manner we were obliged to escape as we could." [56]

Thomas paused at Deschambault, where a high bluff overlooked the Richelieu Rapids and where vessels sailing upstream could be halted by shore-based artillery. At a hurriedly summoned council of war, he asked his officers if they considered it "prudent" to make a stand. All but three voted against it, urging an immediate retreat to Sorel. In explaining the vote to Washington and the commissioners, Thomas said that he had neither the guns nor the ammunition to command the rapids and that his troops would "labour under the same disadvantages at Deschambault as before Quebec; the men-of-war would run up the river, intercept our resources, and soon oblige us to decamp." [57] Remaining at Deschambault with a rear guard of 500 men, he ordered the army to continue upstream, the sick by bateau, the rest on foot.

Not everyone was happy with Thomas' decision. "I have but just time, by an express that goes to New York, to acquaint you of our unfortunate, and I must add, disgraceful retreat," one officer wrote home. "The General and officers halted here, and held a council of war, to determine whether they should stop the troops and engage the enemy. It was determined almost unanimously against the proposal, although I was of the opinion, from the best accounts I received from the officers, that the British troops might have been driven back into the town. In vain was every argument of disgrace attending a retreat urged. They had determined not to make a stand till they got to the mouth of the Sorel." [58]

Chaplain Robbins, afflicted with sore eyes and an upset stomach, was assigned to a bateau. He described the journey as "enough to destroy the strongest constitution." As the crewmen coped with head winds and heavy rain they sang "Row the boat, row," Robbins

said, until it "ran in my head when half asleep, nor could I put it
entirely out of mind amid all our gloom and terror, with water up
to my knees as I lay in the boat." At one point the bateau rode out
a small gale. Twice it grounded on reefs. "Our days are days of
darkness," Robbins wrote. At Sorel, he caught up with several other
chaplains, among them Samuel Spring, who may have given heart to
his fellow clergy with stories of the march to Quebec and the hardi-
hood of those who made it.[59]

In Montreal, Arnold had called his own council of war, attended
by the commissioners and several of his officers. They had voted
for a stand at Deschambault and at the mouth of the Jacques Cartier.
"These are the only posts that secure the river until you approach
near Montreal," he had written Washington, "and of such consequence that nothing but superior numbers will oblige us to abandon
them."[60] When he heard that Deschambault might be evacuated,
he hurried off arms and supplies and prepared to go there himself.
Although the commissioners had voted with him, they had serious
doubts that a stand could be brought off.[61]

When Arnold reached Sorel, he learned that Deschambault had
been evacuated. Thomas had held out for six anxious days, down
to "only three pounds of meal per man and not an ounce of meat."
On his retreat upriver he had stopped at Trois Rivières to notify the
commissioners by letter and to detach Maxwell's troops as a rear
guard. In his letter he described his struggles to curb the spread of
smallpox — "notwithstanding which," he said, "and the most express
orders to the contrary, both officers and soldiers privately inoculate
themselves."[62]

Reinforcements were filtering into Canada. Colonel Arthur St.
Clair had come with the rest of the 2nd Pennsylvania. An artillery
unit led by Captain Ebenezer Stevens, one of General Knox's officers, had gone as far as Trois Rivières before turning back when
Deschambault was evacuated. The first of two brigades detached
from Washington's command was on its way from New York. Led
by Brigadier General William Thompson, it included four regiments of Continentals — the 8th under Colonel Enoch Poor of New
Hampshire; the 15th, 24th, and 25th under Colonels John Paterson,
John Greaton, and William Bond, respectively, all from Massachu-

setts; a Pennsylvania rifle company and a detail of artificers under
Colonel Jeduthan Baldwin, an engineer who had been in charge of
fortifications during the siege of Boston.

Thompson, an Irishman by birth, came from Carlisle, Pennsylvania, where he had served on the Committee of Safety and commanded a rifle company. Early in March he had been advanced to
brigadier, but he had rough edges — a brashness and a mean temper
— that made Washington slow to assign him major responsibilities.
On May 18, he joined Thomas at Sorel, detaching Paterson's regiment to Montreal.

Thomas found his army ridden with smallpox and depleted by
expired enlistments. Returns were sketchy. He could only guess at
how many effectives he could count on. Supplies were so low that
the commissioners had advised Schuyler to halt further reinforcements until the men already in Canada were cared for. "We are
unable to express our apprehension of the distress our Army must
soon be reduced to from want of provisions and the small-pox,"
they wrote. "If further reinforcements are sent without pork to
victual the whole Army, our soldiers must perish or feed on each
other." [63] *Habitants* who had wheat to sell demanded hard money.
Arnold requisitioned 2700 bushels from a reluctant *seigneur* and
rounded up twenty head of cattle, but this could not feed an army.

Thomas could envision the disintegration of his entire command.
He wrote the commissioners that there were "great murmurings and
complaints" among his men, whom he described as "destitute of
almost every necessary to render their lives comfortable or even
tolerable ... Unless some effectual spirited steps are immediately
taken for our relief," he said, "it will not be possible to keep the
Army together but we must unavoidably be obliged to abandon a
country of infinite importance to the safety of the Colonies and to
leave our friends here a prey to those whose mercies are cruelties." [64]

Smallpox had reached epidemic proportions. Even Arnold had
advised some of the troops to inoculate themselves. "A great part of
the Army are, or speedily will be, unfit for duty by means of inoculation, notwithstanding everything I have been able to do to prevent
it," Thomas wrote the commissioners, who had urged him — vainly
— to submit to inoculation for his own protection.[65]

Not the least of Thomas' problems were the commissioners themselves. Accustomed to the ways of the committee room and town meeting, they advised on military matters, passed on personnel, and, ignoring his chain of command, were an impromptu court of appeal where his decisions could be questioned and undercut. He found himself a lieutenant to three civilians who, without military training or experience, were placed in charge of a floundering campaign.

Thomas called in Maxwell's regiment from Trois Rivières. Maxwell was indignant, believing with General Thompson that Deschambault could have been held until the arrival of reinforcements. But John Thomas was in no condition to debate the matter. He had contracted smallpox.

X

"The First Stain
Upon American Arms"

1

THE COMMISSIONERS and Father Carroll waited nearly a
month for Congress to define the scope of their assignment
and issue their instructions. They did not leave Philadelphia until
the end of March. At New Brunswick they caught up with a
Prussian soldier of fortune, Baron Friedrich de Woedtke, also on
his way to Canada. "Though I had frequently seen him before,"
Father Carroll wrote his mother, "yet he was so disguised in furs,
that I scarce knew him, and never beheld a more laughable object
in my life. Like other Prussian officers, he appears to me as a man
who knows little of polite life, and yet has picked up so much of
it in his passage through France, as to make a most awkward appearance." The baron had served with Frederick the Great and
had so impressed Congress with his claims that he was commissioned
a brigadier. Unhappily, Congress could not know that de Woedtke,
like various other Europeans enrolled in the Continental Army,
was given to rarely interrupted drunkenness.

New York had been turned into an armed camp by Washington's
army and, according to Father Carroll, was "no more the gay,
polite place" of pre-Revolutionary days.[1] He and his fellow travelers were glad to set sail for Albany on April 2, starting a journey

that Charles Carroll of Carrollton would describe in an informative and sprightly diary. Carroll took note of the scenery, the weather, the fertility of farmlands, geological phenomena, waterfalls, and forts. He told of a fire on Bedloe's Island that he thought had been set by one of Washington's detachments. He compared the Catskills to "bluish clouds" on the horizon. He described an excursion made by Chase and himself to a sylvan waterfall, not concealing his annoyance that Chase, whose mind seems to have been less occupied with the gems of nature than with the dinner being prepared in their sloop's galley, had become "very apprehensive about the leg of mutton being boiled too much" and had cut the excursion short.[2] He was conscientious in his inspection of military installations and wrote careful reports. He described Fort Constitution as so weakly defended that had General Howe been "a man of enterprise," he could have taken it "with sixty men and without cannon." [3]

The commissioners took pleasure in one another's company. Samuel Chase and the Carrolls were old friends, and all three warmed instantly to Franklin, who delighted them with his erudition and unfailing wit. Charles Carroll described him as "a most engaging & entertaining companion of a sweet & lively temper full of facetious stories & always applied with judgment & introduced apropos . . . a man of extensive reading, deep thought & curious in all his enquiries . . . even his age makes all these happy endowments more interesting, uncommon & captivating." [4] Although in poor health and conscious of the sometimes crushing weight of his seventy years, Franklin was at his best, holding forth on many subjects and making lifelong friends of the two Carrolls. To be sure, their religious orthodoxy had no parallel in his own thinking, but he could applaud their politics.

The travelers were met at Albany by Philip Schuyler, who drove them to his family mansion and entertained them royally. Charles Carroll, accustomed to good things himself, was impressed with Schuyler's "pretty style" of living and with his daughters, Betsy and Peggy, whom he described as "lively, agreeable, black-eyed girls." [5] * Next day, the Schuyler family accompanied their guests

* Betsy became the wife of Alexander Hamilton.

to Saratoga, joined by General Thomas, who had been waiting for open water on the lakes. The journey, made miserable by wet weather, muddy roads, and abominable ferry service, left Franklin so weary and shaken that he feared he might not survive the mission.

Charles Carroll has left a glowing account of the Schuylers' country house at Saratoga, with its sweep of river and rich bottom-lands. He found Schuyler a congenial host, "a man of good understanding improved by reflection and study," and wrote appreciatively of "the ease and affability" of the Schuyler family.[6] After Schuyler and General Thomas had left for Fort George, a spring snowstorm blanketed the countryside, allowing the travelers a few extra days at Saratoga. Charles Carroll extolled "the lively behavior of the young ladies," whose presence contributed to "a most pleasant sejour."[7] He could not resist mention of them in letters he wrote home. "G. Schuyler has two fine girls," he said. "They are lively & sensible, & appear to be blessed with sweet tempers."[8] One wonders if his wife, Molly, after a little of this, remained equally sweet-tempered.

With improved weather, the travelers took leave of Saratoga and followed the Hudson to Fort Edward, where their inn was crowded with "stout fellows" from the 2nd Pennsylvania. They rejoined Schuyler at Lake George, boarding a troop boat equipped with awnings that allowed them to sleep on deck in their own beds. Charles Carroll was impressed with the rugged grandeur of the lake. "The country is wild and appears utterly incapable of cultivation," he wrote. "It is fine deer country, and likely to remain so, for I think it never will be inhabited." At the lake's northern tip, more than fifty bateaux were waiting to be portaged to Lake Champlain, and Carroll took advantage of the delay to make his own inspection of Fort Ticonderoga. He deemed it poorly located to fend off an attack from the north and "of no other use than an entrepot or magazine for stores."[9] Three schooners and a sloop stood at anchor, including *Royal Savage*, raised from the riverbed at St. Jean and in need of a new mainmast. He hoped all four vessels would be speedily rigged and armed so that they might "defy the enemy on Lake Champlain for this summer and fall at least, even should we unfortunately be driven out of Canada."[10]

Parting with Schuyler at Ticonderoga, the travelers sailed down Lake Champlain in the same troop boat with its awninged deck and comfortable beds, although Charles Carroll and Chase followed the example of the troops one night and slept on the ground with a log fire at their feet. Carroll praised the lake's potential as a future trade route and thought its shores well suited to agriculture. On reaching Ile aux Noix, he took note of the island's strategic location. Properly fortified, with gunboats on the river and a row of pickets stretched from shore to shore, it could serve as a barricade if the rest of Canada had to be evacuated.

At St. Jean the travelers were quartered in Moses Hazen's house, so vandalized by the troops that hardly a door or window remained intact. Across the Richelieu, Charles Carroll could see the battered fort where Major Preston had held off Montgomery's army for so many weeks. The buildings had been much damaged by artillery fire, but the earthen redoubts looked practically unscathed. A messenger was dispatched to notify Arnold and to arrange for transportation to La Prairie. Presently, word came back that he had been refused passage on a ferry when he tried to negotiate with paper money and that if a friend of the colonies had not provided him with silver he might never have arrived in Montreal. The incident was not lost on the commissioners, who carried only a small reserve of hard money.

Traveling by calash to La Prairie over roads muddier than any Charles Carroll had ever seen in Maryland, the four crossed to Montreal, where they were met by Arnold and escorted to headquarters in the Château de Ramezay. Father Carroll described their welcome in a letter to his mother:

We came hither the night before last, and were received at the landing by General Arnold, and a great body of officers, gentry, &c, and saluted by firing of cannon, and other military honors. Being conducted to the general's house, we were served with a glass of wine, while people were crowding in to pay their compliments, which ceremony being over, we were shown into another apartment, and unexpectedly met in it a large assemblage of ladies, most of them French. After drinking tea, and sitting some time, we went to an elegant supper, which was followed with the singing of the ladies, which proved very agreeable, and would have been more so, if we had not been so much fatigued with our journey.[11]

They were indeed exhausted, especially Franklin. It was almost a month since they had left New York.

The travelers were lodged in Thomas Walker's house — "the best built, and perhaps the best furnished in this town," Charles Carroll said.[12] All of them admired Arnold. "If this war continues, and Arnold should not be taken off pretty early," Carroll wrote, "he will turn out a great man; he has great vivacity, perseverance, resources, & intrepidity, and a cool judgment." [13] The day after their arrival, the commissioners took part in Arnold's council of war, voting in favor of a stand at Deschambault.

In their first letter to Congress, the commissioners asked for £20,000 in hard money to pay off debts and re-establish the army's credit. They could neither beg nor borrow from allies in Montreal. "Many of our friends are drained dry," they wrote. "Others say they are so, fearing, perhaps, we shall never be able to reimburse them. They show us long accounts, no part of which we are able to discharge, of the supplies they have furnished our Army, and declare they have borrowed and taken up credit so long for our service, that they can now be trusted no longer, even for what they want themselves."

Canadians were demanding "instant pay in silver or gold" for even "the most trifling service," the commissioners continued. "If money cannot be had to support your Army here with honour, so as to be respected, instead of being hated by the people, we report it as our firm and unanimous opinion that it is better immediately to withdraw it." They were "pestered hourly" by creditors, they said, and must appease angry citizens from whom the army had exacted provisions or services without pay. Before they could ask Canadians to name delegates to Congress, they must produce hard money to show that Congress was not bankrupt. "Till the arrival of money," they wrote Hancock, "it seems improper to propose the Federal union of this Province with the others." Congress sent them a little more than £1600 — "all that was in the Treasury," Hancock said.[14]

The commissioners also had to undo Wooster's mistakes. One

of their first acts was to order the return of exiled loyalists and the release of those held captive at Chambly, signaling an end to the flouting of the very liberties that Congress had promised to bestow on the Canadians. But it came too late to win new friends or change public opinion.

Father Carroll found the Montreal clergy almost unanimously pro-British. They questioned the sincerity of Congress's pledge to allow them "the full, perfect, and peaceful possession and enjoyment of all their estates." They challenged him to name a single colony where the Church and her clergy were given privileges equal to those spelled out in the Quebec Act. They reminded him of the Acadians, sent into exile by colonial troops. They asked him how he reconciled the Address to the People of Great Britain, which had accused the Church of "impiety, bigotry, persecution, murder and rebellion throughout every part of the world," with Congress's promise to allow Canadians "the free and undisturbed exercise of their religion." [15] They were aware, too, of the low regard shown the Church by American troops. Chaplain Robbins spoke for many of his fellow colonists when he described Canada as "the dwelling place of Satan" and expressed disdain for wayside shrines and chapels. " 'Tis grievous and affecting to see the superstition," he wrote, "every mile and sometimes oftener I find a cross fixed, and on some the spear, sponge, hammer, nails, &c." [16] To him and others like him such symbols of the faith were signs of the Antichrist.

Father Carroll quickly recognized the hopelessness of his mission. He spent more and more time with Father Floquet, the errant Jesuit who was chaplain to Hazen's regiment, meeting with him surreptitiously at the home of Pierre Du Calvet, another collaborator. On one occasion he was given permission by the Abbé Montgolfier to say mass in Father Floquet's house, but he was treated less as a fellow priest than as a spokesman for the enemy.

No less frustrated was Fleury Mesplet, the French printer sent by Congress to shape public opinion. He had installed his presses in the basement of the Château de Ramezay, but the time was past when any newspaper, even in the French language, could restore faith in a shattered army and an apparently bankrupt Congress.

On May 10, the commissioners learned that the army had fled

Quebec. So shaken by the news that they considered terminating their mission, they wrote Congress that all of Canada might have to be abandoned except a possible toehold at St. Jean. "We are afraid it will not be in our power to render our country any further service in this Colony," they said, urging Schuyler to assemble bateaux for evacuating the army.[17]

Next day Benjamin Franklin left for home. His health had worsened. He considered the mission a failure and was anxious to alert Congress to the magnitude of what had happened. He was accompanied by Father Carroll, who felt that he could be more useful to Franklin than to the two remaining commissioners in Montreal. In the course of their journey, they shared a carriage with Mrs. Thomas Walker, on her way to join her husband in the colonies. She spent much of the time denouncing the commissioners for catering to Montreal Tories instead of showing a proper appreciation for the colonies' friends and supporters. When her husband met them at Saratoga, he was even more vituperative. "They both took such liberties at taunting our conduct in Canada that it came almost to a quarrel," Franklin said. "We continued our care of her, however, and landed her safe in Albany with her three wagon-loads of baggage brought hither without putting her to any expense." [18] It marked a sorry end to what for him had been a thankless mission.

Chase and Charles Carroll felt they must remain in Montreal, if only to set an example for the troops and their Canadian allies. "Tho' our stay can be of no great service," Carroll wrote home, "yet as in the present circumstances our departure would discourage our troops & friends in the country we have resolved to remain here till further advices from below . . ." [19] On the 12th, they left for a tour of inspection that took them to St. Jean and Chambly. While at La Prairie, they wrote General Thomas, advising the use of force, when necessary, to obtain provisions for the troops. "We think force regulated by proper authority not only justifiable in this case," they said, "but that it will prevent the horrors arising from the licentiousness of a starving and, of course, uncontrollable soldiery." [20]

On their way northward, the commissioners had met with representatives from several Canadian tribes and had been given assurance that the Indians would lay aside the hatchet urged on them the previous autumn by Guy Johnson. They had conferred with them again at Montreal, where they made them a small present and promised a larger one "when the hatchet is delivered up." [21] However, when Chase and Carroll returned from Chambly, they learned that a task force of Indians and British regulars was advancing on the Cedars (Les Cèdres), an American outpost some forty miles upstream from Montreal. Colonel Timothy Bedel, in command at the Cedars, had hurried to the city to report that more than 100 Indians and an unknown number of regulars were within nine miles of the post. A contingent of 140 men under Major Henry Sherburne, a Rhode Islander attached to the 15th Continentals, was sent to reinforce the garrison, but Chase and Carroll were surprised that Bedel had come in person when he could easily have sent word by a subordinate. "This intelligence . . ." they wrote Congress, "might have been communicated to the commanding officer here by any other person, as well as Colonel Bedel." [22]

2

Carleton had a third British regiment, the 8th, deployed in the western hinterland. Garrisoning military posts from Oswegatchie (Ogdensburg) to Detroit and Michilimackinac, the troops maintained close ties with the Indians. Early in the winter, Arnold had warned Congress of enemy activities at Detroit and Niagara. Wooster suspected Montreal merchants of corresponding with the British garrisons, and rumor had it that 5000 tribesmen would come to "the relief of their father [Carleton]." [23] Moses Hazen heard the Indians would mount a spring offensive along the western frontier. "They keep aloof from us," he wrote Schuyler. "We are to expect little or no friendship from them, and, indeed, little or no precaution has been taken for that purpose. It is expected by some that numbers will come from the interior country, and fall on our frontiers, early in the spring." [24] His fears were shared by many others when it became known that three noted loyalists, including François de Lorimier, had left secretly for the hinterland.

Montreal merchants and their Indian dependents had kept pressure on Congress for a prompt reopening of the fur trade. Indeed, among the terms submitted to Montgomery had been a request that trade with the Indians be allowed to continue "as freely as heretofore." [25] In February, a deputation of merchants had gone to Philadelphia to plead their cause. Nor did the Indians conceal their resentment, threatening to make war unless the trade was reopened and they were permitted the guns, ammunition, and other articles of exchange that could be supplied more cheaply and in greater quantity from Montreal than from the colonies. Reports reached Philadelphia of a great Indian assemblage scheduled for early May at Fort Niagara. Congress was alarmed. Among the commissioners' instructions was a directive to reopen the fur trade and issue permits to those engaged in it "as far as it may consist with the safety of the troops and the public good." [26] Congress and the commissioners hoped the change of policy would placate the Indians and win friends among the merchants, but they were quickly disappointed. In less than a fortnight Arnold would refer to the citizens of Montreal as "our bitter enemies." [27] Of the Canadian tribes, only the Caughnawagas seemed other than hostile. The time had passed when any measure, however well intended, could mitigate the smoldering resentment toward Congress and its ragtag army.

In mid-April, Lorimier was reported at the Cedars, a site commanding the second rapid between two broad expanses in the St. Lawrence known as Lake St. Francis and Lake St. Louis. He was said to be collecting supplies for newly mustered troops and was quoted as threatening to return "in twenty days time" with a strike force of British regulars, French volunteers, and 800 Indians.[28] Moses Hazen, who had been left in charge at Montreal during the hiatus between Wooster and Arnold, dispatched Colonel Bedel to the Cedars with orders to build a stockade and mount two artillery pieces. Bedel was already involved in negotiations with the Caughnawagas and seems to have resented this additional assignment, complaining that it was "an undeserved responsibility," both "difficult and disagreeable." [29] He deputized his second in command, Major

Isaac Butterfield, to erect the stockade and take charge during his absence.

Butterfield had nearly 400 men, including Bedel's troops and part of Burrall's command. According to Private Zephaniah Shepardson, a private in Bedel's regiment, the officers were "ignorant of the art and policy of war," the rank and file "not very well disciplined, being young in the military art." The troops went about their tasks casually, he said, "like a company of sportsmen at play." Strangers were admitted to the post. Two who passed for Indians and were subsequently found to have been white men in disguise were allowed access to the magazine.[30] The fact that both Bedel and Butterfield had smallpox, probably contracted by inoculation, may account in part for their failure to impose stricter rules and discipline.

When Bedel arrived, he found shortages of both food and ammunition. "In vain did I frequently apply to Genl. Arnold the then Commanding officer at Montreal for the most necessary supplys of ammunition provisions, Intrenching tools and Batteaus," he said. He was often absent, pursuing further negotiations with the Caughnawagas and supervising other outposts. "I never Conceived that by my writen orders or any other verbal Instructions from Genl. Arnold, that I was to remain at the Cedars and at that post only," he said, "but on the Contrary that I was to establish, over see, & have an eye to the several Different posts and to protect all that part of the Country — and in Particular to attend to the Cultivation of a friendship with the savages." On May 15, he crossed to the Caughnawagas' village, leaving the Cedars "in as perfect tranquillity as it had ever before been," and learned that a force of redcoats and Indians had been sighted a few miles upstream. Instead of returning to his command, he continued to Montreal to alert the city in person — "an error in Judgement," he would subsequently admit, "a Defect in the head and not in the heart." [31]

Word of the stockade spread swiftly through the fur country. Lorimier, who was busy enlisting western tribesmen, already had Canadian allies in the neighborhood. During his search for supplies he had been assisted by the Reverend Pierre Denaut, the village *curé* and a future Bishop of Quebec. Jean Baptiste Pierre Louvigny, Sieur de Montigny, had enrolled a band of thirty Canadians in the vicinity of the Cedars, and Pierre Fortier of Montreal had delivered gunpowder and fifteen sacks of bullets to a local *curé*, who had buried them in a pasture to await Montigny's bidding.

With Lorimier's tribesmen as a nucleus, the post commander at Oswegathcie, Captain George Forster of the 8th, assembled a strike force of 160 Indians, several officers, and thirty-six rank and file from the 8th, and eleven French and British volunteers. On May 12, he started downstream with a fleet of bateaux and bark canoes to "relieve Montreal from the oppressive tyranny of the rebels," pausing at St. Régis to enroll an additional fifty-four Indians.[32] Early on the 18th, he put in three miles above the Cedars and ordered a detachment of Indians to engage the enemy on the left while he opened fire from the right flank. As the detachment approached the stockade, it intercepted an enemy supply train, killing one of Burrall's men and capturing another.

On reaching the stockade, the Indians came "skiping and runing out of the woods," according to Private Shepardson, with "nothing but a sort of wildgrass to secrete or hide them from us."[33] Butterfield and his men had the wherewithal for a stout defense — two fieldpieces, half a barrel of gunpowder, fifteen pounds of shot. One officer, Captain Daniel Wilkins, thought that, with a wise use of ammunition, they could hold out until the arrival of reinforcements.

Before starting hostilities, Forster advised the garrison that a prompt capitulation could prevent what might be unavoidable "acts of cruelty" on the part of his Indians.[34] Butterfield showed a willingness to comply — something not lost on Forster — but asked that his men be allowed to keep their guns. This Forster refused, and shots were exchanged. Butterfield's two artillery pieces, manned by inexperienced crews, were yards off target. Enemy musket fire took a negligible toll, although one American sustained a shoulder wound, and another, whose name was Bacon, got the fright of his life when a bullet struck the button on his cocked hat. "A musket ball met against his head and knocked him down," Private Shepardson wrote. "He sprang up and run crying out, 'I'm a dead man, dead man' . . . I must confess I never see a dead man run before now. The ball struck a large button on his cocked up hat and drove through two thicknesses [of hat] into his skin towards the skull. So the button saved his Bacon."[35]

At one point, Captain Wilkins sallied from the stockade with a small task force to set fire to a barn in which some of the enemy had taken cover. He was anxious to make another sally, but Butterfield forbade it. Shots were traded to little purpose all afternoon. When Forster heard that an American relief column was at Quinze Chiens (Vaudreuil), a village a few miles distant on the Ottawa, he ordered Montigny to reconnoiter and to harass the column if he could.

War whoops and a random musket fire continued after sundown, striking fear in the hearts of Butterfield and some, but not all, of his men. By daybreak he was ready to capitulate. He indicated his willingness to Forster, who urged him to surrender before the Indians got out of hand and to "take advantage of their present favourable turn." [36] In his diary, Private Shepardson described a "schism" in the American command, with Butterfield favoring surrender but with Daniel Wilkins and several others vehemently against it. At the last minute some of the men talked of replacing Butterfield with Wilkins, but before they could do so, Butterfield had capitulated. "Alas, we are too late to accomplish our design," Shepardson wrote. "This moment the flag is coming into our garrison to take possession of our garrison and us." [37]

Butterfield turned over his artillery, ammunition, food supplies, and small arms. The men were allowed only the clothes they had on. However, when they marched out of the stockade, under the scrutiny of six watchful chiefs, some took their knapsacks with them — a breach of the surrender terms sure to incense the Indians, who had been promised everything in the fort. In short order the prisoners were dispossessed not only of their knapsacks but of watches, money, and, according to Captain Andrew Parke of the 8th, "perhaps a laced hat or two." [38] They were then herded into the village church, where they could hear the surge of war whoops as Lorimier's Indians prepared to intercept the relief column at Quinze Chiens.

Major Henry Sherburne, who had left Montreal with a reinforcement of 140 men, had detached several of his troops to cover his line of march and guard supplies. He had lost others to sickness, including Colonel Bedel, who had accompanied the relief column although still weakened by smallpox but had turned back at Lachine. By the time Sherburne reached the western tip of Montreal Island, he was down to a little over 100 men. Crossing the Ottawa to Quinze Chiens, he ordered Captain Theodore Bliss to round up carts to transport supplies and the men's baggage. However, Bliss had not returned by sundown, and that evening word reached the encampment that he had been captured by the enemy and that 500 Indians and Canadians were in the vicinity. Fearful of a nocturnal attack, Sherburne ferried his troops back to Montreal Island and encamped at Ste. Anne, a fortified post occupied by Lieutenant Samuel Young of Bedel's command with a garrison of twenty-five men.

When gale winds delayed a second crossing, Captain Ebenezer Sullivan, brother of New Hampshire's Brigadier General John Sullivan, went to Bliss's rescue with a few volunteers. Putting in at Quinze Chiens, he succeeded in locating his fellow officer, freeing him from a token guard and returning him to the encampment. On the 20th, Sherburne recrossed the Ottawa and began a cautious advance toward the Cedars. He had gone about five miles when a detachment of Indians and Canadians led by Lorimier took aim from behind trees bordering the road. Pinned down in an open field, Sherburne and his troops held their ground for most of an hour, withdrawing when they were about to be outflanked and managing an orderly retreat until they were surrounded by what they thought were hundreds of Canadians and Indians, including Montigny's command. "A large body of them rushed on our front and made them prisoners," Sherburne reported later, "while the rest of the enemy (about five hundred in number) seized the rear and center." He surrendered unconditionally, with twenty-eight men killed, wounded, or "carried off by the savages." [39] British casualties were light, although a chief of the Senecas had been killed and his braves clamored for retribution.

Because Sherburne had surrendered unconditionally, the Indians laid claim to all the prisoners' possessions, including the clothes they wore. One warrior shouted to Lorimier, "Guard the bird and I'll defeather him!" and, singling out Sherburne, proceeded to divest him of nearly all he had on, from his cocked hat to his shirt and breeches. Lorimier sought to make amends by volunteering some of his own apparel, but Sherburne was so broad of girth that nothing would suffice except a voluminous cape that covered him in part. [40]

Presently, all the prisoners were stripped, in a melee that nearly led to bloodshed. Lorimier was thankful when he had delivered the prisoners, alive if short of apparel, to Captain Forster at the Cedars.

Sherburne would assert that several of his men had been tomahawked and scalped. "The barbarity with which we were treated by the savages," he said, "together with our sufferings for want of provisions and clothes, is beyond anything which can be imagined or described." [41] Presumably, the men he cited were tomahawked in the heat of battle. Captain Andrew Parke, Forster's aide, denied that any were killed after they were taken prisoner, although he acknowledged that the Indians were kept in check "only with the utmost difficulty." [42]

With more prisoners than he could handle, nearly 500 in all, Forster could not keep his Indians from stripping Butterfield's men, too, in violation of the surrender terms. Starting with silver buckles, buttons, silk handkerchiefs, and other articles easy to pocket, they soon graduated to coats, breeches, boots, and stockings. Some of the prisoners were peeled to the buff. Private Benjamin Stevens of Burrall's regiment, left with more apparel than most, gave his coat to his commanding officer, who had been "stripped naked to his shirt." [43]

Forster herded his prisoners to Quinze Chiens, where some of the rank and file were billeted in an open field, exposed to the wind and wet of a cold spring. "We lay on the ground for our bed," Shepardson said. "Nothing but mud and mire for our downy feather'd beds; clouds to cover us, with wind, hail and rain. We had no fires ... nor meat to cook nor bread to eat ... No spirits but the spirit of war." [44] Others were taken to Ste. Anne, which had been hastily evacuated by Captain Young and his small garrison. But these were temporary measures, and soon the rank and file were ferried to an island in the Ottawa, where they slept in the open without blankets or sufficient clothing. The officers were consigned to the custody of two priests in the Indian village of Conosadaga at Lac des Deux Montagnes.

More Canadians enrolled at Pointe Claire. Continuing toward Montreal, Forster was within three miles of Lachine when he heard that 600 Americans were already there and would soon be joined by 300 riflemen. One informant said the number could swell to 2500. After conferring with aides, Forster ordered a retreat, first to Pointe Claire, then back to the Cedars. Many of his troops deserted, until he was left with only eighty men. However, nearly 200 returned when it was learned that earlier reports had been mistaken and that the enemy had come in much smaller numbers than had been feared.

Unable to provide for so many captives, Forster must have been hugely relieved when the American officers proposed a cartel that would permit an exchange of the prisoners for a like number of British prisoners of war. He dispatched Lorimier, Montigny, and Captain Parke to confer with the officers at Lac des Deux Montagnes. In a meeting that seems to have gone more smoothly than anyone could have expected, terms were agreed upon whereby an equal number of British would be exchanged, rank for rank, for Forster's 497 Americans. It was stipulated that the prisoners should return home "without committing any waste or spoil on their march thither," that Canadians should be reimbursed for "all the waste and spoil" attributed to Bedel's troops, and that bateaux used in the exchange should be sent back undamaged. The prisoners were to pledge not to divulge any military secrets picked up during their captivity, and hostages were to be left with the British as a guarantee that the cartel would be honored "without any equivocation whatsoever." A requirement imposed only on the American prisoners forbade them ever to bear arms in the war with the mother country. Parke, Lorimier, and Montigny signed for Captain Forster. Signing for the Americans were Majors Butterfield and Sherburne, Captains Bliss, Sullivan, and Wilkins, and Captain John Stevens of Burrall's regiment.[45]

Arnold was still at Sorel when he learned of Butterfield's surrender. Hurrying to Montreal, he started upstream with about 100 men. He was reinforced by a small detachment at Lachine and awaited Colonel John De Haas of the 1st Pennsylvania with an additional 400 men. He mounted artillery in a stone farmhouse and stationed his command athwart the Montreal road. On the night of the 24th, enemy drums could be heard. "The morning dawns," wrote Captain James Wilkinson of the 2nd Continentals, "that morn, big with the fate of a few, a handful of brave fellows." [46] When the enemy unexpectedly withdrew, Arnold started in pursuit, dispatching several Caughnawagas to warn Forster's Indians that if they failed to surrender the prisoners or if an American lost his life while in their custody, he would "follow them to their towns and destroy them by fire and sword." [47]

Arnold was at Ste. Anne by late afternoon. A mile offshore he could see bateaux ferrying American prisoners to Quinze Chiens from an island in the Ottawa. As he watched the men being hurried out of reach, he received a message from Forster warning him that if he attacked, the Indians would massacre all the prisoners. "Words cannot express my feelings at the delivery of this message," he wrote the commissioners. "Torn by the conflicting passions of revenge and humanity, a sufficient force to take ample revenge, raging for action, urged me on one hand; and humanity for five hundred unhappy wretches, who were on the point of being sacrificed if our vengeance was not delayed, plead equally strong on the other." [48]

Forster had ordered the prisoners transferred from the island to Quinze Chiens, where they would be less accessible to the enemy. Privates Stevens and Shepardson were among them, herded with their comrades through swamps and waist-high streams to the island's tip, where the bateaux were assembled. Stevens was told that a man had drowned when trying to cross a swift-running rivulet, that two others, too weak to march, had been put to death. As his bateau approached Quinze Chiens, he could see Arnold's fleet starting across the Ottawa. He thought he could count fifteen craft. Shepardson also saw the boats, "about as large as chestnut burs floating on the water." [49] He counted seventeen, each carrying fifteen or twenty men.

Arnold had set forth with fifteen bateaux and three canoes loaded to capacity. It was a tranquil autumn night, which would prompt a flight of eloquence in Captain Wilkinson's memoirs. "The sun was setting," he wrote, "the sky unclouded, the atmosphere serene, the surface on which we floated as smooth as a mirror, and the spire of the church at Quinze Chiens, together with the white Canadian houses ranged along the coast, diversified the prospect most agreeably." [50] Arnold crossed first to the island, where he rescued five prisoners left behind by the enemy and whom he found "naked and almost starved." They told him that "one or two" of their comrades had been murdered by the Indians.[51]

As the fleet neared Quinze Chiens, Forster opened fire with small arms and with the two artillery pieces he had captured at the Cedars. Shots freckled the water, narrowly missing some of Arnold's canoes and bateaux. "Our distance was too great for any effect from small arms," Wilkinson would report, "but we were eminently exposed to the artillery, every shot plunging beneath or passing over us, and the slightest touch of our fragile craft, would have sent a crew to the bottom, as we were too deeply laden to furnish the smallest relief to each other." [52] Arnold directed his Caughnawaga paddlers to take his canoe as near shore as enemy gunfire would permit. He was able to determine the location of the two artillery pieces and to distinguish redcoats deployed on the landing beach and Indians spaced along the flat, thickly wooded river bank. An attempt to land would have been suicidal. After a brief reconnoiter, he signaled his fleet to put about.

Returning to Ste. Anne, Arnold called together his officers and proposed a second attempt on Quinze Chiens, this time in the dark of early morning, when he could outflank the enemy. Moses Hazen was against it. He expressed concern for the prisoners' safety and doubted that Forster's Indians could be caught off guard. Colonel De Haas and several others sided with him. Arnold spoke vehemently in defense of his proposal but was outvoted — after an exchange of insults that would add Hazen to his list of enemies.[53]

During the night, Captain Parke and Major Sherburne crossed from Quinze Chiens to acquaint Arnold with the cartel. Sherburne, who had been admitted to a gathering of Forster's tribesmen and had seen for himself that they were not given to empty threats, warned that failure to approve the cartel could mean death for the prisoners. Arnold took the document and spread it under a lantern. As he scanned it his face darkened. He was incensed that the Americans must pledge not to engage in further military service, whereas their British counterparts were put under no such restriction. He told Parke to advise his superior that an exchange could take place only on equal terms. "If he refused," he subsequently wrote the commissioners, "my determination was to attack him immediately, and if our prisoners were murdered, to sacrifice every soul who fell into our hands." [54] Happily, Forster acceded to Arnold's demand "as the only means to avoid the destruction of the prisoners." [55] It was agreed that four hostages would be turned over — Captains Theodore Bliss, Ebenezer Sullivan, and John Stevens, and Captain Ebenezer Green of Bedel's command.

On the night of May 27, five bateaux crossed the St. Lawrence, to start the first prisoners on their journey homeward. The rest followed, some of them harassed by Forster's Indians. "It is true," Captain Parke said, "that on the 30th, in the evening, while they were embarking, the savages amusing themselves by the water side, did fire several muskets, but without the least intention to injure them, nor were any of them injured." [56] Private Shepardson told it differently. "We proceeded down to our boats," he said, "but not without the attendance of a host of Indians with all there weapons of cruelty and the most horrid noise of war. With violence they attempted to rush upon us but were hindered by there superiors, yet they threaten'd us with there tomahawks, spears, knives and fire arms, showing the skalps they took off five of my mates, whom they killed after they were made prisoners." [57] Whether the scalps were indeed those of Shepardson's "mates" is questionable, nor is it certain that the tribesmen intended more than a parting harassment. Some of them fired balls of mud instead of bullets.

The Indians kept ten of the prisoners to adopt into the tribes. Eight were subsequently ransomed by the British, but two seem to have preferred their captors' free-ranging life. "They were during the time of their captivity with the Indians treated more like children than prisoners," Captain Parke said, "and we have reason to believe, those who yet remain in their hands, do so by choice." [58] A few captured Canadians, not included in the cartel, were sent home.

Forster and his troops withdrew to Oswegatchie. Arnold returned to Montreal after leaving orders with Colonel De Haas to burn the blockhouse at Ste. Anne and the Indian village of Conosadaga. De Haas set fire to the blockhouse but, after conferring with his officers, disregarded his superior's order to level the tribal village lest it prompt an Indian uprising. Arnold exploded when he heard about it. "None but cowards would hesitate to obey a positive order!" he thundered.[59] "The orders I sent Colonel De Haas were very positive," he wrote the commissioners. "How he should think of calling a council to determine if he should obey them, appears to me very extraordinary." [60]

The colonies accused the enemy of murdering American prisoners of war in cold blood. In his letter to the commissioners, Arnold spoke of "one or two" deaths. The commissioners put the figure at "five or six." Congress heard that two had been killed on the night after Butterfield's surrender, "four or five" subsequently, and that one was roasted to death "while still retaining life and sensation." [61] The prisoners gave conflicting stories — Private Stevens, for example, spoke of two men killed and one accidentally drowned; Private Shepardson, of five killed and scalped. The British, on the other hand, denied that any prisoners had been put to death. Captain Parke's report cited an investigation that was made of the alleged murder of a prisoner. "On making the strictest inquiry," he said, "we could not find any person who saw this act of cruelty, nor could any of the prisoners name the person so said to have been killed, and we do declare, the prisoners were in every respect treated with all possible attention which humanity could suggest, and our situation admit." [62] Captain Ebenezer Sullivan, one of the four hostages, said that "not a man living could behave with more humanity than Capt. Forster did after the Surrender of the Party I belonged to and whoever says to the contrary let his Station in Life be what it will, he's an Enemy to Peace and a fallacious disturber of mankind." [63]

The Cedars incident, coming so soon after the retreat from Quebec, sent further shock waves through the colonies. Washington ascribed the surrender to "the base and cowardly Behaviour" of Bedel and Butterfield.[64] John Adams called it "the first stain upon American arms," adding that Butterfield deserved "a most infamous death." [65] In a letter to James Warren, he expressed his fears of what would befall the colonies should Canada be evacuated:

The regulars, if they get full possession of that province, and the navigation of St. Lawrence river above Deschambault, at least above the mouth of the Sorel, will have nothing to intercept their communications with Niagara, Detroit, Michilimackinac; they will have the navigation of the five great lakes quite as far as the Mississippi River; they will have a free communication with all the numerous tribes of Indians extended along the frontiers of all the colonies, and, by their trinkets and bribes, will induce them to take up the hatchet, and spread blood and fire among the inhabitants; by which means, all the frontier inhabitants will be driven in upon the middle settlements, at a time when the inhabitants of the seaports and coasts will be driven back by the British navy. Is this picture too high colored? Perhaps it is; but surely we must maintain our power in Canada.[66]

Congress deemed the cartel to be no more binding than "a mere sponsion," for what was done with British prisoners of war was its own prerogative and not that of any military commander. A committee appointed to assess the matter advised against relinquishing any prisoners of war until the persons responsible for the alleged murder of American captives were surrendered to the colonies and made "to suffer such punishment as their crime deserves."[67] Congress concurred in this, which was tantamount to not honoring the agreement. Neither Carleton nor any other British commander could be expected to comply.

"The truth was," said Thomas Jones, a loyalist who wrote a history of the Revolution, "Congress had got their own people, and were determined the British should not be benefitted by an addition of near 500 veterans, then prisoners in the Colonies, who, by the agreement between Foster and Arnold, ought to have been returned; and under the aforesaid false pretences, supported by hearsay evidence, and the testimony of two or three privates, the Congress absolutely refused to ratify the agreement so solemnly made, and of which they had received the full benefit by a return of the whole of the troops taken by Foster and the Indians. Punica fides!"[68]

"Such is the Treaty enter'd into by the Party concern'd," said a correspondent in the *Quebec Gazette*, "and which has been as religiously observed by the Savages as wickedly broke through by the Promoters of this unnatural Rebellion — I say, the Promoters, for the poor, deluded multitude are more the objects of our Pity than of our Vengeance. To such a height of political Frenzey are our infatuated Countrymen in the refractory Colonys now arrived, that it is become not only an Act of Justice but of Mercy to enforce Submission." [69]

That summer Timothy Bedel, Isaac Butterfield, and Samuel Young were duly court-martialed. Bedel, found guilty of "quitting his post," was cashiered but not barred from further military service. The court accepted his claim that his had been "an error in Judgement, a Defect in the head and not in the heart." [70] He would serve again, on New Hampshire's northern frontier. Butterfield was found guilty, cashiered, and forbidden to hold another commission in the Continental Army. Young, who had fled Ste. Anne with his small garrison, was acquitted. [71]

All four hostages eventually returned home, Captain Sullivan still incensed that Congress had failed to honor the cartel. "I am surprised to hear that instead of Redeeming us according to the Cartel," he had written his brother while still a hostage, "the Congress have not only refused to do it, but have also demanded to have Captain Forster to be given up to answer for his Conduct in what they are pleased to term the Massacre of the Cedars. I cannot think that the Congress would ever have thought of such unheard of Proceedings had they not had a wrong Representation of the Matter . . . If you suspect I write this for the sake of getting my own Liberty your suspicion wrongs me; it is not my own Confinement but the breach of a Treaty which even the Savages have ever held sacred that causes me to write." [72] Both Green and Bliss agreed with him. We are not told what Stevens thought.

XI

An Irishman's Luck

1

"I LONG MOST ARDENTLY to be at home," Charles Carroll had written his father on May 16, "and am quite sick of the confused state of things in this province." [1] By now, both he and Chase were convinced of the futility of their mission. They had come too late to achieve their primary goal of forging an alliance between the Canadians and the thirteen colonies. "In the present situation of our affairs," they wrote Congress, "it will not be possible for us to carry into execution the great object of our instructions, as the possession of this country must finally be decided by the sword. We think our stay here no longer of service to the publick." They were unhappy, too, with their involvement in a military campaign they were not qualified to direct. "We have no fixed abode," they wrote Schuyler, "being obliged to follow your example and become Generals, Commissaries, Justices of the Peace; in short, to act in twenty different capacities." [2]

At the end of May, they left for home. Their last letter to Congress spoke of food shortages, lack of ammunition and hard money, and an army so ridden with smallpox that more than 400 men were unfit for duty. "We cannot find words strong enough to describe our miserable situation," they wrote. "You will have a faint idea of

it if you figure to yourself an Army broken and disheartened, half
of it under inoculation, or under other diseases; soldiers without
pay, without discipline, and altogether reduced to live from hand to
mouth, depending on the scanty and precarious supplies of a few
half-starved cattle and trifling quantities of flour, which have
hitherto been picked up in different parts of the country." [3]

To the commissioners' dismay, the ailing Thomas had turned over
the command to David Wooster. "General Wooster is, in our
opinion, unfit, totally unfit, to command your Army, and conduct
the war ..." they wrote Congress. "His stay in this Colony is unnecessary, and even prejudicial to our affairs; we would therefore
humbly advise his recall." [4] Wooster was soon replaced, but in
Congress he would have a formidable defender in John Adams, who
was ever on the alert for an "anti New England Spirit" among his
fellow delegates. "In Woosters case," he said, "there was a manifest
Endeavour to lay upon him the blame of their own misconduct in
Congress in embarrassing and starving the War in Canada. Wooster
was calumniated for Incapacity, Want of Application and even for
Cowardice, with[out] a Colour of Proof of either." [5] A congressional committee exonerated Wooster, but this would be his last
assignment in the Continental Army.

John Thomas lay mortally ill. By now he was blind, semicon-
scious, and in the last throes of smallpox. Early on Sunday morning,
June 2, he died at the old fort in Chambly. General John Sullivan
had arrived that same day from the colonies and was given charge
of the campaign. In a hurry to show that he, as senior brigadier,
could turn the campaign around, he left immediately for Montreal
and did not attend his predecessor's burial in the small cemetery
outside the fort.

"He is active, spirited, and Zealously attach'd to the Cause,"
Washington said of Sullivan. "But he has his wants, and he has his
foibles. The latter are manifested in a little tincture of vanity, and
in an over desire of being popular, which now and then leads him
into some embarrassments." [6] Contentious and cocky, Sullivan
nursed ambitions that outreached his abilities. The son of inden-
tured servants who had settled near the New Hampshire coast,
he was unmistakably Irish, with black hair and ruddy good looks.

He had read law, married, and started a family, and he had built himself a thriving practice in Durham, where he was known for taking a hard line with defaulting clients. One day shots were fired through his window. More than 100 petitioners addressed the General Court to protest his "Oppressive Extortive Behaviour." He was accused of having "a View of making his Fortune, out of the Ruin of the poor harmless people, taking of them Unreasonable Fees from such as were not able to Command Cash enough to pay their publick Tax, or to provide Bread for their Families." [7]

Sullivan had been among the first New Hampshiremen to espouse the Revolution. He had represented his province at the First Continental Congress and, in December 1774, was an instigator of one of two raids on Fort William and Mary in Portsmouth Harbor, where he and his fellow patriots seized the artillery and more than 100 barrels of gunpowder. He was a delegate to the Second Continental Congress and, although his military credentials were modest, was named a brigadier in the Continental Army — to the surprise of some New Hampshiremen, who thought the appointment should have gone to Colonel John Stark of Derryfield, a soldier of proven worth and a hero at Bunker Hill.

Sullivan served without distinction during the siege of Boston, quarreling with the New Hampshire legislature over its right to appoint officers in the provincial militia. However, in the spring he was given command of one of the two brigades assigned to Canada. Among his field officers were Colonel Anthony Wayne of the 4th Pennsylvania and the same Colonel Stark who, if military performance had been the chief criterion, would have occupied Sullivan's place as brigadier. Wayne, darkly handsome and given to a swagger, was a martinet who commanded the intense loyalty of his troops. Stark, hard-bitten, crusty, often impolitic, had served with Rogers' Rangers in the French and Indian War and had prevented Howe's redcoats from turning the American flank at Bunker Hill. The brigade had been held up nearly three weeks in Albany while food supplies were hurried to Thomas' army and had been deprived of the 3rd New Jersey, detached to suppress a Tory uprising on the Mohawk. The troops were crossing into Canada when Sullivan took charge.

Sullivan believed he could salvage the campaign. "I am Surprized that an Army Should Live in Continual fear & even Retreat before an Enemy which no person among them has seen," he wrote Hancock, declaring it his "fixed Determination" to regain Deschambault. He fortified Sorel, installed a three-gun battery on the north shore of the St. Lawrence, and ordered the return of ordnance that had been removed for safekeeping. "More work has been done here today," he wrote Washington, "than has been in Canada Since the Surrender of St. John's." He was encouraged by the welcome given him by French Canadians. The Richelieu had been "Lined with men Women & Children Leaping & Clapping their hands for Joy to See me arrive," he wrote the commander-in-chief. Volunteers, he said, were "Flocking by Hundreds" into his encampment. He was even more gratified when some of the *habitants* appeared willing to supply his troops in return for his promise of future payment. "What gives me Still greater Evidence of their Friendship," he said, "is that they have Voluntarily Offer'd to Supply us with what Wheat, flour &c we want & ask nothing in return but Certificates." [8]

General Thompson had heard that Colonel Maclean was at Trois Rivières with a small contingent of regulars and Canadians. On June 3, he had ordered Colonel St. Clair to occupy Nicolet, across the St. Lawrence from Trois Rivières, and, if he saw fit, mount a surprise attack on Maclean's command, thought to number no more than 300 men. St. Clair had already left when Sullivan joined Thompson at Sorel. After conferring with his officers, Sullivan agreed to an attack on Trois Rivières and ordered Thompson to join St. Clair with the 4th and 6th Pennsylvania and the 2nd New Jersey. Thompson's officers would include Colonel Wayne, Colonel Maxwell of the 2nd New Jersey, and Colonel William Irvine of the 6th Pennsylvania. His little army, after uniting with St. Clair, would total nearly 2000 men. In his instructions, Sullivan expressed confidence that the enemy could be rolled back, even to Quebec. "I have the highest Opinion of the Bravery & Resolution of the Troops you Command," he wrote Thompson, "& Doubt not but under the Direction of a kind providence you will Open the way for our Recovering that Ground which former Troops have so Shamefully Lost." Already he had his eye on Deschambault, where British vessels had been sighted. "The Ships are now above that place," he wrote Washington, "but if General Thompson Succeeds at three Rivers, I will Soon Remove the Ships below Richelieu falls & after that Approach Toward Quebeck as fast as possible." [9]

Thompson left Sorel on the afternoon of June 6, reaching Nicolet at midnight. Next morning he learned that ten British vessels had been seen above Trois Rivières and that as many as fifteen hundred men might have debarked. He gave orders for a crossing, that same night, three miles above the enemy ships. To conceal his plans from local citizens, he had his men dig trenches and erect redoubts.

Sullivan had hoped to join Thompson with De Haas's regiment, but Arnold wanted it in Montreal. "By Some Strange kind of Conduct in General Arnold," he wrote Washington, "he had kept that Detachment dancing between this & Montreal ever Since my Arrival." [10] He sent Colonel William Winds downstream with the 1st New Jersey. By the time the reinforcement reached Nicolet, Thompson had already crossed. Winds and his men could hear gunfire across the river.

2

General Burgoyne had debarked at Quebec on June 1, bringing with him seven British regiments of foot,* a British artillery corps, and more than 3000 German mercenaries, including a Hesse-Hanau artillery unit. His troops swelled Carleton's army to about 11,000 men and were a blaze of color as they came ashore to the salute of artillery. The British infantry wore scarlet coats; the artillery, blue. The grenadiers, many of them six-footers, wore the high bearskin caps that made them look even taller. Most of the Germans had blue coats, but the sharpshooters, known as "jaegers," were in green with red facing. German grenadiers wore brass-faced caps embossed with the royal cipher of the Duke of Brunswick.

Except for the Hesse-Hanau troops, Burgoyne's mercenaries came from Brunswick, a small duchy impoverished by the Seven Years'

---

* The 9th, 20th, 24th, 31st, 34th, 53rd, and 62nd Regiments of Foot.

War. To shore up the economy, Duke Karl I had arranged with King George the Third to turn over several thousand able-bodied males to the British army at thirty crowns a head. Some were professional soldiers enrolled in the ducal army. Many were guileless farm boys grabbed off by the duke's recruiting agents. Others were the flotsam of towns and cities. Their appearance in the British army infuriated the colonists, changing the Revolution from a family quarrel to a war with strangers.

Burgoyne had won recognition in the Seven Years' War as a young officer of promise. In Portugal, which was England's ally, he had been given the local rank of brigadier and, at the head of the 16th Light Dragoons, had halted an attempt by Spain to invade and subjugate her smaller neighbor. More versatile than most of his military colleagues, he had sat in Parliament and had written a comedy, *The Maid of the Oaks*, that David Garrick produced in London. He had married above his station, but his wife, a daughter of the Earl of Derby, had recently fallen ill, and Burgoyne would be widowed that very June. He was now in his mid-fifties, still handsome although prone to flesh. Horace Walpole dubbed him "General Swagger," and in dress uniform he must have glittered. Adored by women and a favorite with the rank and file, he was the antithesis of Carleton. Lieutenant William Digby of the 53rd deemed Carleton "one of the most distant, reserved men in the world" but praised Burgoyne for "a winning manner in appearance and address, far different from the severity of Carlton, which caused him to be idolized by the army, his orders appearing more like recommending subordination than enforcing it." [11] Accompanying Burgoyne were Major General William Phillips, of the Royal Artillery, and Baron Friedrich von Riedesel, who was in charge of the German troops.

Carleton sent Lieutenant Colonel Simon Fraser of the 24th to Trois Rivières with four battalions, followed by Lieutenant Colonel William Nesbitt of the 47th with an additional brigade. Fraser took his men ashore, but Nesbitt kept his brigade aboard ship and anchored three miles upstream. "Troops were joining us fast," Digby said. "I suppose we might then have about 1000 with some field pieces & many of our ships off the town. We posted strong guards, the enemy being so very near, and intended to halt there until the coming up of the rest of the army." [12] Major Griffith Williams of the Royal Artillery estimated that as many as 2000 men were on hand, including Colonel Maclean's Canadians and regulars.

Thompson had organized his troops into four divisions under St. Clair, Wayne, Maxwell, and Irvine, with Lieutenant Colonel Thomas Hartley of the 6th Pennsylvania in charge of a reserve. His boats had skirted the British vessels safely, and he had detached 250 men to watch over them after he had touched shore at Pointe du Lac. He had enlisted one Antoine Gautier, a local *habitant*, as guide, apparently without making sure of his dependability. Thompson seems to have harbored doubts about the timing of his expedition. He had written Washington that if he had come only two weeks sooner, he could have held Deschambault and retained control of the St. Lawrence. "Three thousand men could have defended Canada at that place better than ten thousand now we are out of possession of it," he had said. [13]

Thompson followed the river to a crossroads, where he could have branched from the St. Lawrence and been out of sight of the British ships. However, he was told that the enemy had occupied a house two miles down the river road, and he decided to clear it before advancing on Trois Rivières. When he reached the house he found it empty. Gautier persuaded him to cut through the woods to the branch road, rather than retrace his steps, but after advancing only a short distance he found himself in a nearly impenetrable swamp. As his troops waded to their knees in muck, he suspected Gautier of leading him in the wrong direction. With the sky brightening and his chances of a surprise attack rapidly diminishing, he ordered a return to the river road. When he regained it, an enemy gunboat sighted his column and sped downstream.

The gunboat belonged to sloop-of-war *Martin*, whose captain had hauled his ship close to shore to debark units of the 29th and 47th. When he saw Thompson's troops, he raked them with artillery fire until they took cover in the woods. Thompson found a cart road at a safe distance from the river, but it soon led him into another bog, which Colonel Wayne would describe as "the most Horrid swamp that ever man set foot in" [14] and which Colonel St.

Clair thought was at least three miles long.[15] With Wayne's troops in the lead, the column pushed through waist-high water. "Nature, perhaps, never formed a place better calculated for the destruction of an army," Colonel Irvine would recall. "It was impossible to preserve any order of march, nay, it became at last so difficult, and the men so fatigued, that their only aim was how to get extricated." [16] Nearly three hours were lost before Wayne's division set foot on dry ground and was met by a small detachment of light infantry and Indians. Wayne attacked on both flanks and after a brief skirmish drove the enemy into headlong retreat. Across an open meadow he could see the church spire, monastery, and squat log houses of Trois Rivières. He could detect freshly built ei. ⸰nchments and, near the river, columns of British regulars formed for a counterattack.

Major Griffith Williams had spent the night aboard ship. "At half past 3 the next morning," he would remember, "much was I surpris'd to hear Colo Fraser hail me, & beg for God's sake I would send what Artillery on Shore I possibly could, assuring me the Rebels were within a mile of the Town, to the amount of two or three thousand. I could scarce believe it; however as I had 2 six pounders mounted on the Deck with 80 rounds of Case & round Shot, I had them on Shore in less than Twenty minutes." [17] He stationed one gun north of Trois Rivières, another to the west.

Wayne's skirmish with the patrol prompted a swift counterattack by light infantry companies from the 20th and 62nd and by two grenadier battalions from the 9th. Major Williams joined the 62nd with a pair of six-pounders, and the ships swept the meadows with gunfire. Maxwell hurried to Wayne's support, but his ranks broke, retreating "in such disorder," Irvine said, "that there was no possibility of rallying them." [18] Wayne, too, fell back. He was joined by Thompson with the other two divisions and Hartley's reserve. Several counterattacks were attempted, shots were traded at close range, but there could be no defense against ship-based artillery. "Under all those disadvantages our men would fight, but we had no ground for it," one officer would explain. "We had no covering, no artillery, and no prospect of succeeding, as the number of the enemy was so much superior to ours." [19] Thrown back into the swamp, Thompson tried to rally what men he could. Fewer than fifty responded. Within minutes, his entire command had broken ranks and dispersed.

Major Williams thought the Americans might have succeeded had they arrived an hour sooner. "The King of Prussia," he said, "when he had been on the brink of ruin never plann'd beter than what the Rebels did by endeavouring to Surprize the Troops, & burn the Shipping at the Three Rivers. Nothing but the 6 pounders prevented their Succeeding. Nay, had they not lost their road they would have been an hour sooner, & must have Carried their point." [20]

Denied access to the road, Thompson and his men struggled through the same swamps that Antoine Gautier had led them into a few hours before. Although ranks were broken, Wayne managed to assemble part of his command. When he spied a squad of British regulars, he would have attacked had his men been in any shape for it. At Pointe du Lac, St. Clair caught sight of Nesbitt's troops. The bateaux were gone. Warned of Nesbitt's approach, the guard had retreated to Sorel.

The men crossed Rivière du Loup and continued to Berthier, where they were picked up and ferried to Sullivan's encampment. They had not eaten since leaving Nicolet and had been devoured by mosquitoes that one sufferer described as of "Monsterous size and innumerable numbers." [21] Some had marched all night; others had grabbed a few hours' sleep while their comrades kept watch. "The mantle of Heaven was our only cover," one of them remembered. "No fire, and bad water our only food. We mounted a quarter-guard, fixed our alarm post, and made every man lay down ... I slept a little by resting my head on a cold bough of spruce." [22] Before they reached Berthier, more than 200 had been captured by enemy patrols. No one could be sure how many had been killed. One officer put the number at "between thirty and fifty," but Lieutenant Digby said that "upwards of 50 were found killed in the woods." British losses had been light. Carleton wrote Lord Germain that "Twelve or Thirteen soldiers only" had been killed or wounded.[23]

When Carleton reached Trois Rivières that night, he dismayed some of his officers by calling in a detachment sent to halt the enemy at Rivière du Loup. Professionals like Fraser and Nesbitt were baffled at his failure to put his seal on a resounding victory by cutting off the entire rebel detachment.

Among the prisoners were both Thompson and Irvine, who had turned themselves over to Colonel Nesbitt after facing certain capture. They had quickly realized their mistake. Nesbitt, no respecter of rebels, denied their request for a carriage or a pair of horses to take them to Trois Rivières, and lumped them with the rank and file for the six-mile march. His sole concession was to place them near the front of the long, closely guarded column. However, they fared better at headquarters. Both Carleton and Burgoyne received them cordially, showing them a proper respect and offering them refreshments, which were served by General Burgoyne himself.[24]

3

Although shaken by the defeat, Sullivan vowed to hold Sorel or die in the attempt. "I now think only of a glorious Death or a victory obtained against superior numbers," he wrote Schuyler.[25] In a letter to Washington he cited reports of large British reinforcements. "I am every Moment Inform'd of the Vast number of the Enemy which have arrived," he said. "Some Indeed Say that great Numbers have Arrived from England & all the Troops from Halifax; this I do not believe but I apprehend their numbers are now very Great." [26] His encampment, described by Dr. Senter as "a low, unhealthy place," teemed with smallpox patients.[27] Sullivan called it "the General Hospital of America." [28] Whole regiments were laid low. All of Greaton's and Bond's men were under inoculation; Stark had only forty fit for duty; Paterson, only six. "Out of eight thousand men that we have in this country," Arnold said, "not five thousand effectives can be mustered." [29]

Nevertheless, both Congress and the commander-in-chief expected Canada to be held. Sullivan was informed that "the Congress are fully convinced of the absolute necessity of keeping possession of that country." [30] He was told by Hancock that if

Canada was lost, the enemy would have a base from which to "harass the adjacent country" and make "the preservation of American liberty . . . much more difficult and precarious." [31] Washington urged a stand "as far down the river as possible." [32] "I hope our vigorous exertions will be attended with success, notwithstanding the present unpromising appearances," he wrote Sullivan, "and that we shall yet acquire and maintain possession of that country, so important to us in the present conflict." [33]

Arnold knew better. He urged that the army evacuate Canada and devote its energies to defending the adjacent colonies. "Shall we sacrifice the few men we have by endeavouring to keep possession of a small part of the country which can be of little or no service to us?" he wrote Sullivan. "The junction of the Canadians with the Colonies — an object which brought us into this country — is now at an end. Let us quit them, and secure our own country before it is too late." Lest he be thought faint-hearted, he declared himself "content to be the last man who quits this country, and fall, so that my country may rise." [34]

As if the sorry state of the campaign were not enough, Arnold was having his troubles with Moses Hazen. Before leaving Canada, the commissioners had directed Arnold to confiscate blankets, linens, and other merchandise from Montreal merchants and distribute them among the troops. He had issued certificates promising future payment for what was taken, but many of the parcels bore no other proof of ownership than the merchant's name. Having confiscated what was needed, he had directed a Major Scott to deliver the packages to Hazen, then commandant at Chambly. Hazen, still smarting from the tongue-lashing Arnold had given him at the strategy session at Ste. Anne, had refused house room to the merchandise. Instead of placing the packages under lock and key, he had left them on the river bank, where they were rifled by thieving soldiers. When Arnold heard what had happened, he accused Hazen of insubordination, arrogance, and habitual disobedience. "The guard was ordered to return," he wrote Sullivan, "and the goods to be delivered to Colonel Hazen to be stored. He refused receiving or taking care of any of them, by which means, and Major Scott's being ordered away, the goods have been opened and plundered,

I believe to a large amount. It is impossible for me to distinguish each man's goods, or ever settle with the proprietors . . . This is not the first or last order Colonel Hazen has disobeyed. I think him a man of too much consequence for the post he is in." [35] He made sure that Hazen received a copy of the letter. Hazen, equally irate, asked for a court-martial to clear his name.

In preparation for a retreat, Arnold urged Schuyler to begin construction of an inland navy and to send boats to St. Jean to evacuate the troops, whom he described as "sick, ragged, undisciplined and unofficered." [36] During a visit to St. Jean, he had found the frames of a British vessel that had been left on her stocks by Carleton's shipwrights. He had had the planks and timbers numbered and then sent to Crown Point. He hoped Schuyler would hurry them to completion.[37] "I make no doubt the enemy will pass Sorel," he said, "and as soon as in possession of Montreal, march immediately for St. Johns, and endeavour to cut off our retreat. All craft on your side of the Lake, in my opinion, ought immediately to be sent to St. Johns, and a number of gondolas built as soon as possible to guard the Lake. You may expect soon to hear of our evacuating Canada, or being prisoners." [38] This was on June 13.

That same day, British regulars were sighted on the north shore of the St. Lawrence — part of Simon Fraser's corps of 1200 men. At a hastily called staff meeting, Sullivan was warned by his colleagues to abandon Sorel or be prepared to take sole blame for what might occur. Both Hazen and Antill, who had much to lose, favored a retreat. Sullivan still wanted to hold out, even if it led to that "glorious death" mentioned in his letter to Schuyler, but after pondering the matter further he agreed, reluctantly, to a retreat. "I Soon found that however Strongly I might fortify Sorell my men would in general Leave me upon appearance of the Enemy," he wrote Schuyler.[39] Artillery, baggage, and supplies were loaded into bateaux. The campsite was picked clean — not a spade was left behind. The sick were started up the Richelieu by boat; the men fit for duty were ordered to follow them on shore. There was no time to notify the troops stationed at Berthier, who would have to escape by way of Montreal.

Carleton's fleet had lifted anchor on the 13th, fanning across the broad waters below Sorel in a cloud of canvas that stirred the heart of Lieutenant Enys. "Our fleet being now all together on Lake St. Peter made a Most beautyfull appearance," he wrote. "At the End of this Lake is a very great Number of Small Islands thro which the fleet were obliged to pass. I think it was one of the most Agreable prospects I ever saw, the Islands and Shiping being so interspersed one with another." [40] An officer of the 47th was similarly affected. "The object was the finest I ever beheld," he wrote. "Upwards of Eighty Sail, with near 8000 Troops on Board, appeared like a moving Forest." [41] Within an hour of Sullivan's leave-taking, an advance guard of British grenadiers and light infantry debarked at Sorel, followed by Nesbitt, now advanced to brigadier, with part of the 47th. Next morning Burgoyne came ashore with 4000 men and half a dozen fieldpieces. He had orders to pursue the retreating rebels cautiously, allowing Carleton time to land his troops farther up the St. Lawrence, cross to the Richelieu, and, it was hoped, intercept the enemy at St. Jean.

Carleton continued upstream with the fleet. Near Varennes, the wind dropped and he cast anchor. The Richelieu was only twelve miles away, but no road led to it from where he anchored. When the calm persisted he disembarked his troops and, after a night's rest, marched eight miles upstream — as far as he thought prudent for men who had just completed a long sea voyage in crowded transports. He was still more than forty miles from St. Jean. Although Burgoyne made faster time at first, his troops tired and he allowed them a day's rest at St. Denis. Lieutenant Digby has testified to "the great heat of the day" and to the men's fatigue, "owing chiefly to their being so long confined on ship board." [42]

Carleton was beset with supply problems. His commissary was inexperienced and short of trained assistants. Victualer *Swift*, carrying most of the provisions for Burgoyne's advance troops, had burned in the English Channel. Much of what came from England had spoiled during the weeks at sea. Flour had turned moldy, casks of pickled foods had sprung leaks. What reached Canada untainted was consumed by early summer, before most of the crops could be harvested. By scouring the countryside, the commissary managed to collect enough foodstuffs to keep the army on the move, but the necessity of feeding not only the regulars but also Canadian troops, Indians, ships' crews, and civilian assistants slowed the pace and intensified Carleton's innate caution. His commissary estimated that about 20,000 men had to be fed.[43]

Arnold was still unaware of the retreat and had ordered Captain James Wilkinson to deliver some messages to Sullivan. Wilkinson left for Sorel by bateau, beating into a head wind that caught his craft in an ugly swell and obliged him to keep close to the south shore. As he neared Varennes he heard two bursts of artillery fire. He beached his bateau and, with his men under arms, approached Varennes on foot. At a turn in the road, he caught sight of a platoon of British regulars. Taking cover in some woods, he chanced on an unattended horse, left his men in charge of a subordinate, and went on a gallop to Longueuil. By late afternoon he was at headquarters, breaking the news to Arnold.

Arnold had just learned of Sullivan's retreat. He was preparing to quit Montreal next morning, but after a few minutes with Wilkinson he ordered an immediate evacuation. Within two hours, his troops had crossed to Longueuil and were forming for the march to St. Jean. He sent Wilkinson to Chambly for reinforcements.

Wilkinson reached Chambly late that night and threaded his way through sleeping soldiers stretched on the grass outside the old stone fort. He was surprised that no sentries had been posted and that he was not challenged when he knocked at headquarters. He found Sullivan in conference with three colleagues. At first none would believe what Wilkinson told them, but after a few minutes he convinced them that the enemy was indeed at the threshold of Montreal. They directed him to seek out Baron de Woedtke, who had been assigned to the rear guard, and request him to detach 500 men.

It had begun to rain. Wilkinson lost his way in the rain and darkness and, abandoning his mount, continued the search on foot. In every farmhouse and outbuilding men were sleeping on floors and in entryways and haylofts. Toward daybreak, he learned that de Woedtke had wandered to the front and was probably drunk. He was advised to check with Anthony Wayne, who shared command of the rear guard with John Stark.

When Wilkinson located Wayne, he found him "as much at ease as if he was marching to a parade of exercise." Indeed, Wayne offered to lead the detachment himself and, posting guards at a bridge, buttonholed every man who crossed. In less than an hour, he had collected the 500 men and was ready to march. He would not go far before learning that Arnold was out of danger, but Wilkinson never forgot how quickly Wayne had raised the reinforcements and how eager the men were to serve under him. "By one of those caprices of the human mind which baffles inquiry," he said, "it was observable that those very men, who had been only the day before retreating in confusion before a division of the enemy, now marched with alacrity against his main body!" [44]

Before evacuating Chambly, Sullivan had his troops set fire to the fort and destroy all watercraft that could not be taken upstream. Three cannons had to be left behind, but he dismissed them as "bad pieces of ordnance at best." [45] He kept close to the bateau crews, who had come into a long surge of fast water. Some of the boats were loaded into carts and hauled overland. Others were wrestled upstream. Immersed to their armpits, the crews strained at towlines and heaved against a current that Colonel St. Clair likened to a churning millrace. Some locked their arms over gunwales and grappled with the boats, steadying them against the onrush, inching forward over slithery rocks and drowned tree trunks. Others guided the bateaux with long poles or pulled on towlines. Sullivan himself joined in, assisting at the towlines, shouting encouragement to his crews. Prodded by their commander, men with rope-burned hands and throbbing arm muscles struggled in the hot June sun until the last bateau was above the rapids. "But for the general's own personal exertions and directions it would not have been accomplished," St. Clair said. [46] With the rapids behind them, the bateau crews continued to St. Jean, followed by the men on foot. Colonel Porter and his Massachusetts regiment joined Stark and Wayne at the rear, poking up stragglers and pausing at intervals to scan the countryside for the telltale scarlet of Burgoyne's advance troops. They made sure that every bridge was demolished between Chambly and St. Jean.

Arnold was already at St. Jean. At a council of war, he and

Sullivan agreed that the army should fall back to Crown Point, behind the fleet on Lake Champlain. As at Chambly, Sullivan had the fort set on fire and ordered the destruction of all watercraft that could not be taken upstream. Two and a half tons of lead roofing were stripped from the stone house inside the fort, to be converted one day into bullets. Across the Richelieu, Moses Hazen's house was burned to the ground, together with its barns and outbuildings. The sick went first, followed by the men fit for duty. Although they did not know it, the last troops to leave were barely ahead of Lorimier and his Indians, who had hoped to intercept them while it was still light enough to take aim.

Before quitting St. Jean, Arnold made a final reconnoiter. He had reserved a boat for himself and Wilkinson. After the rear guard had gone, the pair readied their craft for a quick leave-taking, then mounted their horses and rode past the burning fort toward Chambly. Their eyes smarted in the smoke that stretched like a black veil across the road. They had not gone far when they caught sight of Burgoyne's advance troops. They could see the glint of bayonets and could distinguish the snug leather caps of the British light infantry. Wheeling about, they galloped back to the landing, where they were met by Chief Louis of the Caughnawagas. A friend of the Americans, he had come to wish them Godspeed.

Arnold stripped and shot his horse and ordered Wilkinson to do the same. Taking the saddles with them, the two climbed into their boat. It was Arnold who pushed the craft from shore, an act that would one day prompt Wilkinson to accuse him of having "indulged the vanity" of being the last American to leave mainland Canada.[47] Chief Louis waved them off before vanishing into the woods.

4

No one would forget the days at Ile aux Noix. Wilkinson described the wet little island with its malarial swamps and solitary farmhouse as "scarcely above the surface of the water."[48] Captain John Lacey of Pennsylvania noticed an ugly scum on the river that by noonday became "Peutrified by the heat of the Sun" and "very offensive to the smell." [49] Another officer said that the island, with its clutter of unsanitary campsites, "stunk enough to breed an infection." [50] Malaria and other ailments invalided many of the men, but it was smallpox that carried them off in droves. Dr. Samuel Meyrick, surgeon with a Massachusetts regiment, found the sick lying exposed to the hot sun and nighttime dews. His medicine chest was empty. "Great numbers could not stand, calling on us for help, and we had nothing to give them," he would remember. "It broke my heart, and I wept till I had no more power to weep." [51]

Language cannot describe nor imagination paint, the scenes of misery and distress the Soldiery endure, [wrote Dr. Lewis Beebe, a Connecticut surgeon]. Scarcely a tent upon this Isle but what contains one or more in distress and continually groaning, & calling for relief, but in vain! Requests of this Nature are as little regarded as the singing of Crickets in a Summers evening. The most shocking of all Spectacles was to see a large barn Crowded full of men with this disorder, many of which could not See, Speak, or walk — one nay two had large maggots, an inch long, Crawl out of their ears . . . No mortal will ever believe what these suffered unless they were eye witnesses.[52]

Captain Lacey visited an encampment that had been ravaged by smallpox. He found the sick crowded into foul-smelling tents or left unattended in the open. No doctors were in evidence, no medicines available. Lacey went to see the big, fly-buzzing pit where the dead were taken. The stench got to his stomach as he watched four soldiers bring a dead man from the encampment and toss him into the pit. They told Lacey that each night they covered the bodies with a few spadefuls of earth, starting another layer the next day.

Sullivan wrote Schuyler that his men were "Dropping off Like the Israelites before the Destroying Angel," that "Heaven Seems at present to frown upon us in this Quarter & take off those by pestilence who have Escaped the Sword." [53] But he remembered the expectations of Congress and the commander-in-chief, and he was reluctant to leave Ile aux Noix without the approval of a superior. He sent Arnold to consult with Schuyler at Crown Point and began to evacuate the sick, warning Schuyler to expect "the most Dismal Spectacle Ever furnished from one army in This Quarter of the Globe." [54] Colonel John Trumbull, a son of the Connecticut governor and subsequently an artist of wide repute, watched as the bateaux laden with sick men put in at Crown Point. "The boats were leaky and without awnings," he said. "The sick being laid on their bottoms without straw, were soon drenched in the filthy water of that peculiarly stagnant muddy lake, exposed to the burning sun of July, with no sustenance but raw pork, which was often rancid, and hard biscuit or unbaked flour; no drink but the vile water of the lake, modified perhaps, not corrected, by bad rum, and scarcely any medicine." [55]

Men who crossed to the mainland unarmed or in small groups risked being waylaid by Carleton's Indians. A foraging detail lost several of its number. A party of Pennsylvanians, crossing in search of spruce beer, was ambushed in a farmhouse. Four men were killed and scalped, six captured. "This happen'd in both cases for want of that care that Should ever be taken in an Enemys Country," Sullivan wrote Washington.[56] He was under mounting pressure to quit the death-ridden little island.

By the end of June, Sullivan felt authorized to evacuate Ile aux Noix, a measure urged by both Washington and Schuyler. Some of the men marched through the woods to embark in bateaux near the tip of Lake Champlain. Others made the long journey by boat. It took most of a week to get everyone to Crown Point, where Sullivan hoped his army would be restored to health. But the number of smallpox cases seemed to multiply. "Death is now become a daily visitant in the Camps . . . as Little regarded as the singing of birds," Dr. Beebe wrote. "The Generals have their hands full in riding about the camp — prancing their Gay horses. The Field officers set much of their time upon Court martials. The Capts. & Subs may generally be found at the grog shops, the Soldiers either sleeping, swimming, fishing, or Cursing and Swearing most generally the latter." He was troubled by the absence of religious orthodoxy. "In general the Regt. is composed of Deists, Arminians, and a few who ridicule the Bible, and everything of a sacred nature. In short they Laugh at death, mock at Hell and damnation; & even challenge the Deity to remove them out of this world by Thunder and Lightning." It was too much for the pious doctor. "God seems to be greatly angry with us," he said. "He appears to be incensed against us for our abominable wickedness." [57]

Colonel Trumbull, ordered to make a return of Sullivan's troops, found the army "so totally disorganized by the death or sickness of officers, that the distinction of regiments and corps was in a great degree lost." All ranks were crowded into the same tents, board shacks and brush lean-tos. "I did not look into a tent or hut," he said, "in which I did not find either a dead or dying man." He reported that out of 5200 men some 2800 were unfit for duty.[58]

Word of the retreat left the colonies stunned and disbelieving. Citizens wanted to know what had gone wrong, who was to blame, why more had not been done for the undersupplied and woefully handicapped army. A congressional committee attributed what had happened to the smallpox, to short enlistments, and to the lack of hard money.* Thomas Jefferson questioned the choice of commanders. Samuel Adams hinted at "secret Enemies" and "Seeds of Discord and Faction." John Adams cited the smallpox as a factor — "ten times more terrible than Britons, Canadians and Indians," he wrote Abigail. But he declared, too, that there were those "in high station and of great influence" who by their "slow and languid" response to the campaign had helped foster "obstructions, embarrassments and studied delays." He would never forgive the moderates, both in and out of Congress, whose hopes for a reconciliation with the mother country had slowed the war effort. Earlier in the spring, John Hancock had acknowledged the colonies' unpreparedness for the attempt on Canada. "We were compelled, unprepared, hastily to take up the weapons of self-preservation," he wrote Schuyler, "and have consequently had numberless difficulties to struggle with; of which the expedition into Canada has been a continued scene." [59] Isaac Senter, more qualified than most to speak, blamed the outcome on "an unpardonable neglect either in our commanders, in not giving Congress a true representation

---

* In 1776, Washington submitted a plan to enlist men for the duration of the war. The response was so poor, however, that a term of three years was permitted. Anything was preferable to the short enlistments that had plagued the American commanders throughout the Canadian campaign.

of the state of the army from time to time, or if so represented to them, the fault may be sought in the non-attention of the latter." [60]

Sullivan believed that he had brought off a praiseworthy retreat. "It is Seldom that an officer can Claim any merit from a Retreat & I am far from Laying in a Claim of the kind," he wrote Hancock, "yet it gives me Some Satisfaction That with all our Disadvantages we Saved the whole of the Publick Stores ... & Left not one of our Sick behind us. This I hope will at Least Convince Congress that we did not retreat in hurry & Confusion." [61] Nevertheless, he had no more than set foot on Crown Point when Congress notified him that he would be replaced by Major General Horatio Gates, a former British officer with a gift for administration. Deeply aggrieved, he left for Philadelphia, where he tendered his resignation from the Continental Army. He would be persuaded to rescind it, but the hurt lingered. He felt that he deserved something better from his country's leaders.

Sullivan had had his share of luck in extricating his pox-ridden army. If Carleton's fleet had not been becalmed, if Burgoyne had been given freer rein, if Carleton had succeeded in intercepting the retreating column, Sullivan might never have made it to Crown Point. But this does not detract from his handling of the retreat. Whatever Congress may have thought, he was appreciated by his field officers, including Wayne and Stark, who in a parting testimonial credited him with having "comforted, supported and protected the shattered remains of a debilitated army." [62]

XII

A Play for Time

1

CARLETON PUT GENERAL PHILLIPS in charge at St. Jean, which was turned into a bustling shipyard, with sailors and carpenters crowding the reactivated barracks and with new vessels on the ways. Phillips, by training an artilleryman, was assisted by several naval officers, including Captains Douglas and Pringle and Lieutenants James Dacres and John Schanck. Carleton already had the makings of a fleet. When Pringle had returned to England in the fall, he had relayed a request for boats, building materials, and shipwrights. The Admiralty had forwarded ten flat-bottomed boats, together with the marked sections of fourteen gunboats that could be reassembled in Canada. Although fewer than Carleton had hoped for, they were a start. Moreover, vessels in service on the St. Lawrence could be dismantled and brought in sections past the Chambly rapids.

During the summer, scouting parties reconnoitered on both sides of the border. Carleton's patrols ventured as far as Crown Point. Americans penetrated to Ile aux Noix and St. Jean. Sometimes shots were exchanged. A detail led by Captain James H. Craig of the 47th skirmished with the enemy on Isle La Motte, killing two Americans and capturing thirty. Late in July, Brigadier General

Patrick Gordon of the 29th was shot from ambush near St. Jean by an American, Lieutenant Benjamin Whitcomb of Bedel's command.* Outraged by what he deemed murder in cold blood, Carleton put a price on Whitcomb's head, but the New Hampshireman eluded capture and was advanced in rank.

In a general order on August 7, Carleton cautioned his troops against blaming "the Provincials at large" for the Gordon murder as well as for Congress's "late notorious breach of faith" in refusing to exchange British prisoners of war for the Americans taken at the Cedars. Both acts, he said, could be traced to the machinations of "a few wicked and designing men, who first deceived, then, step by step, misled the credulous multitudes to the brink of ruin, afterwards usurped authority over them, established a despotick tyranny not to be borne, and now wantonly and foolishly endeavour to provoke the spilling the blood of our unhappy countrymen of this Continent, in hopes of covering their own guilt, or confirming their Tyranny by the general destruction of their Country." [1] He continued to believe that a small knot of agitators and opportunists was responsible for the Revolution.

Carleton spent a busy summer tending to the affairs of both the army and the provincial government. He discharged his Canadian militia, cantoned his regulars in villages bordering the Richelieu, designated Chambly as a supply depot, and posted Simon Fraser, now a brigadier, at Ile aux Noix with the advance troops. He reorganized the provincial courts and filled vacancies on the Council. At Montreal, he met with delegations of friendly Indians and welcomed Sir John Johnson and 200 recruits from the Mohawk Valley. Johnson, who said the valley teemed with loyalists, was authorized to raise a battalion that would be known as the King's Royal Regiment of New York.

Carleton appointed commissions in both Montreal and Quebec to circulate through the parishes, inquire into the conduct of suspected collaborators, rescind military commissions issued by the rebels, and replace doubtful militia captains with men known to be

* Carleton lost two brigadiers during the campaign. William Nesbitt, advanced with Gordon and Simon Fraser from lieutenant colonel, died of natural causes at Quebec.

loyal. He chose his commissioners with care — Saint-Georges Du-pré, Pierre Panet, and Edward William Gray in Montreal, François Baby, Gabriel Taschereau, and Jenkin Williams in Quebec, all men of high repute. After weeks of interrogation they would learn that the great majority of *habitants* had remained neutral during the conflict and that only a minority had given active support to either side. The findings confirmed Carleton's belief that for most Canadians the ties with Britain were tenuous at best. "As to my opinion of the Canadians," he wrote Lord Germain, "I think there is nothing to fear from them while we are in a state of prosperity, and nothing to hope for when in distress. I speak of the people at large; there are some among them who are guided by sentiments of honour, but the multitude is influenced by hopes of gain, or fear of punishment." [2]

Losing no opportunity to support the governor, Bishop Briand chastised the collaborators in pastorals and from the pulpit and ruled that they repent or be denied the sacraments. He accused them of violating their oaths and informing on their countrymen, of insulting their clergy and disobeying their bishop, of theft and arson. Most of the collaborators submitted to his edict and recanted publicly in the presence of their clergy and the local congregation, but a hard core refused. Years afterward, isolated gravestones could be seen in some of the parishes, reminders that there had been those who had defied their bishop to the death and been consigned in perpetuity to unconsecrated ground.

Much of the governor's time was spent with his naval officers and shipwrights. Although pleased with their progress, he feared that he was already too late to push deep into the colonies in support of General Howe. "Unfortunately the season is so far advanced," he wrote Germain, "that I dare not flatter myself we shall be able to do more this summer than to draw off their [the colonists'] attention and keep back part of their forces from General Howe, who, I doubt not, is exerting himself to the southward tho' I have heard nothing from him since he left Halifax." [3] The summer had its reward, however. In July, he was nominated for knighthood, an honor accorded him by a grateful homeland, although in the judgment of at least a few at Whitehall, "some parts of his conduct

were doubtful." [4] He had saved Quebec, but there were those who
blamed him for the escape of the rebel army.

In taking over from Sullivan, General Gates had been promised
nearly dictatorial powers. Ambitious and not above political ma-
neuvering, he was a favorite with New Englanders. His command
was disputed, however, by Philip Schuyler, who maintained that it
was contingent on the army's still being in Canada. Now that the
troops had crossed into New York, Schuyler laid claim to the supreme command by virtue of his position as head of the Northern
Department. Happily, Gates acquiesced when Congress upheld
Schuyler, thereby resolving what could have become another disruptive quarrel in the high command. Schuyler would supply the
army while keeping watch on Sir John Johnson and his Tory ad-
herents on the Mohawk. Gates would take charge on Lake Champlain.

Early in July, Schuyler and Gates called a council of war to
debate whether to hold Crown Point. Arnold was present, and
Sullivan, still in the vicinity nursing his wounded feelings, and
Baron de Woedtke, with his memories of happier campaigning under Frederick the Great. All agreed that Crown Point was obsolete
and should be evacuated. Their decision was warmly disputed by
Colonel Stark and some of the other field officers. Even Washington was dismayed, until Schuyler persuaded him that Crown Point
was indeed a burned-out ruin and could be by-passed by a fleet
ascending the lake from Canada.

Colonel Trumbull, who was at Crown Point when it was evacuated, was appalled at the condition of the troops:

At this place I found not an army but a mob [he wrote his father],
the shattered remains of twelve or fifteen very fine battalions, ruined
by sickness, fatigue, and desertion, and void of every idea of discipline
or subordination... We have now three thousand sick, and about the
same number well; this leaves five thousand to be accounted for. Of
these, the enemy has cost us perhaps one, sickness another thousand,
and the others, God alone knows in what manner they are disposed of.
Among the few we have remaining, there is neither order, subordination, nor harmony; the officers as well as men of one colony, insulting
and quarreling with those of another. [5]

Gates had the sick transferred to the military hospital at Fort George, where they were crowded into malodorous, ill-ventilated wards. Chaplains Robbins and Spring circulated among the beds, comforting the apprehensive, praying over the very ill. "Never saw such a portrait of human misery," Robbins wrote. "Deaths have been about five a day, for some days past." Late in July, Baron de Woedtke was brought to the hospital. Mortally ill, he lay all but unnoticed among the rank and file. He begged Robbins and Spring to give him the last rites of the Church, but neither felt authorized to accommodate him. "I endeavoured to show him that God did not require it," Robbins said. Apparently, the dying baron was too weak to press the matter.[6]

Like Crown Point, Fort Ticonderoga had been built to repulse an attack from the south and now faced in the wrong direction. It was in serious disrepair, although by no means to the same degree as the scorched ruin at Crown Point. Moreover, Schuyler pointed out that he had "no men, and, I would add, no implements, even to put Ticonderoga in a state of defence."[7] Across the narrows, however, facing Ticonderoga, was a craggy, cedar-studded promontory that looked north. Bounded by deep water on both north and west, by a swamp and creek to the east, and with access on the south to Skenesboro and the New Hampshire Grants, it rose — in places almost perpendicularly — to a plateau that would allow a clear line of fire and accommodate extensive battleworks. Early in July, Schuyler and Gates inspected the site with Colonel Jeduthan Baldwin, the engineer who had accompanied Thompson's brigade with a detail of artificers. They liked what they saw, and Baldwin was ordered to clear and fortify the promontory.

With a crew of more than 200, Baldwin laid out an artillery park, began work on a redoubt, and chose the site for a barbette battery. On the west shore, he improved defenses and started new fortifications that would command the portage to Lake George. Troops were hurried north to man the forts. Four regiments of Continentals, several artillery units, and eight militia regiments, including a company of Stockbridge Indians, checked in during the summer.

On July 18, word spread that Congress had declared the colonies

a free and independent nation. Ten days later, a copy of the Declaration of Independence was brought by courier from Philadelphia.
Colonel St. Clair read it to the assembled troops. When he finished,
a salute of thirteen guns echoed off the mountains, and men who
had retreated from Canada in rags and misery broke into three
reverberating cheers. The freshly cleared promontory, soon to
bristle with fortifications, was named Mount Independence.[8]

It was an irksome July for Arnold. Moses Hazen had his court-
martial and won acquittal. The court had refused to admit the
testimony of Major Scott, Arnold's star witness, declaring him
an interested party, even though it was he who had delivered the
confiscated goods to Hazen. When Arnold denounced the ruling
as "unprecedented" and "unjust," Colonel Enoch Poor, president of
the court, asked for an apology. This, Arnold would not make.
Reminding the court that it was "not infallible," he offered to take
on any of its members, as soon as the war was ended, with dueling
pistols. "As your very nice and delicate honour, in your apprehension, is injured," he told them, "you may depend, as soon as this
disagreeable service is at an end (which God grant may soon be the
case) I will by no means withhold from any gentleman of the
Court the satisfaction his nice honour may require."

Poor and his colleagues demanded Arnold's arrest for contempt,
charging that "the whole of the General's conduct during the
course of the trial was marked with contempt and disrespect" and
that "by his extraordinary answer he has added insult to injury."
Gates did not arrest Arnold, but he sent a transcript of the proceedings to Congress. In a letter to John Hancock, he acknowledged
that "the warmth of General Arnold's temper might possibly lead
him a little further than is marked by the precise line of decorum to
be observed before and towards a Court-Martial," but he left no
doubt that he needed Arnold on Lake Champlain. "The United
States must not be deprived of that excellent officer's services at
this important moment," he wrote Hancock.[9]

Congress took no action on the court-martial. Hazen and John
Brown, however, continued to malign Arnold, accusing him of
having confiscated the merchandise for his own profit and causing
him so much grief that he asked for a court of inquiry to clear his

name. "I cannot but think it extremely cruel," he wrote Gates, "when I have sacrificed my ease, health, and a great part of my private property, in the cause of my country, to be calumniated as a robber and a thief — at a time, too, when I have it not in my power to be heard in my own defense." [10] He was eventually exonerated, but there were those in Congress who questioned his fitness for higher rank.

2

Schuyler had picked Skenesboro as his shipyard, turning it into the American counterpart of St. Jean. The humid, mosquito-infested hamlet at the southernmost tip of Lake Champlain, once the base of operations for Philip Skene and his Tory retainers, was well endowed for the purpose, with timbered hillsides, two sawmills, and a forge. Schuyler had put thirty men to work felling trees, reactivating the mills, and laying the keel for the first gondola. He had appointed a bumbling Dutchman, one Jacobus Wyncoop, commander of the fleet, but he was depending increasingly on Arnold, whose drive won the plaudits of both Washington and himself. "The enemy . . . will doubtless become masters of the Lake," Arnold had written the commander-in-chief, "unless every nerve on our part is strained to exceed them in a naval armament." [11]

David Waterbury, formerly with Montgomery and now a brigadier, was put in charge at Skenesboro. High wages and hard money were needed to attract carpenters from the seacoast, where shipwrights received unheard-of sums for building privateers. By offering as much as five dollars a day, Waterbury had assembled about 200 carpenters by late July. Many of the men were soon sidelined with malaria and other ailments — one day in August only ten showed up out of a company of fifty. Waterbury was plagued, too, with dawdlers who allowed half-built vessels to linger on the stocks. Gates complained about "the laziness of the artificers" and "the neglect of those whose duty it is to see them diligent in their work." [12] To speed the effort, he named Arnold commander of the fleet, although no one seems to have informed Jacobus Wyncoop.

Arnold drove the men twelve and fourteen hours a day, ending idleness and keeping a close check on sick leaves. When he was not riding herd on his shipwrights, he bombarded Schuyler with requests for oakum, pitch and tar, for sailcloth and cordage, for cables and anchors, guns and ammunition. Somehow, Schuyler managed to come up with what was needed, calling on both Congress and the neighboring states, and the fleet took shape, to the hum of saws and ring of axes.

Arnold had three ships already in service: *Enterprise*, the sloop he had captured at St. Jean before the start of the campaign; schooner *Liberty*, formerly Philip Skene's and confiscated by some of Ethan Allen's men; and schooner *Royal Savage*, salvaged at St. Jean by Montgomery's troops. A third schooner, *Revenge*, was still on the stocks at Fort Ticonderoga. Four new row-galleys would be his mainstays. Christened *Washington, Congress, Trumbull*, and *Gates*, each measured some seventy feet in length, was of shallow draft, and had twin masts and lateen sails, a rig introduced on Lake Champlain by the French. Each carried eight or ten guns, including twelve- and eighteen-pounders and several swivels. A smaller galley, *Lee*, nearly forty-four feet long and cutter-rigged, was constructed from the frames that Arnold had numbered and sent in sections from St. Jean. She carried a twelve-pounder, five lighter guns, and swivels. There were eight gondolas — *New York, Jersey, Connecticut, Philadelphia, New Haven, Boston, Providence,* and *Spitfire* — flat-bottomed, single-masted craft that were able to sail only before the wind and at other times had to be propelled with oars. Each carried a twelve-pounder in her bow, two nine-pounders amidships, and several swivels.

Arnold assembled his fleet at Crown Point. "The carpenters go on with great spirit," he wrote Schuyler on August 8. "Eight gondolas will be completed in a few days. One row-galley is gone to Ticonderoga and will soon be fitted and armed." [13] To man his ships, he sent recruiting officers to New England seaports, only to learn that men making fat profits aboard privateers could not be lured to his inland navy and that most of his sailors must be drafted from the ranks. The schooners and sloop called for large crews, each row-galley needed eighty men, a gondola required forty-five men to pull at the oars and work the guns. Arnold had to take what he could get, although presently he would implore Gates to spare him further "land lubbers." [14] "We have a wretched, motley crew in the fleet," he complained, "the marines the refuse of every regiment, and the seamen few of them ever wet with salt water." [15] All his ships were undermanned. "I am much surprised so little attention is paid us by the good people below," he said. "I should have imagined two hundred seamen could have been sent us in three or four months, after they were so pressingly wrote for." [16] But even appeals to patriotism could not lure men from the privateers.

Jacobus Wyncoop, who still deemed himself commodore of the fleet, paced the quarter-deck of his flagship, *Royal Savage*. When two schooners left Crown Point without his knowledge, to check on enemy activities, he fired across their bows. "I know of no orders but what shall be given out by me, except sailing orders from the commander-in-chief," he announced. "If the enemy is approaching I am to be acquainted with it, and know how to act in my station." As soon as Arnold heard what had happened, he boarded *Royal Savage* and, in language no eavesdropper would forget, informed Wyncoop that he was no longer in charge on Lake Champlain and was as subject to orders as any other subordinate. "You must surely be out of your senses to say no orders shall be obeyed but yours," he added in a stiff letter.[17] Wyncoop was hustled off to Albany. "Although I believe him brave," Schuyler said, "yet I do not think him equal to the command of such a fleet as we now have." [18] Everyone looked to Arnold.

In late August, Arnold cruised northward with eleven sail. Although short of food, ammunition, and men, he was anxious to reconnoiter the lower lake and keep watch on the enemy. A day out of Crown Point, he ran into gale winds that drove him back through the narrows and forced him to find shelter in an inlet. *Spitfire*, separated from the fleet, rode out the storm on the open lake, battling waves that must have chilled the hearts of the landlubbers who manned her. Arnold had given her up for lost when she hove in sight under full sail, to all appearances unscarred.

When the storm subsided, Arnold dispatched scouts to spy on

Carleton's shipyard. He believed the presence of his fleet could discourage the enemy from venturing into the lake. "I hope no time will be lost in forwarding the three galleys," he wrote Gates. "When they have joined us, I am very confident the enemy will not dare attempt crossing the lake." [19] One of the scouts was the same Benjamin Whitcomb who had killed General Gordon. Another, Eli Stiles, followed Whitcomb to Canada a day later.

After permitting his men a pig roast embellished with wine and hard cider, Arnold set sail for the far tip of the lake. At Isle La Motte, he sent a work crew ashore to cut fascines. As the men left their bateau and started into the woods, they were met by a burst of musket fire. All got back to the bateau, but offshore they were caught in a stream of bullets that killed three of their number and wounded six. Arnold immediately ordered the island searched. A laced beaver hat was picked up, carrying a button stamped with the mark of the 47th Foot, but there was no sign of the enemy.

Although Gates had warned him to avoid any "wanton risk or unnecessary display of the power of the fleet," Arnold continued nearly to the Richelieu, where he was joined by an additional gondola and by *Lee*, his smallest galley, and where he formed his ships in a battle line across the channel.[20] During the night, he could see the play of lanterns on shore and suspected that the enemy were readying batteries. He withdrew his fleet when early daylight revealed several felled trees within artillery range of the lake.

Off Isle La Motte, Arnold was rejoined by his scouts. Whitcomb had two British regulars in tow. Sullen and uncommunicative, they conceded that a ship mounting twenty guns was under construction at St. Jean. Eli Stiles reported two vessels launched, a third nearly planked. Two professed allies brought even grimmer news. Antoine Girard, who had just come from St. Jean, spoke of a floating battery, two schooners mounting a dozen twelve-pounders each, four gondolas, and a whole fleet of bateaux. Thomas Day, a deserter from the Royal Highland Emigrants, said that two schooners had been brought overland from the St. Lawrence and that a floating battery, now on the stocks, would mount two dozen eighteen-pounders as well as mortars.

The reports convinced Arnold that the enemy had the firepower to annihilate his fleet. He had sent scouts to reconnoiter Valcour Island, located off the west shore nearly halfway up the lake. They had described it as a secluded harbor, and he wrote Gates that he would retreat to Valcour and lie in wait for the enemy. "I intend first fair wind to come up as high as Isle Valcour," he said, "where is a good harbour, and where we shall have the advantage of attacking the enemy in the open lake, where the row-galleys, as their motion is quick, will give us a great advantage over the enemy; and if there are too many for us we can retire." [21] He asked for fifty more sailors, "three or four good gunners," and several swivels. And he needed warm clothing for his men. "The season is coming on severe," he wrote, "and more so on the water than land." He could do with "a watch-coat or blanket and one shirt" for each man.[22] As he set sail from Isle La Motte, he ordered *Liberty* to reconnoiter the lower lake and rejoin the fleet near Cumberland Head.

During her reconnoiter, *Liberty* was hailed from shore by a solitary white man, who asked to be taken aboard. The captain lowered a boat, boarding it himself with a small crew, but became suspicious as he scrutinized the man, who had waded out into the lake to beckon them in. He ordered his crew to stop rowing. A sudden volley struck the boat, wounding three of his oarsmen. As his crew pulled toward the schooner, a large number of regulars and Indians showed themselves on the beach, but their shots fell short and the boat reached *Liberty* without being hit again.

Arnold found Valcour Island a strategic hiding place, with wooded bluffs that concealed his fleet on the north. "We are moored in a small bay on the west side of the island, as near together as possible," he wrote Gates, "and in such a form that few vessels can attack us at the same time, and those will be exposed to the fire of the whole fleet." [23] The big row-galleys were slow in coming, and as the days passed and the headlands flamed with autumn color, he wrote Gates that "the want of those galleys may decide the contest against us." [24] *Trumbull* was the first to arrive, joining the fleet in late September but so weakly armed that Arnold assigned her two four-pounders and three swivels from schooner *Liberty*. *Congress* and *Washington* followed. *Gates*, the last of the galleys, was

still under construction in early October, and *Liberty*, sent to Ticonderoga for supplies, had not yet returned. Arnold assigned
Washington to General Waterbury, his second in command. He
was still short of sailors, and those he had, shivered in the cold. "I
hope to be excused," he wrote Gates, "if with five hundred men,
half naked, I should not be able to beat the enemy with seven thousand men, well clothed, and a naval force, by the best accounts, near
equal to ours." [25]

3

Carleton's shipwrights had turned out a fleet that included *Carleton*, a schooner mounting twelve guns; schooner *Maria*, named for
the governor's lady and mounting fourteen guns; *Loyal Convert*,
an American gondola captured on the St. Lawrence and mounting
six nine-pounders; and a ponderous floating battery, radeau *Thunderer*, manned by a crew of 300 and mounting six twenty-four-
pounders, six twelve-pounders, and two howitzers. *Inflexible*, a
ship-rigged sloop-of-war brought in sections from the St. Lawrence,
was reassembled at St. Jean under the supervision of her commander, Lieutenant John Schanck. Carleton had waited four extra
weeks to include her in his armada.

On October 4, watchboats led the British ships into the widening
corridor of Lake Champlain. Because the lake must first be cleared
of enemy vessels, General Burgoyne debarked his troops near Point
au Fer on the west shore. The men took advantage of the wait to
feast on passenger pigeons culled from the huge flocks winging
southward. One day they heard Arnold's crews scaling artillery —
exploding small charges of powder to remove rust from gun barrels.
They watched as *Inflexible* made her appearance a few days after
the other vessels. She looked incongruous, Lieutenant Digby said,
on "a fresh water lake in the very heart of the Continent of America & so great a distance from the sea." [26] Her eighteen twelve-
pounders followed in flat-bottomed boats. They were to be
mounted when she reached deeper water, where she would not risk
touching bottom under the added weight.

Early on the 11th, the fleet debouched onto the lake, commanded by Captain Pringle, who had designated *Maria* as his flagship. Together with *Carleton* and *Inflexible*, *Maria* led the armada, powered by a north wind. Twenty gunboats came next, each with a cannon in her bow, followed by four longboats and a fleet of bateaux bringing supplies. Bobbing in their wake were war canoes packed with Carleton's Indians. *Loyal Convert* and *Thunderer* trailed, the radeau wallowing far astern. Units from the 29th served as marines aboard the larger ships, and artillerymen, both British and German, had been assigned to the gunboats. Carleton had no counterparts of the "wretched, motley crew" that Arnold complained of.

Dr. Robert Knox, an army surgeon, shared *Maria*'s quarterdeck with Carleton and Captain Pringle. About ten that morning, he spied a sail off Valcour Island, a white flutter that quickly vanished. A boat was lowered. When it rounded the tip of the island, its crew fired a warning shot and hurriedly put about. Pringle signaled his fleet and, tacking to starboard, caught sight of Arnold's entire squadron formed in a tight crescent across the channel between Valcour and the mainland. He tried to beat upwind but failed to bring his ship within artillery range. As he tacked repeatedly, a schooner he recognized as *Royal Savage* nosed from the channel with three smaller craft.

Pringle's gunboats took after *Royal Savage* like angry birds of prey while *Inflexible* splintered her mast and bowsprit with three solid hits. The schooner yawed to leeward. Pursued closely by the gunboats, she was run ashore and abandoned by her green crew. Subsequently, Lieutenant Edward Longcroft, captain of *Loyal Convert*, boarded her with a small task force and, turning her guns on the enemy, maintained a brisk cannonade until driven off by artillery fire that killed three of his men.

As the Indians swarmed from their canoes to fire from both shores, Pringle's gunboats spread across the mouth of the channel, advancing to open fire, dropping back to redeploy. Arnold's gondolas joined with the enemy, sometimes with telling effect. As Captain George Pausch was sighting his cannon aboard a German gunboat, an explosion ripped through a craft commanded by Captain Dufais, a fellow Hessian, and manned in part by German gunners. Speeding to its side, Pausch found that a chance shot had exploded the magazine. Three men were dead; a fourth had lost a leg. He pulled the survivors aboard his already crowded gunboat and hurried them away.

Of Pringle's larger vessels, only *Carleton* managed to beat upwind into the channel. Her commander, Lieutenant James Dacres, fought Arnold's fleet at close quarters, taking punishment that severed *Carleton*'s aft cable and left two feet of water in her hold. After trading broadsides for nearly an hour, Dacres was knocked senseless by a head wound. Eight of his men had been killed, six wounded. The command devolved on Edward Pellew, a young midshipman who, like Dacres, would one day advance to admiral and leave his mark in naval annals. When the jib fouled, Pellew crawled to the tip of the bowsprit and struggled to release the foresail amid a flurry of gunfire. Two longboats approached, sent to his aid by Lieutenant Schanck of *Inflexible*. Pellew tossed a line from the bowsprit, and *Carleton* was towed out of artillery range.

Late in the afternoon, *Inflexible* beat upwind far enough to hurl five broadsides at Arnold's squadron, then fell back as Pringle formed his ships across the mouth of the channel. He had locked in the enemy fleet, as he supposed, until morning, when he was sure Arnold would surrender. He ordered *Royal Savage* set afire where she lay beached on Valcour Island. She went up in a swirl of flame, steam billowing from her waterline.

Pringle had had comparatively few casualties. Although he had lost a gunboat, of his larger ships only *Carleton* was severely damaged. Arnold's losses were much greater, with about sixty killed and wounded. *Washington* reported her first lieutenant killed, her captain wounded. Of the officers aboard *New York*, only the captain remained alive. *Washington* had been hulled repeatedly. "The *Congress*," Arnold reported, "received seven shot between wind and water; was hulled a dozen times; had her mainmast wounded in two places, and her yard in one." [27] One gondola, *Philadelphia*, hulled by a twenty-four-pound shot, sank that evening.*

Arnold had noted a gap between Pringle's battle line and the

* *Philadelphia* was raised in 1935 and is now at the Smithsonian.

mainland. A night fog had begun to shroud the channel, and he proposed trying to slip through the gap, which was large enough to permit the passage of ships in single file. Arnold's captains agreed that the attempt should be made, however dim its prospects. At seven that evening, oars were muffled. Lights were extinguished except a hooded lantern at the stern of each ship, to guide those that followed. *Trumbull* led the way, commanded by Colonel Edward Wigglesworth. She passed noiselessly through the gap, spectral in the fog and darkness. The gondolas and smaller vessels followed, edging close to shore, with *Congress* and *Washington* coming last. Unchallenged, they slipped one by one past the British fleet. By daybreak, all fourteen were off Schuyler's Island, eight miles south, where the crews spent the morning mending canvas, making what repairs they could, and scuttling two shot-ridden gondolas.

At midday Arnold lifted anchor and beat upwind. Soon his crews had to man the oars, rowing most of the afternoon and throughout the night. At daybreak he was still twenty-eight miles below Crown Point. He could see enemy ships astern, gaining steadily. Carleton, who had been frustrated the preceding day by head winds, awoke on the morning of the 13th to a northeast gust. Fickle wind conditions denied Arnold a similar assist, and he looked on helplessly as the gap narrowed between his limping fleet and the fast-moving enemy ships. Off Split Rock, Carleton's swiftest under sail, *Maria*, *Carleton*, and *Inflexible*, overhauled *Washington*, slowed by her battering at Valcour Island. Arnold watched from his quarterdeck as the wallowing row-galley took three mighty broadsides and struck her colors. *Lee* fared no better. Cut off and closely pressed, she was run ashore by her crew.

Inflexible and the two schooners turned the full weight of their artillery on Arnold's flagship. "We were then attacked in the *Congress* galley," he would report, "by a ship mounting twelve eighteen-pounders, a schooner of fourteen sixes, and one of twelve sixes, two under our stern, and one on our broadside, within musket shot." [28] Chased through the narrows of the lake, *Congress* fought all three of her pursuers, with round shot and grape whistling across her decks. Arnold took charge of the artillery, shouting orders to his inexperienced gunners, often working the guns himself. More than a third of his men were killed or wounded. Hulled in many places, her canvas cut to ribbons, *Congress* won time for four ships that had gone ahead. *Trumbull, Revenge, Enterprise,* and one gondola made it to Crown Point.

Arnold was determined that his flagship would never strike her colors. After a pounding of more than two hours, he broke free of the British ships and, signaling his four remaining gondolas, steered for the east shore. Head winds slowed the enemy, and, by dint of hard rowing, he herded the gondolas into a shallow cove, where he ordered his men to abandon ship. *Congress* and the gondolas were then set afire. He kept his men in formation until the fire had engulfed *Congress* and consumed the flag still fluttering at her masthead. Then he and his weary sailors struck off through the woods for Crown Point.*

4

The campaign for Canada ended on the lake. Sir Guy Carleton showed his customary indulgence toward American prisoners of war, sharing his table with General Waterbury and returning all 110 officers and men to Fort Ticonderoga on condition that they refrain from further military service until formally exchanged. The prisoners spoke so warmly of their treatment that Gates hurried them off before they contaminated some of his none too resolute militiamen.

Carleton remained on the upper lake another two weeks, his fleet immobilized by adverse winds. A detachment from Simon Fraser's advance corps reconnoitered Ticonderoga and found both forts aswarm with troops. "Ticonderoga must have had a very imposing aspect that day, when viewed from the lake," Colonel Trumbull said. "The whole summit of cleared land, on both sides of the lake,

---

* A rumor would circulate through the British army that Arnold had left his wounded to perish aboard the abandoned ships. General Riedesel heard it from General Phillips. In his account of the battle, Dr. Knox, the surgeon aboard Pringle's flagship, accused Arnold of "burning the wounded and sick."²⁹ There is no mention of this in American sources.

was crowned with a splendid show of artillery and flags. The number of troops under arms that day (principally however militia) exceeded thirteen thousand." [30] Early in November, Carleton set sail for the Richelieu with his entire fleet. The risks involved in storming the forts, compounded by the approach of winter and by logistical problems of appalling scope, had discouraged him from attempting further military action in 1776. He considered establishing a toehold at Crown Point but decided against posting troops in that ruined bastion so many snow-swept miles from the Richelieu.

Apparently Carleton never questioned the soundness of his course. He was not sure that the forts could be taken before the descent of winter or, if won, that they could be supplied and held. He lacked the draft animals to transport provisions and haul artillery in a push southward and had already advised Lord Germain that he could give no more than peripheral support to General Howe. He had accomplished what he set out to do — ridding Canada of the invader, gaining control of Lake Champlain, and tying down troops that otherwise could have reinforced Washington in southern New York, where Howe had won the battle of Long Island and occupied New York City.

Nevertheless, there were those who disagreed, both in the military and at Whitehall. Burgoyne and Phillips had hoped for something more. Policy-makers at home would accuse him of excessive caution — particularly Lord Germain, who would assign the command of next year's expedition to Burgoyne. Nor could Carleton foresee that his failure to take the forts and his inability to push southward would allow the Americans a whole year of grace, crucial to the success of the Revolution. By compelling the British to assemble their own armada, the shipwrights at Skenesboro had won their fellow countrymen an extra summer. By waiting for *Inflexible* to leave the ways, Carleton had handed the enemy four additional weeks. General Riedesel believed that if the British had left the Richelieu only a month earlier, Ticonderoga would have fallen.

Billeting his troops on both shores of the St. Lawrence and on the Richelieu below Chambly, Sir Guy Carleton hastened to Quebec, where he was reunited with Lady Maria and the children, now back from England. He received the plaudits of his thankful subjects, none of whom was more jubilant than Bishop Briand. As the year neared its end, the bishop ordered solemn high mass with a sung Te Deum for December 31, the first anniversary of Montgomery's defeat. On that winter morning, the cathedral blazed with candles. Every pew was filled, and members of the Quebec militia came in a body. At the bishop's bidding, twelve erstwhile collaborators were herded to a cleared space at the church door, each with a knotted rope around his neck. When mass was finished, the twelve implored the forgiveness of God and of King George the Third, their act of contrition witnessed by all who flowed past them into the street.[31] It was a sight the faithful would not readily forget.

NOTES

BIBLIOGRAPHY

Notes

Full information about sources will be found in the Bibliography.

Chapter I

(*pages 1–20*)
1. *Quebec Gazette,* September 22, 1774.
2. Public Archives of Canada, Q, X, p. 120.
3. Ibid., V, p. 260.
4. Archives of the Archbishopric of Quebec, *Copies des Lettres,* III, p. 503.
5. Henry Cavendish, *Debates of the House of Commons,* p. 102.
6. Ibid., p. 106.
7. Ibid., pp. 288–90.
8. Justin H. Smith, *Our Struggle for the Fourteenth Colony,* I, p. 74; Reginald Coupland, *The Quebec Act,* pp. 102–103.
9. W. P. M. Kennedy, ed., *Statutes, Treaties and Documents,* pp. 156–59.
10. Public Archives of Canada, Q, X, p. 120.
11. Ibid., p. 122.
12. A. Shortt and A. G. Doughty, eds., *Documents Relating to the Constitutional History of Canada, 1759–91,* p. 668.
13. Francis Masères, *Additional papers,* p. 375.
14. Public Archives of Canada, Q, XI, p. 290.
15. A. Shortt and A. G. Doughty, p. 458.
16. Public Archives of Canada, Shelburne Correspondence, LXVI, pp. 32–33.
17. *Journal of the Continental Congress,* September 17, 1774.
18. Peter Force, ed., *American Archives,* 4, II, p. 1556.
19. Charles H. Metzger, *The Quebec Act,* pp. 109–110.
20. Charles F. Adams, ed., *The Works of John Adams,* III, pp. 448–64.
21. Ibid., II, p. 395.
22. Lyman H. Butterfield, ed., *Adams Family Correspondence,* I, p. 147.
23. Frederick L. Gay, *Gay Transcripts of Material in the Public Record Office, London, 1630–1776,* XIII, pp. 104–105.

24. Harold C. Syrett and Jacob E. Cooke, eds., *Papers of Alexander Hamilton*, I, pp. 68, 175.
25. *Journal of the Continental Congress*, October 21, 1774.
26. Ibid., October 26, 1774.
27. H. A. Cushing, ed., *The Writings of Samuel Adams*, III, pp. 182–88.
28. Public Archives of Canada, Q, XI, p. 167.
29. Lucius E. Chittenden, *The Capture of Ticonderoga*, Letter of John Brown to Boston Committee of Correspondence, pp. 97–99.

CHAPTER II

(pages 21–42)

1. *Connecticut Historical Society Collections*, I, Journal of Captain Edward Mott, p. 171.
2. Allen French, *The Taking of Ticonderoga in 1775*, p. 53.
3. Ethan Allen, *Narrative*, p. 9.
4. *Conn. Hist. Soc. Coll.*, I, Journal of Captain Edward Mott, p. 172.
5. Force, *American Archives*, 4, II, p. 645.
6. Ibid.; "Benedict Arnold's Regimental Memorandum Book," *Pennsylvania Magazine of History*, VIII, pp. 367–68.
7. *Journal of the Continental Congress*, May 18, 1775.
8. Force, *American Archives*, 4, II, pp. 732–33.
9. Ibid., p. 735.
10. Ibid., p. 714.
11. Ibid., p. 733.
12. Ibid., pp. 976–77.
13. Ibid., pp. 1085–87.
14. Ibid., p. 1087.
15. *Conn. Hist. Soc. Coll.*, I, p. 247.
16. *Proceedings of the Massachusetts Historical Society*, First Series, XII, pp. 226–27.
17. E. C. Burnett, ed., *Letters of Members of the Continental Congress, August 29, 1774–July 4, 1776*, p. 113.
18. Public Archives of Canada, Q, XI, pp. 233–34.
19. Jared Sparks Manuscripts, XXIX, pp. 284–85.
20. Force, *American Archives*, 4, II, p. 1133.
21. *Journal of the Continental Congress*, May 29, 1775.
22. Public Archives of Canada, Q, XI, p. 184.
23. *Journal of the Massachusetts Provincial Congress*, pp. 751–52.
24. *Journal of the Continental Congress*, June 27, 1775.
25. "Letterbook of Philip Schuyler," Philip Schuyler Papers, June 28, 1775, to February 24, 1776: Schuyler to Wooster, July 3, 1775.
26. Public Archives of Canada, Q, XI, p. 184.
27. Colonial Office 42/34, Carleton to Dartmouth, June 7, 1775, Public Record Office, London.
28. *Quebec Gazette*, June 15, 1775.
29. H.-A. Verreau, ed., *Invasion du Canada*, p. 39.
30. Ibid., p. 54; Masères, *Additional papers*, pp. 76–77.

31. Verreau, pp. 170–71; Masères, *Additional papers*, pp. 77–78.
32. Archives of the Archbishopric of Quebec, *Copies des Lettres:* Montgolfier à Briand, November 1775.
33. Verreau, p. 168.
34. Henri Têtu and C. O. Gagnon, eds., *Mandements, Lettres Pastorales et Circulaires des Evêques de Québec*, II, pp. 264–65.
35. Masères, *Additional papers*, pp. 112–17.
36. Public Archives of Canada, Claus Papers, I, p. 209.
37. Ernest Cruikshank, ed., *A History of the Organization, Development and Services of the Military and Naval Forces of Canada*, II, pp. 96–99.
38. Gage Papers: Gage to Carleton, June 3, 1775.
39. Public Archives of Canada, Q, XI, p. 267.
40. Force, *American Archives*, 4, III, pp. 493–95.
41. Ibid., II, pp. 1880–83.
42. Ibid., p. 1123.
43. Ibid., pp. 891–93.
44. Ibid., pp. 1594–96.
45. Ibid., p. 315.

Chapter III

(*pages 43–61*)
1. Force, *American Archives*, 4, II, pp. 1685–86.
2. Ibid., p. 1668.
3. Ibid., pp. 1788–89.
4. Jared Sparks, ed., *Correspondence of the American Revolution*, I, pp. 13–16.
5. Force, *American Archives*, 4, III, p. 1527, and 4, II, p. 1734.
6. For a definitive study of the New York regiments and their supply problems, see Alan and Barbara Aimone, "Organizing and Equipping Montgomery's Yorkers in 1775," *Military Collector and Historian*, XXVIII, no. 2.
7. John Armstrong, *Life of Richard Montgomery*, p. 191.
8. Livingston Papers, Richard Montgomery to Robert R. Livingston, August 6, 1775.
9. John C. Fitzpatrick, ed., *The Writings of George Washington*, III, pp. 436–39.
10. Force, *American Archives*, 4, III, pp. 442–30.
11. Bayze Wells, "Journal," *Conn. Hist. Soc. Coll.*, VII, pp. 241–48.
12. Force, *American Archives*, 4, III, pp. 135–36; *Boston Gazette*, September 18, 1775.
13. Force, *American Archives*, 4, III, p. 468.
14. Philip Schuyler Papers, Montgomery to Schuyler, August 25, 1775.
15. Force, *American Archives*, 4, III, pp. 442–43.
16. Rudolphus Ritzema, "Journal," *Magazine of American History*, I, pp. 98–107.
17. Public Archives of Canada, Q, XI, p. 258; Force, *American Archives*, 4, III, p. 671.

18. Verreau, pp. 248–49.
19. Ritzema, p. 99.
20. Force, *American Archives*, 4, III, pp. 669–70.
21. Ibid., p. 740.
22. Ibid., pp. 743–44.
23. Ibid., pp. 740–41.
24. *Bulletin of Fort Ticonderoga Museum*, I, no. 1, p. 17.
25. Catharina V. R. Bonney, *A Legacy of Historical Gleanings*, p. 44.
26. Harry Parker Ward, ed., *Follett-Dewey-Fassett-Safford Ancestry*, p. 216.
27. Sparks, *Correspondence of the American Revolution*, I, pp. 53–54.
28. Thomas Jones, *History of New York During the Revolutionary War*, p. 342.
29. H. P. Ward, p. 217.
30. Force, *American Archives*, 4, III, p. 797.
31. H. P. Ward, p. 217.
32. Force, *American Archives*, 4, III, p. 797.
33. Verreau, p. 45.
34. Force, *American Archives*, 4, III, p. 754.
35. A. Shortt and A. G. Doughty, p. 459.
36. Force, *American Archives*, 4, II, p. 1649.
37. Ethan Allen, p. 16.
38. Ibid., pp. 12–28, for Ethan's account of his capture.
39. Mrs. Thomas Walker, "Journal," Collections of the *New Hampshire Antiquarian Society*, II, pp. 45–52.
40. Louise L. Hunt, *Biographical Notes concerning General Richard Montgomery*, pp. 12–13.
41. Force, *American Archives*, 4, III, pp. 952–53.
42. Ibid., pp. 953–54.
43. Ibid., pp. 951–52.
44. Verreau, pp. 54–55.
45. Public Archives of Canada, Q, XI, pp. 267, 274.
46. Gustave Lanctot, *Canada and the American Revolution*, p. 85.
47. Ibid., p. 84.

CHAPTER IV

(*pages 62–81*)
1. Public Record Office, London, W. O. 34, Murray to Amherst, August 2, 1761.
2. Justin H. Smith, *Arnold's March from Cambridge to Quebec*, pp. 75–76.
3. Force, *American Archives*, 4, III, pp. 761, 763.
4. Justin H. Smith, *Arnold's March*, p. 56.
5. Kenneth Roberts, ed., *March to Quebec*, Morison, pp. 507–508.
6. Justin H. Smith, *Our Struggle*, I, p. 511.
7. Roberts, *March to Quebec*, Henry, p. 302.
8. North Callahan, *Daniel Morgan, Ranger of the Revolution*, p. 25.

9. John Quincy Adams, *Life in a New England Town*, *1787–88*, p. 63.
10. Herbert S. Parnet and Marie B. Hecht, *Aaron Burr, Portrait of an Ambitious Man*, p. 18.
11. Force, *American Archives*, 4, III, pp. 765–67.
12. Ibid., p. 764; Fitzpatrick, *Writings of George Washington*, III, pp. 478–80.
13. Force, *American Archives*, 4, III, pp. 213–14.
14. Roberts, *March to Quebec*, Stocking, p. 546.
15. Ibid., Fobes, p. 581.
16. Force, *American Archives*, 4, III, p. 960.
17. Ibid., pp. 961–62.
18. Justin H. Smith, *Arnold's March*, pp. 80–81.
19. Force, *American Archives*, 4, III, p. 960.
20. Ibid., pp. 1084–85.
21. Roberts, *March to Quebec*, Senter, p. 199.
22. Parnet and Hecht, p. 21.
23. Roberts, *March to Quebec*, Henry, p. 303.
24. Force, *American Archives*, 4, III, pp. 960–61.
25. *Maine Historical Society Collections*, I, pp. 357–58; Roberts, *March to Quebec*, Arnold, p. 67.
26. Roberts, *March to Quebec*, Senter, pp. 200–201.
27. *Maine Hist. Soc. Coll.*, I, p. 362; Roberts, *March to Quebec*, Arnold, pp. 71–73.
28. Roberts, *March to Quebec*, Haskell, p. 474.
29. Ibid., Stocking, p. 548.
30. Ibid., Thayer, p. 250.
31. Ibid., Morison, p. 511.
32. Ibid., Morison, p. 514.
33. Ibid., Arnold, pp. 49–50.
34. Ibid., Senter, p. 205.
35. *Maine Hist. Soc. Coll.*, I, pp. 359–62; Roberts, *March to Quebec*, Arnold, pp. 69–71.
36. Roberts, Arnold, p. 51.
37. *Maine Hist. Soc. Coll.*, I, pp. 362–63; Roberts, *March to Quebec*, Arnold, p. 73.
38. Roberts, *March to Quebec*, Henry, p. 309.
39. Ibid., Morison, p. 515.
40. Ibid., Arnold, p. 52; Montresor, p. 20.
41. Ibid., Senter, pp. 207–208.
42. Ibid., Morison, pp. 515–16.
43. Ibid., Senter, pp. 209–210.
44. Ibid., Arnold, p. 55.
45. Ibid., Stocking, p. 551.
46. Ibid., Thayer, p. 256.
47. *Maine Hist. Soc. Coll.*, I, pp. 364–65; Roberts, *March to Quebec*, Arnold, pp. 75–76.
48. Roberts, *March to Quebec*, Senter, p. 210.
49. Ibid., Thayer, p. 257.

50. Ibid., Stocking, p. 552.
51. Ibid., Dearborn, p. 137.
52. *Maine Hist. Soc. Coll.*, I, pp. 370–71; Roberts, *March to Quebec*, Arnold, pp. 82–84.
53. Roberts, *March to Quebec*, pp. 642–45.

CHAPTER V

(pages 82–100)

1. Livingston Papers, 1775–77, p. 51, Montgomery to Robert R. Livingston, October 5, 1775.
2. Force, *American Archives*, 4, III, pp. 135–36.
3. Benjamin Trumbull, "A Concise Journal or Minutes of the Principal Movements Towards St. John's," *Conn. Hist. Soc. Coll.*, VII, p. 146.
4. Force, *American Archives*, 4, III, p. 1124.
5. Hunt, p. 13.
6. Force, *American Archives*, 4, III, p. 826.
7. Ibid., p. 1094.
8. *Conn. Hist. Soc. Coll.*, II, p. 288.
9. Force, *American Archives*, 4, III, p. 972.
10. Ritzema, p. 101.
11. *Report of Public Archives of Canada for 1914–15*, App. B, pp. 21–22.
12. Justin H. Smith, *Our Struggle*, I, p. 432.
13. Force, *American Archives*, 4, III, p. 1197.
14. Ibid., p. 1374.
15. Sparks, *Correspondence of the American Revolution*, I, pp. 469–71.
16. Henry Livingston, "Journal," *Pennsylvania Magazine of History and Biography*, XXII, pp. 16–17.
17. While researching *The Traitor and the Spy*, James T. Flexner identified the handwriting in the journal as André's. I had pages from the journal and samples of André's handwriting professionally analyzed. All the documents were declared to have been written by the same person, John André.
18. Public Archives of Canada, M.G., B 43, Samuel Mackay Papers, p. 2.
19. *Report of Public Archives of Canada for 1914–15*, App. B, p. 18.
20. Ibid., p. 19.
21. Ibid., pp. 20–21.
22. Ibid., pp. 22–23.
23. Ibid., pp. 10–12.
24. Force, *American Archives*, 4, III, pp. 1195–96.
25. Cruikshank, *Military and Naval Forces of Canada*, II, pp. 104–105.
26. Masères, *Additional papers*, p. 92.
27. Force, *American Archives*, 4, III, pp. 962–63.
28. Hunt, pp. 13–14.
29. Force, *American Archives*, 4, III, p. 1132.
30. Ibid., p. 1195.
31. Verreau, p. 60.

32. Ibid., pp. 259–62.
33. H. P. Ward, pp. 223–28; Verreau, pp. 65–66, 230–33, 260–62.
34. Ritzema, p. 102.
35. Cruikshank, *Military and Naval Forces of Canada*, II, p. 114.
36. *Report of Public Archives of Canada for 1914–15*, App. B, p. 15–17.
37. Force, *American Archives*, 4, III, pp. 15–17.
38. *Report of Public Archives of Canada for 1914–15*, App. B, p. 25.
39. Force, *American Archives*, 4, III, p. 1401.
40. Benjamin Trumbull, p. 159.
41. Force, *American Archives*, 4, III, pp. 1207–08.
42. Ibid., pp. 1596–97.
43. Public Archives of Canada, Q, XI, p. 274.
44. Ibid., p. 323.
45. Ibid., Sir John Hamilton Papers, M.G. 23, B 11; Verreau, pp. 176–77; *Gentlemen's Magazine*, 1776, p. 39.
46. Lewis A. Leonard, *Life of Charles Carroll of Carrollton*, p. 309.
47. Hunt, p. 15.
48. Verreau, pp. 79–82; Force, *American Archives*, 4, III, p. 1597.
49. Force, *American Archives*, 4, III, pp. 1597–98.
50. Benjamin Trumbull, p. 164.
51. Force, *American Archives*, 4, III, pp. 973–74.
52. Ibid., p. 1695.
53. Ibid., pp. 1683–84.
54. Benjamin Trumbull, p. 166.
55. Ritzema, p. 103.
56. Force, *American Archives*, 4, III, pp. 1681–82.
57. Benjamin Trumbull, pp. 160, 167.
58. Force, *American Archives*, 4, III, p. 1603.
59. Hunt, pp. 14–15.
60. Force, *American Archives*, 4, III, pp. 1638–39.
61. Roberts, *March to Quebec*, Arnold, pp. 82–84; Force, *American Archives* 4, III, p. 1634.
62. Hunt, p. 15.

CHAPTER VI

(*pages 101–120*)
1. Roberts, *March to Quebec*, Arnold, p. 57.
2. Ibid., Morison, p. 523.
3. Ibid., Arnold, p. 58.
4. Ibid, Arnold, p. 59.
5. *Maine Hist. Soc. Coll.*, I, pp. 366–67; Roberts, *March to Quebec*, Arnold, pp. 77–78.
6. *Maine Hist. Soc. Coll.* I, pp. 367–68; Roberts, *March to Quebec*, Arnold, pp. 79–80.
7. Roberts, *March to Quebec*, Arnold, p. 60.
8. Ibid., Senter, p. 213.

9. Ibid., Morison, p. 523.
10. Ibid., Henry, pp. 335–36.
11. Ibid., Senter, pp. 215, 218.
12. Ibid., Dearborn, p. 137.
13. Ibid., Henry, pp. 336–38; Stocking, p. 556.
14. Ibid., Stocking, p. 554.
15. Ibid., Thayer, p. 259.
16. Ibid., Stocking, p. 554.
17. Ibid., Stocking, p. 554.
18. Ibid., Senter, p. 217.
19. Ibid., Meigs, p. 181.
20. Ibid., Stocking, p. 555; Morison, p. 526.
21. Ibid., Senter, p. 219.
22. Ibid., Morison, p. 526.
23. Ibid., Stocking, p. 556; Fobes, p. 608.
24. Ibid., Senter, p. 219.
25. Ibid., Henry, p. 346.
26. Ibid., Dearborn, p. 141.
27. *Maine Hist. Soc. Coll.*, I, pp. 368–69; Roberts, *March to Quebec*, Arnold, pp. 80–81.
28. Roberts, *March to Quebec*, Senter, pp. 220–21.
29. Ibid., Morison, p. 531.
30. Ibid., Senter, p. 222.
31. *Maine Hist. Soc. Coll.*, I, pp. 370–71; Roberts, *March to Quebec*, Arnold, pp. 82–84.
32. *Quebec Gazette*, October 5, 1775; Cruikshank, *Military and Naval Forces of Canada*, II, p. 85.
33. A. Shortt and A. G. Doughty, pp. 455–56.
34. Sheldon S. Cohen, ed., *Canada Preserved*, p. 19.
35. Masères, *Additional papers*, pp. 102–103; Cruikshank, *Military and Naval Forces of Canada*, II, p. 121.
36. Cohen, *Canada Preserved*, pp. 20–21.
37. Masères, *Additional papers*, pp. 101, 107; Cruikshank, *Military and Naval Forces of Canada*, II, pp. 121–22.
38. *Dalhousie Review*, XLVII, no. 1, p. 60; Henry Caldwell Letter, Literary and Historical Society of Quebec, *Historical Documents*, Second Series, pp. 4–5; Cohen, *Canada Preserved*, p. 21.
39. Cohen, *Canada Preserved*, p. 23.
40. Public Archives of Canada, Q, XI, pp. 349–50; Cruikshank, *Military and Naval Forces of Canada*, II, pp. 132–33.
41. Roberts, *March to Quebec*, Henry, p. 352.
42. Caldwell, Letter, p. 6.
43. *Maine Hist. Soc. Coll.*, I, p. 376; Roberts, *March to Quebec*, Arnold, pp. 89–90.
44. *Maine Hist. Soc. Coll.*, I, p. 375; Roberts, *March to Quebec*, Arnold, pp. 88–89.
45. Public Archives of Canada, Q, XI, pp. 342–44; Cruikshank, *Military and Naval Forces of Canada*, II, pp. 128–29.

46. Roberts, *March to Quebec*, Henry, pp. 356–60.
47. *Maine Hist. Soc. Coll.*, I, pp. 379–80; Roberts, *March to Quebec*, Arnold, pp. 93–94.
48. *Maine Hist. Soc. Coll.*, I, pp. 377–79; Roberts, *March to Quebec*, Arnold, p. 101.
49. *Maine Hist. Soc. Coll.*, I, p. 386; Roberts, *March to Quebec*, Arnold, pp. 90–92.
50. Force, *American Archives*, 4, III, pp. 1639–40.

Chapter VII
(*pages 121–142*)
1. Roberts, *March to Quebec*, Thayer, p. 270.
2. Ibid., Morison, p. 534.
3. Force, *American Archives*, 4, IV, p. 189.
4. Ibid.
5. Public Archives of Canada, Q, XII, pp. 18–19; Cruikshank, *Military and Naval Forces of Canada*, II, pp. 136–37.
6. *Quebec Gazette*, March 21, 1776; Cruikshank, *Military and Naval Forces of Canada*, II, p. 138.
7. Public Archives of Canada, Q, XII, pp. 18–19; Cruikshank, *Military and Naval Forces of Canada*, II, pp. 136–37.
8. Public Archives of Canada, Q, XI, p. 318; Cruikshank, *Military and Naval Forces of Canada*, II, pp. 133–34.
9. Cohen, *Canada Preserved*, p. 28.
10. Ibid., pp. 27, 29.
11. Roberts, *March to Quebec*, Fobes, p. 588.
12. W. T. P. Shortt, ed., *Journal of the Principal Occurrences During the Siege of Quebec*, p. 5.
13. Cohen, *Canada Preserved*, p. 29.
14. W. T. P. Shortt, p. 7.
15. Cohen, *Canada Preserved*, p. 30.
16. Ibid.
17. Roberts, *March to Quebec*, Henry, p. 374.
18. Force, *American Archives*, 4, IV, pp. 464–65.
19. Roberts, *March to Quebec*, Senter, p. 231.
20. *Almon's Remembrancer*, 1776, part I, p. 134; Force, *American Archives*, 4, IV, pp. 202–203.
21. Force, *American Archives*, 4, IV, pp. 442–60.
22. Ibid., III, pp. 1717–18.
23. Ibid., IV, pp. 309–310.
24. Ibid., III, pp. 1717–18.
25. Sparks Manuscripts, no. 52, II, p. 60: Montgomery to Wooster, December 16, 1775.
26. Roberts, *March to Quebec*, Stocking, p. 562.
27. Public Archives of Canada, Q, XII, pp. 20–21; Cruikshank, *Military and Naval Forces of Canada*, II, p. 137.

28. Force, *American Archives*, 4, IV, p. 290.
29. Roberts, *March to Quebec*, Morison, p. 535.
30. Cohen, *Canada Preserved*, p. 32.
31. Roberts, *March to Quebec*, Thayer, p. 273.
32. Cohen, *Canada Preserved*, pp. 31–32; W. T. P. Shortt, pp. 17–20.
33. Cohen, *Canada Preserved*, p. 27.
34. Ibid., pp. 37–38.
35. James M. LeMoine, *Quebec Past and Present*, p. 210.
36. Force, *American Archives*, 4, IV, pp. 706–707.
37. Hunt, p. 16.
38. Force, *American Archives*, 4, IV, pp. 188–90.
39. Roberts, *March to Quebec*, Henry, p. 375.
40. Livingston Papers, 1775–76, p. 145: Donald Campbell to Robert R. Livingston, March 28, 1776.
41. Ibid.
42. Roberts, *March to Quebec*, Henry, p. 376.
43. Ibid., p. 377.
44. Caldwell, Letter, p. 10.
45. Roberts, *March to Quebec*, Dearborn, p. 150.
46. W. T. P. Shortt, pp. 30–31.
47. James Graham, *Life of General Daniel Morgan*, p. 103.
48. Robert R. Livingston Papers, 1775–76, p. 145; Donald Campbell to Robert R. Livingston, March 28, 1776.
49. "Chalmers Journal," Sparks Manuscripts, no. 42, p. 19.
50. Caldwell, Letter, p. 13.
51. Roberts, *March to Quebec*, Arnold, pp. 102–109.
52. Cohen, *Canada Preserved*, pp. 36–37.
53. W. T. P. Shortt, p. 33.

CHAPTER VIII

(*pages 143–167*)
1. Roberts, *March to Quebec*, Arnold, p. 105.
2. Ibid., p. 108.
3. Force, *American Archives*, 4, IV, pp. 668–70.
4. Ibid., p. 805.
5. Fitzpatrick, *The Writings of George Washington*, IV, p. 255.
6. Force, *American Archives*, 4, IV, p. 1681, as quoted in the oration by the Reverend William Smith.
7. Fitzpatrick, *The Writings of George Washington*, IV, pp. 123–27.
8. Ibid., p. 76.
9. Force, *American Archives*, 4, IV, p. 188.
10. *Journal of the Continental Congress*, January 19–22, 1776.
11. Force, *American Archives*, 4, IV, pp. 1675–83.
12. *Journal of the Continental Congress*, January 24, 1776.
13. Force, *American Archives*, 4, III, pp. 1011–13.

14. Edmund C. Burnett, ed., *Letters of Members of the Continental Congress*, I, p. 354.
15. Annabelle M. Melville, *John Carroll of Baltimore*, p. 44, Charles Lee to John Hancock, February 27, 1776.
16. Charles F. Adams, ed., *The Works of John Adams*, III, p. 36.
17. *Journal of the Continental Congress*, March 20, 1776.
18. Ibid.
19. Thomas O. Hanley, ed., *The John Carroll Papers*, I, p. 46.
20. Force, *American Archives*, 4, IV, p. 588.
21. Justin H. Smith, *Our Struggle*, II, p. 186.
22. H. P. Ward, p. 243.
23. Force, *American Archives*, 4, IV, pp. 869–70.
24. Ammi Robbins, *Journal*, p. 3.
25. Force, *American Archives*, 4, IV, p. 781.
26. Sgt. Samuel Hodgkinson, Letter: "Before Quebec, 1776," *Pennsylvania Magazine*, X, p. 159.
27. Force, *American Archives*, 4, IV, pp. 813, 897.
28. Ibid., p. 1146.
29. Cruikshank, *Military and Naval Forces of Canada*, II, pp. 145–46.
30. Ibid., p. 141.
31. Force, *American Archives*, 4, IV, p. 874; Fitzpatrick, *The Writings of George Washington*, IV, p. 281.
32. Cohen, *Canada Preserved*, pp. 45, 48.
33. Ibid., p. 44.
34. Roberts, *March to Quebec*, Haskell, p. 487.
35. Ibid., pp. 487, 489, 490.
36. Force, *American Archives*, 4, IV, p. 1147.
37. Cohen, *Canada Preserved*, p. 50.
38. Force, *American Archives*, 4, V, pp. 549–50.
39. Seth Warner Papers, *Proceedings of the Vermont Historical Society*, XI, no. 2, pp. 111–12.
40. Fitzpatrick, *The Writings of George Washington*, III, p. 495.
41. Justin H. Smith, *Our Struggle*, II, pp. 235–37.
42. Public Archives of Canada, Haldimand Papers, MG 21, vol. B 27, Antill to Hazen, March 28, 1776.
43. *Quebec Gazette*, October 5, 1775.
44. Force, *American Archives*, 4, V, pp. 751–53.
45. Verreau, p. 196.
46. Force, *American Archives*, 4, IV, pp. 751–53.
47. Roberts, *March to Quebec*, Haskell, pp. 488–89.
48. Force, *American Archives*, 4, IV, pp. 907–908.
49. J. E. A. Smith, *History of Pittsfield, Massachusetts*, I, p. 259.
50. Cruikshank, *Military and Naval Forces of Canada*, II, pp. 139–40.
51. Force, *American Archives*, 4, IV, pp. 601–03.
52. *Continental Congress Papers*, no. 41, III, p. 151, Judge John Fraser Memorial.
53. Force, *American Archives*, 4, IV, p. 796.
54. Ibid., V, p. 481.

55. Ibid., IV, pp. 851–52, 1001–04.
56. Auguste Gosselin, *L'Eglise du Canada après la Conquête,* II, pp. 72–73.
57. Lanctot, pp. 118–19.
58. Verreau, pp. 103–105.
59. Ibid., pp. 105–106.
60. Lanctot, pp. 130–31; "Journal of the Baby-Taschereau-Williams Commission," *Rapport de l'Archiviste de la Province de Québec,* 1927–28, pp. 435–99; and 1929–30, pp. 138–40.
61. Roberts, *March to Quebec,* Dearborn, p. 158.
62. Force, *American Archives,* 4, V, pp. 549–50.
63. Cohen, *Canada Preserved,* pp. 71–72.
64. Force, *American Archives,* 4, V, pp. 1098–99.
65. Ibid.

CHAPTER IX

(pages 168–187)

1. Caldwell, Letter, p. 14.
2. Cohen, *Canada Preserved,* p. 54.
3. "Journal of the Siege and Blockade of Quebec," Literary and Historical Society of Quebec, *Historical Documents,* Fourth Series, p. 23.
4. Cohen, *Canada Preserved,* p. 95.
5. Ibid., p. 86.
6. Justin H. Smith, *Our Struggle,* II, p. 248.
7. Roberts, *March to Quebec,* Henry, pp. 392–93; Morison, p. 538.
8. Cohen, *Canada Preserved,* p. 41.
9. Roberts, *March to Quebec,* Henry, p. 408.
10. Ibid., Fobes, p. 595.
11. Ibid., Henry, p. 409.
12. W. T. P. Shortt, p. 76.
13. Ibid., pp. 77–78.
14. William Heth, "Diary," *Annual Papers of Winchester, Virginia, Historical Society,* I, p. 46.
15. Cohen, *Canada Preserved,* pp. 75, 83; "Journal of the Siege and Blockade of Quebec," p. 23.
16. Cohen, *Canada Preserved,* p. 77.
17. Ibid., p. 81.
18. W. T. P. Shortt, p. 87.
19. Heth, p. 45.
20. Cohen, *Canada Preserved,* p. 81.
21. "Journal of the Siege and Blockade of Quebec," p. 21.
22. Cohen, *Canada Preserved,* p. 55.
23. Ibid., p. 82.
24. Ibid., p. 88.
25. Elizabeth Cometti, ed., *The American Journals of Lt. John Enys,* pp. 3–5.

26. William J. Morgan, ed., *Naval Documents of the American Revolution*, IV, p. 1451.

27. Cohen, *Canada Preserved*, p. 88.

28. "Journal of the Most Remarkable Occurrences in Quebec," *New-York Historical Society Collections*, III, 1880, p. 235.

29. Cometti, p. 12.

30. Public Archives of Canada, M.G. 13, W.O. 1, II, part 2, Maclean to Barrington, May 21, 1776.

31. Robbins, p. 17.

32. Cohen, *Canada Preserved*, p. 91.

33. Cruikshank, *Military and Naval Forces of Canada*, II, p. 157; Public Archives of Canada, Q, XII, p. 7.

34. Caldwell, Letter, p. 18.

35. Cruikshank, *Military and Naval Forces of Canada*, II, p. 152.

36. Ibid., p. 155; *Quebec Gazette*, May 12, 1776; Cohen, *Canada Preserved*, p. 95.

37. Cohen, *Canada Preserved*, p. 95.

38. Cruikshank, *Military and Naval Forces of Canada*, II, p. 152.

39. Roberts, *March to Quebec*, Thayer, p. 287.

40. Ibid., p. 283.

41. Ibid., Henry, p. 413.

42. Callahan, p. 112; Henry Lee, *Memoirs of the War in the Southern Department of the United States*, p. 429.

43. Roberts, *March to Quebec*, Dearborn, p. 161.

44. Andrew Parke, *An Authentic Narrative of Facts Relating to the Exchange of Prisoners Taken at the Cedars*, p. 18.

45. Callahan, p. 115; Jared Sparks, ed., *The Writings of George Washington*, III, p. 268.

46. Force, *American Archives*, 4, V, p. 84.

47. Ibid., p. 822.

48. Ibid., p. 1104.

49. Ibid., p. 1166.

50. Ibid., VI, pp. 453–54, 589.

51. Roberts, *March to Quebec*, Senter, p. 238.

52. Force, *American Archives*, 4, VI, p. 453.

53. Ibid., pp. 453–54.

54. Roberts, *March to Quebec*, Senter, p. 238.

55. Elisha Porter, "Diary," ed. by Appleton Morgan, *Magazine of American History*, XXX, pp. 192–93.

56. Roberts, *March to Quebec*, Senter, p. 239.

57. Force, *American Archives*, 4, VI, p. 454.

58. Ibid., pp. 398–99.

59. Robbins, pp. 17–20.

60. Force, *American Archives*, 4, VI, p. 389.

61. Ibid., pp. 588–89.

62. Ibid.

63. Ibid., p. 481.

64. Ibid., p. 592.

65. Ibid.

CHAPTER X

(*pages 188–208*)
1. Hanley, *John Carroll Papers*, I, p. 47.
2. Leonard, p. 279.
3. Ibid., p. 281.
4. Ellen H. Smith, *Charles Carroll of Carrollton*, p. 140.
5. Leonard, p. 282.
6. Ibid., p. 284.
7. Ibid., p. 285.
8. Ellen H. Smith, p. 141.
9. Leonard, p. 295.
10. Ibid., p. 296.
11. Hanley, *John Carroll Papers*, I, p. 47.
12. Leonard, p. 306.
13. Ellen H. Smith, p. 146.
14. Force, *American Archives*, 4, V, pp. 1166, 1237; VI, p. 558.
15. *Journal of the Continental Congress*, March 20, 1776.
16. Robbins, pp. 13, 15.
17. Force, *American Archives*, 4, VI, pp. 450–51.
18. Melville, p. 52.
19. Ellen H. Smith, p. 150.
20. Kate M. Rowland, *The Life of Charles Carroll of Carrollton*, pp. 159–60.
21. Force, *American Archives*, 4, V, p. 1214.
22. Ibid., VI, pp. 587–88.
23. Ibid., V, p. 753.
24. Ibid., p. 752.
25. George F. G. Stanley, *Canada Invaded, 1775–1776*, pp. 117–18; Verreau, p. 81.
26. *Journal of the Continental Congress*, March 20, 1776.
27. Force, *American Archives*, 4, VI, p. 580.
28. Cruikshank, *Military and Naval Forces of Canada*, II, p. 146.
29. Bedel Papers, New Hampshire Historical Society, p. 40.
30. Zephaniah Shepardson, "Journal," pp. 3, 5.
31. Bedel Papers, p. 40.
32. Parke, p. 21.
33. Shepardson, p. 7.
34. Parke, p. 23.
35. Shepardson, p. 9.
36. Parke, p. 25.
37. Shepardson, p. 12.
38. Parke, p. 26.
39. Force, *American Archives*, 4, VI, pp. 598–99.
40. Verreau, pp. 278–79.
41. Force, *American Archives*, 4, VI, pp. 598–99.
42. Parke, p. 28.
43. Benjamin Stevens, "Journal," p. 10.
44. Shepardson, p. 13.
45. Parke, pp. 31–34.

46. James Wilkinson, *Memoirs of My Own Times*, I, pp. 43–44.
47. Force, *American Archives*, 4, VI, pp. 595–96.
48. Ibid.
49. Shepardson, p. 15.
50. Wilkinson, *Memoirs*, I, p. 45.
51. Force, *American Archives*, 4, VI, pp. 595–96.
52. Wilkinson, *Memoirs*, I, p. 45.
53. Ibid., p. 46.
54. Force, *American Archives*, 4, VI, pp. 595–96.
55. Parke, p. 36.
56. Ibid., p. 37.
57. Shepardson, p. 17.
58. Parke, pp. 37–38.
59. Wilkinson, *Memoirs*, I, pp. 47–48.
60. Force, *American Archives*, 5, I, p. 165.
61. Ibid., 4, VI, pp. 592, 596, and 5, I, pp. 1571–73; Benjamin Stevens, p. 12; Shepardson, p. 17.
62. Parke, pp. 35–36.
63. Cruikshank, *Military and Naval Forces of Canada*, II, pp. 185–86; Public Archives of Canada, Q, 12, pp. 230–32.
64. Fitzpatrick, *The Writings of George Washington*, V, p. 130.
65. Charles F. Adams, *The Works of John Adams*, IX, p. 407.
66. Ibid., III, p. 399.
67. Force, *American Archives*, 5, I, pp. 1571–73.
68. Thomas Jones, *History of New York during the Revolutionary War*, p. 94.
69. Cruikshank, *Military and Naval Forces of Canada*, II, p. 182.
70. Bedel Papers, p. 40.
71. Force, *American Archives*, 5, I, p. 801.
72. Cruikshank, *Military and Naval Forces of Canada*, II, pp. 185–86; Public Archives of Canada, Q, 12, pp. 230–32.

CHAPTER XI
(*pages 209–228*)
1. Ellen H. Smith, p. 151.
2. Force, *American Archives*, 4, VI, pp. 587–88.
3. Ibid., pp. 589–90.
4. Ibid.
5. Lyman H. Butterfield, ed., *Diary and Autobiography of John Adams*, pp. 408–409.
6. Fitzpatrick, *The Writings of George Washington*, V, p. 152.
7. Charles P. Whittemore, *A General of the Revolution*, p. 5.
8. Otis G. Hammond, ed., *Letters and Papers of Major-General John Sullivan*, I, Sullivan to Hancock, June 1, 1776, p. 212; Sullivan to Washington, June 5–6, 1776, pp. 218–19.
9. Ibid., Sullivan to Washington, June 6, 1776, pp. 219–21; Instructions to Thompson, p. 222.
10. Ibid., Sullivan to Washington, June 8, 1776, p. 227.

11. James P. Baxter, ed., *The British Invasion from the North*, pp. 156–57.
12. Ibid., p. 106.
13. Force, *American Archives*, 4, VI, p. 684.
14. Justin H. Smith, *Our Struggle*, II, p. 405.
15. Arthur St. Clair, *Narrative*, p. 237.
16. William Irvine, "Journal of the Canadian Campaign, 1776," *Historical Magazine*, VI, pp. 115–17.
17. Morgan, *Naval Documents*, V, p. 693.
18. Irvine, pp. 115–17.
19. Force, *American Archives*, 4, VI, pp. 826–28.
20. Morgan, *Naval Documents*, V, p. 694.
21. John Lacey, "Memoirs," *Pennsylvania Magazine of History and Biography*, XXV, p. 201.
22. Force, *American Archives*, 4, VI, pp. 826–28.
23. Baxter, p. 108; Force, *American Archives*, 4, VI, pp. 826–28; Cruikshank, *Military and Naval Forces of Canada*, II, p. 174.
24. Irvine, pp. 115–17.
25. Hammond, *Letters and Papers of Major-General John Sullivan*, I, Sullivan to Schuyler, June 12, 1776, p. 234.
26. Ibid., Sullivan to Washington, June 12, 1776, p. 230.
27. Roberts, *March to Quebec*, Senter, p. 240.
28. Hammond, *Letters and Papers of Major-General John Sullivan*, I, Sullivan to Washington, June 8, 1776, p. 228.
29. Jared Sparks Manuscripts, no. 60, p. 93, Arnold to Schuyler, June 6, 1776; Justin H. Smith, *Our Struggle*, II, p. 417.
30. *Journal of the Continental Congress*, May 24–25, 1776.
31. Force, *American Archives*, 4, VI, p. 559.
32. Ibid., p. 560.
33. Hammond, *Letters and Papers of Major-General John Sullivan*, I, Washington to Sullivan, May 17, 1776, p. 204.
34. Force, *American Archives*, 4, VI, p. 796.
35. Hammond, *Letters and Papers of Major-General John Sullivan*, I, p. 238; Arnold to Sullivan, June 13, 1776.
36. Force, *American Archives*, 4, VI, p. 1038.
37. Ibid., p. 1039.
38. Ibid.
39. Hammond, *Letters and Papers of Major-General John Sullivan*, I, Sullivan to Schuyler, June 19, 1776, p. 252.
40. Cometti, p. 15.
41. George F. G. Stanley, ed., *For Want of a Horse*, p. 72.
42. Baxter, p. 117.
43. R. Arthur Bowler, "Sir Guy Carleton and the Campaign of 1776 in Canada," *Canadian Historical Review*, June 1974, pp. 131–40.
44. Wilkinson, *Memoirs*, I, pp. 49–53.
45. Hammond, *Letters and Papers of Major-General John Sullivan*, I, Sullivan to Schuyler, June 19, 1776, p. 252.
46. St. Clair, p. 241.
47. Wilkinson, *Memoirs*, I, pp. 54–55.

48. Ibid., p. 55.
49. Lacey, p. 203.
50. Force, *American Archives*, 5, I, p. 131.
51. John Trumbull, *Autobiography*, pp. 299–300.
52. Hammond, *Letters and Papers of Major-General John Sullivan*, I, Sullivan to Schuyler, June 22, 1776, pp. 257–58; June 25, 1776, p. 268.
53. Ibid., June 19, 1776, pp. 253–54.
54. Ibid.
55. John Trumbull, p. 28.
56. Hammond, *Letters and Papers of Major-General John Sullivan*, I, Sullivan to Washington, June 24, 1776, pp. 261–62.
57. Lewis Beebe, *Journal*, pp. 337–39.
58. John Trumbull, p. 28.
59. Justin H. Smith, *Our Struggle*, II, p. 451; *Journal of the Continental Congress*, July 30, 1776; P. L. Ford, ed., *Writings of Thomas Jefferson*, II, p. 39; Samuel Adams Papers, S. Adams to J. Hawley, July 9, 1776; Force, *American Archives*, 4, VI, pp. 1083, 1232; 4, V, p. 1086.
60. Roberts, *March to Quebec*, Senter, p. 241.
61. Hammond, *Letters and Papers of Major-General John Sullivan*, I, Sullivan to Hancock, July 2, 1776, pp. 276–77.
62. Force, *American Archives*, 5, I, p. 127.

Chapter XII

(*pages 229–246*)
1. Force, *American Archives*, 5, I, pp. 987–88.
2. Lanctot, p. 154; Public Archives of Canada, Q, XII, pp. 188–92.
3. Public Archives of Canada, Q, XII, pp. 188–92.
4. Alfred L. Burt, *The Old Province of Quebec*, p. 242; John W. Fortescue, ed., *The Correspondence of King George the Third*, III, p. 386.
5. John Trumbull, pp. 302–303.
6. Robbins, pp. 31–32.
7. Force, *American Archives*, 4, VI, p. 940.
8. John A. Williams, "Mount Independence in Time of War, 1776–1783," *Vermont History*, XXXV, no. 2, April 1967, pp. 89–96.
9. Force, *American Archives*, 5, I, pp. 1272–74.
10. Ibid., II, p. 354.
11. Ibid., pp. 1107–08.
12. Ibid., I, p. 261.
13. Ibid., p. 1033.
14. Morgan, *Naval Documents*, VI, p. 1084.
15. Force, *American Archives*, 5, II, pp. 441, 481.
16. Ibid., p. 982.
17. Ibid., I, pp. 1002–03.
18. Ibid., p. 1221.
19. Ibid., p. 1267.
20. Ibid., p. 826.

21. Ibid., II, p. 481.
22. Ibid., pp. 223, 251.
23. Ibid., p. 591.
24. Ibid., p. 440.
25. Ibid., p. 834.
26. Baxter, p. 153.
27. Force, *American Archives*, 5, II, p. 1038.
28. Ibid., pp. 1079–80.
29. M. Von Eelking, ed., *Memoirs, Letters and Journals of Major-General Riedesel*, I, p. 80; J. Robert Maguire, "Dr. Robert Knox's Account of the Battle of Valcour," *Vermont History*, XLVI, no. 3, Summer 1978, pp. 141–50.
30. John Trumbull, p. 36.
31. Lanctot, pp. 159–60, as described in a letter from Mère Marie Catherine Duchesnay de St. Ignace of the General Hospital; Henri Têtu, *Les Evêques de Québec*, pp. 345–46.

Select Bibliography

Primary sources in the Public Archives of Canada include C.O. 42, Canada, Official Correspondence; Q Series, Correspondence of the Governors of Canada; B Series, Correspondence and Papers of Governor Carleton; M Series, Miscellaneous Documents; and S Series, Sundry Correspondence and Papers. Diaries and other source material have been published in *Reports of the Canadian Archives* and in Literary and Historical Society of Quebec, *Historical Documents*, 1905–06, Second through Fourth and Seventh and Eighth Series. Many pertinent documents have been reprinted in *A History of the Organization, Development and Services of the Military and Naval Forces of Canada from the Peace of Paris in 1763 to the Present Time*, edited by Ernest Cruikshank.

Material relative to the Quebec Bill may be found in *Documents Relating to the Constitutional History of Canada, 1759–1791*, edited by Adam Shortt and Arthur G. Doughty, Francis Masères's writings, and *Debates of the House of Commons in the Year 1774*, as reported by Sir Henry Cavendish. The *Rapport de l'Archiviste de la Province de Québec, 1927–28* contains the journal of the Baby-Taschereau-Williams commission, which investigated pro-American activities in the Quebec district. Journals of Canadian participants in the campaign have been collected in *Invasion du Canada*, edited by Hospice-Anthelme Verreau. Bishop Briand's pronouncements on the American invasion are included in *Mandements, Lettres Pastorales et Circulaires des Evêques de Québec*, II, edited by Henri Têtu and C. O. Gagnon.

Eyewitness accounts by members of the British military include *For Want of a Horse*, edited by George F. G. Stanley; *Canada Preserved, the journal of Captain Thomas Ainslie*, edited by Sheldon S. Cohen; *The Journal of Lieutenant William Digby*, edited by James P. Baxter in *The British Invasion from the North*; the *Journal and Orderly Books of James M. Hadden*, edited by Horatio Rogers; *The American Journals of Lt. John Enys*, edited by Elizabeth Cometti; and the *Journal of Captain Pausch* and the *Memoirs, Letters and Journals of Major-General Riedesel,* translated by William L. Stone. *An Authentic Narrative of Facts Relating to the Exchange of Prisoners Taken at the Cedars,* by Captain Andrew Parke, is invaluable as a contemporary account of a much-debated incident.

American sources include volumes pertinent to the campaign in *American Archives,* edited by Peter Force; the journals of the Arnold expedition, collected by Kenneth Roberts in *March to Quebec;* the Philip Schuyler Papers in the New York Public Library; the Jared Sparks Manuscripts in the Houghton Library at Harvard University; the Gage Papers in the William L. Clements Library at the University of Michigan; and *Letters and Papers of Major-General John Sullivan,* edited by Otis G. Hammond. Among firsthand accounts of the campaign are *The Narrative of Colonel Ethan Allen,* the *Journal of Charles Carroll of Carrollton During His Visit to Canada in 1776,* the *Journal of Dr. Lewis Beebe,* James Wilkinson's *Memoirs of My Own Times,* Chaplain Ammi Robbins's *Journal,* and John Trumbull's *Autobiography.* Journals of several other participants have appeared in publications of state historical societies and *The Bulletin of the Fort Ticonderoga Museum.*

Secondary works include *History of the Campaign for the Conquest of Canada in 1776,* by Charles H. Jones (1882); *Arnold's Expedition to Quebec* by John Codman (1901), *Arnold's March from Cambridge to Quebec,* and *Our Struggle for the Fourteenth Colony,* two volumes, by Justin H. Smith (1903 and 1907 respectively); "Sir Guy Carleton As a Military Leader During the Revolution," two volumes, a doctoral thesis by Perry W. Leroy (1960); *Canada and the American Revolution,* by Gustave Lanctot (1967); *Attack on Quebec,* by Harrison Bird (1968); and *Canada Invaded, 1775–1776,* by George F. G. Stanley (1973). *Sir Guy Carleton,* by A. G. Bradley (1907), and the several biographies of Arnold have much to say about the campaign. Chapters in *The War of the Revolution,* by Christopher Ward, give a comprehensive résumé.

Adams, Charles F., ed. *Familiar Letters of John Adams and His Wife, Abigail Adams, During the Revolution.* New York, 1876.

——. *The Works of John Adams.* Boston, 1850–56.

Adams, John Quincy. *Life in a New England Town: 1787, 1788.* Boston, 1903.

Adams, Samuel, Papers. Bancroft Collection, New York Public Library.

Aimone, Alan and Barbara. "Organizing and Equipping Montgomery's Yorkers in 1775," *Military Collector and Historian,* XXVIII, no. 2, Summer 1976.

Alexander, Holmes. *Aaron Burr, The Proud Pretender.* New York, 1937.

Allen, Ethan. *The Narrative of Colonel Ethan Allen,* Ticonderoga, New York, 1930.

Allen, Gardner W. *A Naval History of the American Revolution.* Boston, 1913.

Allen, Ira. *The Natural and Political History of the State of Vermont.* London, 1798.

Allen, William. "Account of Arnold's Expedition," *Collections of Maine Historical Society*, I, 1861.

Amory, Thomas C. *The Military Services and Public Life of Major-General John Sullivan.* Port Washington, New York, 1868.

Anburey, Thomas. *Travels through the Interior Parts of America.* London, 1789.

Anderson, William J. "Canadian History: The Siege and Blockade of Quebec by Generals Montgomery and Arnold in 1775–6," *Transactions of Literary and Historical Society of Quebec*, New Series, part 9, 1871–1872.

Anonymous. "A Journal of Carleton's and Burgoyne's Campaigns," *Bulletin of the Fort Ticonderoga Museum*, XI, no. 5, December 1964.

Armstrong, John. *Life of Richard Montgomery*, in *Library of American Biography*, Jared Sparks, ed., I, pp. 185–226, Boston, 1834.

Arnold, Benedict. "Letters, September 27–December 5, 1775," *Collections of Maine Historical Society*, I, 1861.

———. "Regimental Memorandum Book," *Pennsylvania Magazine of History and Biography*, VIII, 1884.

Arnold, Isaac N. *The Life of Benedict Arnold.* Chicago, 1880.

Baldwin, Jeduthan. *The Revolutionary Journal of Jeduthan Baldwin, 1775–1778*, ed. Thomas Williams Baldwin, Bangor, 1906; *Bulletin of the Fort Ticonderoga Museum*, IV, January 1938.

Baxter, James P., ed. *The British Invasion from the North. The Campaigns of Generals Carleton and Burgoyne from Canada, 1776–1777, with the Journal of Lieut. William Digby of the 53d, or Shropshire Regiment of Foot.* Albany, 1887.

Bedel Papers. New Hampshire Historical Society, Concord.

Beebe, Lewis. *Journal.* New York, 1971.

Benoit, Pierre. *Lord Dorchester.* Montreal, 1961.

Billias, George A., ed. *George Washington's Generals.* New York, 1964.

Billias, George A., ed. *George Washington's Opponents: British Generals and Admirals in the American Revolution.* New York, 1969.

Bird, Harrison. *Attack on Quebec.* New York, 1968.

———. *Navies in the Mountains.* New York, 1962.

Boatner, Mark M. *Encyclopedia of the American Revolution.* New York, 1966.

Bonney, Catharina V. R. *A Legacy of Historical Gleanings.* Albany, 1875.

Bowler, R. Arthur. *Logistics and the Failure of the British Army in America, 1775–1783.* Princeton, 1975.

———. "Sir Guy Carleton and the Campaign of 1776 in Canada," *Canadian Historical Review*, LV, no. 2, June 1974.

Boylan, Brian R. *Benedict Arnold, The Dark Eagle.* New York, 1973.

Bradley, A. G. *Sir Guy Carleton (Lord Dorchester).* Toronto, 1907.

Bredenberg, Oscar. "The American Champlain Fleet, 1775–1777," *Bulletin of the Fort Ticonderoga Museum*, XII, no. 4, September 1968.

———. "The Royal Savage," *Bulletin of the Fort Ticonderoga Museum*, XII, no. 2, September 1966.

Brent, J. C. *John Carroll*. Baltimore, 1843.

Bull, Epaphras. "Journal," *Bulletin of the Fort Ticonderoga Museum*, VIII, no. 2, July 1948.

Burnett, Edmund, ed. *Letters of Members of the Continental Congress*. Washington, D.C., 1921–36.

Burrall, Charles. "Journal," in manuscript.

Burt, Alfred L. *Guy Carleton, Lord Dorchester*. Canadian Historical Association booklet no. 5, Ottawa, 1905.

———. *The Old Province of Quebec*. Toronto, 1933.

———. "The Quarrel Between Germain and Carleton: An Inverted Story," *The Canadian Historical Review*, vol. 11, September 1930.

Bush, Martin H. *Revolutionary Enigma: A Re-appraisal of General Philip Schuyler of New York*. Port Washington, New York, 1969.

Butterfield, Lyman H., ed. *Adams Family Correspondence*. Cambridge, 1963–73.

Butterfield, Lyman H., Leonard C. Faber, and Wendell D. Garrett, eds. *Diary and Autobiography of John Adams*. Boston, 1961.

Butterfield, Lyman H., Marc Friedlander, and Mary-Jo Kline, eds. *The Book of Abigail and John: Selected Letters of the Adams Family, 1762–1784*. Cambridge, 1975.

Caldwell, Henry. "The Invasion of Canada, Letter Attributed to Major Henry Caldwell," *Literary and Historical Society of Quebec, Historical Documents*, Second Series.

Callahan, North. *Daniel Morgan, Ranger of the Revolution*. New York, 1961.

Campbell, B. U. "Archbishop Carroll," *United States Catholic Historical Magazine*, III.

Canadian Archives Reports, 1904.

Carrington, H. B. *Battles of the American Revolution*. New York, 1876.

Carroll, Charles. *Journal of Charles Carroll of Carrollton during his visit to Canada in 1776 as one of the commissioners from Congress*. Philadelphia, 1845.

Cassedy, Mary, and Sue Perkins. *A Brief History of Early Plainfield*. Plainfield, New Hampshire, 1976. Contains diary of Daniel Kimball of Colonel Bedel's regiment.

Cavendish, Henry. *Debates of the House of Commons in the year 1774*. London, 1839.

Chapelle, Howard I. *The History of the American Sailing Navy*. New York, 1949.

———. *The History of American Sailing Ships*. New York, 1935.

Chipman, Daniel. *Memoir of Colonel Seth Warner*. Middlebury, Vermont, 1848.

Chittenden, Lucius E. *The Capture of Ticonderoga*. Rutland, Vermont, 1872.

Clark, Lyman. "Journal," manuscript in University of Vermont library.

Clarkson, Thomas S. *Clermont, or Livingston Manor*. Clermont, New York, 1869.

Codman, John. *Arnold's Expedition to Quebec*. New York, 1901.

Coffin, Charles. *The Life and Services of Major General John Thomas*. Dearborn, New York, 1845.

Coffin, Robert P. Tristram. *Kennebec, Cradle of Americans*. New York, 1937.

Coffin, Victor. *The Province of Quebec and the Early American Revolution*. Madison, 1896.

Coffin, William F. "On some Additional Incidents in connection with the Siege and Blockade of Quebec in 1775–1776," *Transactions of the Literary and Historical Society of Quebec*, New Series, part 9, 1872–1873.

Cohen, Sheldon S. "Lieutenant John Starke and the Defence of Quebec," *Dalhousie Review*, XLVII, no. 1, Spring 1967.

Cohen, Sheldon S., ed. *Canada Preserved: The Journal of Captain Thomas Ainslie*. New York, 1968.

Collections of the Connecticut Historical Society.

Cometti, Elizabeth, ed. *The American Journals of Lt. John Enys*. Syracuse, 1976.

Commager, Henry Steele, and Richard B. Morris, eds. *The Spirit of Seventy-Six: The Story of the American Revolution as Told by Participants*. New York, 1958.

Coupland, Reginald. *The Quebec Act*. Oxford, 1925.

Creighton, Donald G. *The Commercial Empire of the St. Lawrence, 1760–1850*. Toronto, 1937.

Crockett, Walter H. *Vermont, The Green Mountain State*. New York, 1921.

Cruikshank, Ernest, ed. *A History of the Organization, Development and Services of the Military and Naval Forces of Canada from the Peace of Paris in 1763 to the Present Time*, vols. 1 and 2.

Cullum, George W. *Biographical Sketch of Major-General Richard Montgomery*. 1876.

Cushing, H. A., ed. *The Writings of Samuel Adams*. New York, 1904–1908.

Davis, Matthew L., ed. *Memoirs of Aaron Burr*. New York, 1838.

Danford, Jacob. "Journal of the Most Remarkable Occurrences in Quebec by an Officer of the Garrison," *New-York Historical Society Collections*, 1880.

Dawson, H. B. *Battles of the United States*. New York, 1858.

Deane, Silas. "Letters," *Collections of Connecticut Historical Society*, II, 1870.

Decker, Malcolm. *Benedict Arnold, Son of the Havens*. New York, 1932.

DeFonblanque, Edward B. *Political and Military Episodes in the latter half of the Eighteenth Century derived from the life and correspondence of the Right Hon. John Burgoyne, General, Statesman, Dramatist*. London, 1876.

"Documents relatifs à la reddition du fort Saint-Jean et du fort Chambly

(1775)," *Rapport des Archives Canadiennes pour 1914 et 1915*, Appendice B.

"Documents relating to the War of 1775," *Canadian Archives, Report for 1904*, App. I.

Elting, John R., ed. *Military Uniforms in America in the Era of the American Revolution.* The Company of Military Historians, 1974.

Emmet Collection, New York Public Library.

Everest, Allan S. *Moses Hazen and the Canadian Refugees in the American Revolution.* Syracuse, 1976.

Everett, Edward. *John Stark.* New York, 1902.

Fenton, Walter S. "Seth Warner," *Proceedings of the Vermont Historical Society*, New Series, VIII, no. 4.

Fitzpatrick, John C., ed. *The Writings of George Washington from the Original Manuscript Sources 1745–1799*, vols. III–VI, Washington, D.C., 1931–1944.

Fleming, Thomas. *1776, Year of Illusions.* New York, 1975.

Flexner, James T. *George Washington in the American Revolution.* Boston, 1967.

———. *The Traitor and the Spy.* New York, 1953.

Force, Peter, ed. *American Archives.* Washington, D.C., 1837–1853.

Ford, P. L., ed. *Writings of Thomas Jefferson.* New York, 1892–1899.

Fort Ticonderoga Bulletin.

Fortescue, John W., ed. *The Correspondence of King George the Third from 1760 to December, 1783.* London, 1927.

———. *A History of the British Army*, vol. 3. London, 1899–1930.

Freeman, Douglas S. *George Washington.* New York, 1957.

French, Allen. *The First Year of the American Revolution.* Boston, 1934.

———. *The Taking of Ticonderoga in 1775.* Cambridge, 1928.

Furcon, Thomas B. "Mount Independence, 1776–1777," *Bulletin of the Fort Ticonderoga Museum*, IX, no. 4, Winter 1954.

Gage Papers. William L. Clements Library, University of Michigan.

Gay, Frederick L. *Gay Transcripts of Material in the Public Record Office, London, 1630–1776.* Massachusetts Historical Society.

Gerlach, Don R. *Philip Schuyler and the American Revolution in New York.* Lincoln, Nebraska, 1964.

———. "Philip Schuyler and 'The Road to Glory': A Question of Loyalty and Competence," *New-York Historical Society Quarterly*, XLIX, no. 4, October 1965.

Gipson, Lawrence H. *The Coming of the Revolution.* New York, 1954.

———. *The Triumphant Empire.* New York, 1965.

Gosselin, Auguste. *L'Eglise du Canada après la Conquête.* Quebec, 1917.

Graham, James. *Life of General Daniel Morgan.* New York, 1856.

Guilday, Peter. *The Life and Times of John Carroll.* New York, 1922.

Gurn, Joseph. *Charles Carroll of Carrollton.* New York, 1932.

Hadden, James M. *Journal and Orderly Books.* Ed. by Horatio Rogers. Albany, 1884.

Hamilton, Edward P. *Fort Ticonderoga, Key to a Continent.* Boston, 1964.

Hammond, Otis G., ed. *Letters and Papers of Major-General John Sullivan.* Concord, New Hampshire, 1930.

Hanley, Thomas O., ed. *The John Carroll Papers,* vol. I, 1755–1791. South Bend, Indiana, 1976.

Harriman, Walter. "Seth Warner," *New England Historical and Genealogical Register,* XXXIV, 1880.

Heitman, Francis B., ed. *Historical Register of Officers of the Continental Army.* Baltimore, 1967.

Hendricks, William. "Journal," *Pennsylvania Archives,* Second Series, XV.

Heth, William. "Diary," *Annual Papers of the Winchester, Virginia, Historical Society,* vol. I, 1931.

Higginbotham, Don. *Daniel Morgan — Revolutionary Rifleman,* Chapel Hill, 1961.

———. *The War of American Independence.* New York, 1971.

Hill, Ralph N. *Lake Champlain: Key to Liberty.* Taftsville, Vermont, 1977.

Hitsman, J. Mackay. *Safeguarding Canada, 1763–1871.* Toronto, 1968.

Hodgkinson, Samuel. "Before Quebec, 1776," *Pennsylvania Magazine of History and Biography,* X, p. 159.

Humphrey, William. "Journal," *Magazine of History,* extra number 166.

Hunt, Louise L. *Biographical Notes concerning General Richard Montgomery, together with hitherto unpublished letters.* Poughkeepsie, 1876.

Huot, Lucien. *Siège du Fort de St. Jean en 1775.* St. Jean, Quebec, 1889.

Innis, Harold A. *The Fur Trade in Canada.* Toronto, 1930.

Irvine, William. "Journal of the Canadian Campaign, 1776," *Historical Magazine,* VI, April 1862.

Jellison, Charles A. *Ethan Allen, Frontier Rebel.* Syracuse, 1969.

Jones, Charles H. *History of the Campaign for the Conquest of Canada in 1776.* Philadelphia, 1882.

Jones, Matt B. *Vermont in the Making.* New York, 1968.

Jones, Thomas. *History of New York During the Revolutionary War.* New York, 1879.

Journal of the Massachusetts Provincial Congress, 1775.

"Journal par Messrs. François Baby, Gabriel Taschereau et Jenkin Williams dans le Tournée qu'ils ont faite dans le district de Québec par ordre du General Carleton," *Rapport de l'Archiviste de la Province de Québec,* 1927–1928, pp. 435–99; 1929–1930, pp. 138–40.

Journal of the Continental Congress, 1774–1789. Gaillard Hunt, ed. Washington, 1904–1937.

Keenleyside, Hugh L. *Canada and the United States.* New York, 1929.

Kennedy, W. P M. *Statutes, Treaties and Documents of the Canadian Constitution, 1713–1929.* Toronto, 1930.

Kidder, Frederic. *History of the First New Hampshire Regiment in the War of the Revolution,* Bicentennial edition. Hampton, New Hampshire, 1973.

Kingsford, William. *History of Canada,* V, VI, VII. Toronto, 1892.

Lacey, John. "Memoirs," *Pennsylvania Magazine of History and Biography*, XXV, 1901.

Lanctot, Gustave. *Canada and the American Revolution, 1774–1783.* Cambridge, 1967.

Leacock, Stephen. *Montreal, Seaport and City.* New York, 1942.

Leake, I. Q. *Memoir of the Life and Times of General John Lamb.* Albany, 1850.

Lee, Henry. *Memoirs of the War in the Southern Department of the United States.* New York, 1870.

LeMoine, James M. *Quebec Past and Present.* Quebec, 1876.

Leonard, Lewis A. *Life of Charles Carroll of Carrollton.* New York, 1928.

Leroy, Perry E. "Sir Guy Carleton As a Military Leader During the American Invasion," an unpublished dissertation. Ohio State University, 1960.

Lighthall, W. D. "La Corne St.-Luc," *Canadian Antiquarian and Numismatic Journal*, V, no. 1, January 1908.

Lindsay, William. "Narrative of the Invasion of Canada," *Canadian Review and Magazine*, no. 5, September 1826.

Literary and Historical Society of Quebec, *Historical Documents*, Second, Third, Fourth, Seventh, and Eighth Series. Quebec, 1866, 1871, 1875, 1905, 1906. Journals and other documents relating to the American attempt on Quebec in 1775–1776.

Livingston, Edwin B. *The Livingstons of Livingston Manor.* New York, 1910.

Livingston, Henry. "Journal," *Pennsylvania Magazine of History and Biography*, April 1898.

———. "Letter to Robert R. Livingston," October 6, 1775, *Magazine of History*, XXI, p. 256.

Livingston Papers. Bancroft Collection, New York Public Library.

Lossing, Benson J. *The Life and Times of Philip Schuyler.* New York, 1850.

Lowell, Edward J. *The Hessians.* Port Washington, New York, 1965.

Mackesy, Piers. *The War for America, 1775–1783.* Cambridge, 1965.

Macpherson, John. "Extracts from Letters," *Pennsylvania Magazine of History and Biography*, XXIII, no. 1, April 1899.

Maguire, J. Robert. "Dr. Robert Knox's Account of the Battle of Valcour," *Vermont History*, XLVI, no. 3, Summer 1978.

Mahan, A. T. *The Major Operations of the Navies in the War of American Independence.* Boston, 1913.

———. "The Naval Campaign of 1776 on Lake Champlain," *Scribner's Magazine*, XXIII, 1898.

Maine Historical Society Collections.

Manders, Eric. "Notes on Troop Units in the New York Garrison, 1775–1776," *Military Collector and Historian*, XXV, no. 1, Spring 1973.

———. "Notes on Troop Units in the Northern Army, 1776," *Military Collector and Historian*, XXVII, no. 1, Spring 1975, and XXVII, no. 3, Fall 1975.

Marshall, Douglas W., and Howard H. Peckham, eds. *Campaigns of the American Revolution, An Atlas of Manuscript Maps.* Ann Arbor, 1976.

Masères, Francis. *An Account of the Proceedings of the British and other Protestant Inhabitants of the Province of Quebeck in North America, in order to obtain an House of Assembly in that Province.* London, 1775.
———. *Additional papers concerning the Province of Quebeck.* London, 1776.
———. *Occasional Essays.* London, 1809.
Massachusetts Historical Society Collections.
Melville, Annabelle M. *John Carroll of Baltimore, Founder of the American Catholic Hierarchy.* New York, 1955.
Metzger, Charles H. *The Quebec Act, a Primary Cause of the American Revolution.* New York, 1936.
Military Collector and Historian, Journal of the Company of Military Historians, Washington, D.C.
Monaghan, Frank. *John Jay.* New York, 1935.
Montgomery's Orderly Book. Library of Congress, Peter Force Collection.
"Montgomery's Sword," Note in *Blockade of Quebec in 1775–1776 by the American Revolutionists.* Literary and Historical Society of Quebec, 1905.
Montross, Lynn. *Rag, Tag and Bobtail: The Story of the Continental Army, 1775–1783.* New York, 1952.
———. *The Reluctant Rebels: The Story of the Continental Congress, 1774–1789.* New York, 1950.
Moore, Frank. *Diary of the American Revolution.* New York, 1865.
Moore, Howard P. *General John Stark of New Hampshire.* New York, 1949.
Morgan, William J., ed. *Naval Documents of the American Revolution.* Washington, D.C., 1972.
McCoy, William. *Journal of a March of a Company of Provincials from Carlisle to Boston and thence to Quebec.* Glasgow, 1776.
"Narrative of the Siege of St. Johns," *Canadian Archives Reports* for 1914.
Neatby, Hilda. "Jean Olivier Briand, a 'Minor Canadian,'" *Report of the Canadian Historical Association,* 1963.
———. *Quebec, the Revolutionary Age, 1760–1791.* Toronto, 1966.
New Hampshire Antiquarian Society Collections.
New Jersey Historical Society Proceedings.
New-York Historical Society Collections, III, 1880, p. 235, "Journal of the Most Remarkable Occurrences in Quebec."
Nichols, Francis. "Diary," *Pennsylvania Magazine of History and Biography,* XX, pp. 504–14.
Osler, Edward. "The Battle of Valcour Island," *Bulletin of the Fort Ticonderoga Museum,* II, no. 5, January 1932.
"Papers Relating to the Expedition to Ticonderoga, April and May, 1775," *Collections of the Connecticut Historical Society,* I, 1860.
Parke, Andrew. *An Authentic Narrative of Facts Relating to the Exchange of Prisoners Taken at the Cedars.* London, 1777.
Parnet, Herbert S., and Hecht, Marie B. *Aaron Burr, Portrait of an Ambitious Man.* New York 1967.
Parton, James. *Life and Times of Aaron Burr.* Boston, 1877.

Pell, John. *Ethan Allen*. Boston, 1929.

———. "The Revenge," *Bulletin of the Fort Ticonderoga Museum*, I, no. 4, July 1928.

Pell, Joshua. "Diary," *Magazine of History*, II, part 1, 1878.

Pettengill, Ray W., ed. *Letters from America, 1776–1779*. Boston, 1924.

Porter, Elisha. "Diary," ed. by Appleton Morgan, *Magazine of American History*, XXX, 1893.

Porterfield, Charles. "Diary," *Magazine of History*, XXI, 1889, *Publications of the Southern Historical Society*, VI, 1902.

Potter, Chandler. *Military History of the State of New Hampshire, 1623–1861*. Baltimore, 1972.

Provost, Honorius. *Chaudière-Kennebec, Grand Chemin Séculaire*. Quebec, 1974.

Rhode Island Historical Society Publications.

Rich, E. E. *The Fur Trade and the Northwest to 1857*. London, 1968.

Riddell, William R. "Benjamin Franklin and Canada," *Pennsylvania Magazine of History and Biography*, XLVIII, no. 2, 1924.

Ritzema, Rudolphus. "Journal," *Magazine of American History*, I, part 1, 1877.

Robbins, Ammi. *Journal*. New Haven, 1850.

Roberts, Kenneth, ed. *March to Quebec, Journals of the Members of Arnold's Expedition*. New York, 1938.

Rowland, Kate M. *The Life of Charles Carroll of Carrollton*. New York, 1898.

Ryerson, Egerton. *The Loyalists of America and Their Times from 1620 to 1816*. Toronto, 1880.

Sabine, L. *Loyalists of the American Revolution*. Boston, 1864.

St. Clair, Arthur. *Narrative*. Philadelphia, 1812.

Schachner, Nathan. *Aaron Burr: A Biography*. New York, 1937.

Schuyler Papers. New York Public Library.

Sellers, Charles C. *Benedict Arnold, The Proud Warrior*. New York, 1930.

Shea, John G. *Life and Times of the Most Rev. John Carroll, Bishop and First Archbishop of Baltimore*. New York, 1888.

———. "Why is Canada not a part of the U. S.?," *United States Catholic Historical Magazine*, III, 1890.

Shepardson, Zephaniah. "Journal," manuscript the property of P. Wayne Canaday, Glendale Heights, Illinois. Copy on file at the Vermont Historical Society library, Montpelier.

Shortt, Adam, and Arthur G. Doughty, eds. *Documents Relating to the Constitutional History of Canada, 1759–91*. Ottawa, 1918.

Shortt, W. T. P., ed. *Journal of the Principal Occurrences During the Siege of Quebec by the American Revolutionists under Generals Montgomery and Arnold in 1775–1776*. London, 1824.

Smith, Ellen H. *Charles Carroll of Carrollton*. Cambridge, 1942.

Smith, J. E. A. *History of Pittsfield, Massachusetts*. Boston, 1869.

Smith, Justin H. *Arnold's March from Cambridge to Quebec*. New York, 1903.

——. *Our Struggle for the Fourteenth Colony*. New York, 1907.

Sosin, J. M. "Indians in the American Revolutionary War," *The Canadian Historical Review*, vol. 46, June, 1965.

Sparks, Jared, ed. *Correspondence of the American Revolution: Being Letters of Eminent Men to George Washington*. Boston, 1853.

——. *The Wrtings of George Washington*. Boston, 1834–37.

Sparks Manuscripts. Houghton Library, Harvard University.

Stanley, George F. G. *Canada Invaded, 1775–1776*. Toronto, 1973.

Stanley, George F. G., ed. *For Want of a Horse, a Journal of the Campaigns against the Americans in 1776 and 1777 conducted from Canada, by an officer who served with Lt. Gen. Burgoyne*. Sackville, New Brunswick, 1961.

Stark, Caleb, ed. *Memoir and Official Correspondence of General John Stark*. Concord, New Hampshire, 1877.

Stevens, B. F., ed. *Facsimiles of Manuscripts in European Archives Relating to America, 1773–1783*. London, 1889–1898.

Stevens, Benjamin. "Journal" in manuscript.

Stevens, John. "Journal" in manuscript.

Stillé, Charles J. *The Life and Times of John Dickinson*. Philadelphia, 1891.

——. *Major-General Anthony Wayne and the Pennsylvania Line in the Continental Army*. Philadelphia, 1893.

Stone, William L., ed. *Journal of Captain Pausch*. Albany, 1886.

Syrett, Harold C., and Jacob E. Cooke, eds. *Papers of Alexander Hamilton*. New York, 1961–1977.

Têtu, Henri. *Les Evêques de Québec*. Quebec, 1889.

Têtu, Henri, and C. O. Gagnon, eds. *Mandements, Lettres Pastorales et Circulaires des Evêques de Québec*. Quebec, 1888.

Thacher, James. *A ·Military Journal During the American Revolution*. Boston, 1827.

Topham, John. "Journal," *Magazine of History*, extra number 50.

Trumbull, Benjamin. "A Concise Journal or Minutes of the Principal Movements Towards St. John's of the Siege and Surrender of the Forts There in 1775," *Conn. Hist. Soc. Coll.*, VII, 1899.

Trumbull, John. *Autobiography*. New York, 1841.

Tuckerman, Bayard. *Life of General Philip Schuyler*. New York, 1903.

Turcotte, Louis P. *Invasion du Canada et Siège de Québec en 1775–1776*. Quebec, 1876.

Upton, Richard F. *Revolutionary New Hampshire*. New York, 1971.

Van de Water, Frederic F. *Lake Champlain and Lake George*. Indianapolis, 1946.

Van Doren, Carl C. *Secret History of the American Revolution*. New York, 1941.

Vermont Historical Society Collections.

Verreau, H.-A., ed. *Invasion du Canada, Collection de Memoirs receuillis et annotés par M. l'Abbé Verreau*. Montreal, 1873. Includes journals of Sanguinet, Berthelot, Badeaux, and de Lorimier.

Von Eelking, M., ed. *Memoirs and Letters and Journals of Major General Riedesel*, trans. by W. L. Stone. Albany, 1868.

Vose, Joseph. "Journal," *Publications of the Colonial Society of Massachusetts*, VII, 1905.

Wade, Mason. *The French Canadians, 1760–1967*. New York, 1968.

Walker, Mrs. Thomas. "Fragment of a Journal," *Collections of the New Hampshire Antiquarian Society*, no. 2, 1876.

Wallace, Willard M. *Traitorous Hero: The Life and Fortunes of Benedict Arnold*. New York, 1954.

Ward, Christopher. *The War of the Revolution*. New York, 1952.

Ward, Harry Parker, ed. *The Follett-Dewey-Fassett-Safford Ancestry of Captain Martin Dewey Follett and his wife Persis Fassett*. Columbus, Ohio, 1896.

Warner, Seth. "Papers of Seth Warner," *Proceedings of the Vermont Historical Society*, XI, no. 2.

"Warren-Adams Letters: Being Chiefly a Correspondence among John Adams, Samuel Adams and James Warren," *Collections of Massachusetts Historical Society*, vols. LXXII (1917) and LXXIII (1925).

"The Wayne Orderly Book," *Bulletin of the Fort Ticonderoga Museum*, XI, no. 3, December 1963.

Wells, Bayze. "Journal," *Connecticut Historical Society Collections*, VII.

Whitcher, W. F. *History of Haverhill, New Hampshire*. Concord, New Hampshire, 1919.

Whittemore, Charles P. *A General of the Revolution, John Sullivan of New Hampshire*. New York, 1961.

Wilkinson, James. *Memoirs of My Own Times*. Philadelphia, 1816.

Willett, William M. *A Narrative of the Military Actions of Colonel Marinus Willett*. New York, 1831.

Williams, John A. "Mount Independence in Time of War, 1776–1783," *Vermont History*, XXXV, no. 2, April 1967.

Wilson, Samuel K. "Bishop Briand and the American Revolution," *The Catholic Historical Review*, XIX, no. 2, July 1933.

Winslow, Ola E. *A Destroying Angel: The Conquest of Smallpox in Colonial Boston*. Boston, 1974.

Woedtke, Baron de. Orderly Book (so-called), Library of Congress.

Wood, William. *The Father of British Canada, a Chronicle of Carleton*. Toronto, 1920.

Wrong, George M. *A Canadian Manor and Its Seigneurs*. Toronto, 1926.

———. *Canada and the American Revolution*. New York, 1968.

Newspapers and Periodicals:

Quebec Gazette, Almon's Remembrancer, Boston Gazette, Connecticut Courant, New England Chronicle or Essex Gazette, New York Journal, Pennsylvania Journal, Pennsylvania Packet.

INDEX

Index